SCOTLAND AND THE GREAT WAR

The Scottish National War Memorial, Edinburgh.

SCOTLAND AND THE GREAT WAR

Edited by

Catriona M. M. Macdonald and E. W. McFarland

Forsitan et haec olim meminisse juvabit

First published in 1999
This edition first published in 2014 by
John Donald, an imprint of
Birlinn Ltd
West Newington House
10 Newington Road
Edinburgh
EH9 1QS

www.birlinn.co.uk

ISBN 978 1 906566 81 4

British Library Cataloguing-in-Publication Data
A catalogue record for this book is available
from the British Library

Typeset in Monotype Bell by Carnegie Publishing, Lancaster
Printed and bound in Britain by Bell and Bain Ltd, Glasgow

Contents

List of Illustrations   viii
Acknowledgements   ix

Introduction: 'A Coronach in Stone'   1
E. W. McFarland

1. The Scottish Economy and the First World War   11
   Clive H. Lee

2. The Impact of the First World War on Scottish Politics   36
   I. G. C. Hutchison

3. War Resisters and Anti-Conscription in Scotland:
   an ILP Perspective   59
   William Kenefick

4. Fighting and Bleeding for the Land: the Scottish
   Highlands and the Great War   81
   Ewen A. Cameron and Iain J. M. Robertson

5. 'Be Strong and of a Good Courage': the Royal Scots'
   Territorial Battalions from 1908 to Gallipoli   103
   Ian S. Wood

6. Confrontation and Withdrawal: Loos, Readership and
   'The First Hundred Thousand'   125
   Gordon Urquhart

7. May 1915: Race, Riot and Representations of War   145
   Catriona M. M. Macdonald

8. Piety, Gender and War in Scotland in the 1910s   173
   Callum G. Brown

Contributors   192

Index   194

List of Illustrations

Mark IV Tank with 105hp Daimler engine.

Parkhead Gun Factory.

HMS *Agamemnon* prepared for launch, 1906.

R 34 Airship, laid down at Inchinnan, 1917.

Engraving Department at Barr and Stroud.

Miss J. G. Cadell, 4th Edinburgh Voluntary Aid Detachment.

'The Last Good-bye, 1916'.

1st Battalion, Black Watch, 1914.

Queues at the Recruiting Office, 1915.

Royal Scots on Sunday morning parade, c.1914.

5th Scottish Rifles at pre-war training camp.

Captain Alan G. Cameron, 1st Battalion, 79th Queen's Own Cameron Highlanders.

John Ross of the Lovat Scouts, 1914.

Frontispiece from *The First Hundred Thousand.*

'Jock' by Snaffles.

'A Heilan' Lad' by Snaffles.

Christmas and New Year card, 1918–19.

Acknowledgements

THE EDITORS would like to thank all those who participated in the 'Scotland and the Great War' conference held at Glasgow Caledonian University in November 1997. We are grateful to Mr Bill Laurie, Prof Gordon Dickson, Dr Graham Walker, Dr Margaret Arnott, Laura Wilson and our students, Pauline Grieve, Donald Macdonald and Lee Barnfather for their support on the day. Special thanks go to Mr Charles Macdonald of the Thistle and the Poppy Association and Kate Hutcheson of the Glasgow University Archives and Business Records Centre for their exhibitions.

We are also happy to acknowledge assistance from staff at the United Services Museum, National Museums of Scotland and the Glasgow University Archives and Business Records Centre in the subsequent preparation of the volume.

Extracts from *The First Hundred Thousand*, by Ian Hay, are reprinted by kind permission of Chambers Harrap Publishers Ltd. We are also grateful to the following for permission to use archival and illustrative material: Aberdeen University Library, Department of Special Collections and Archives; The Bodleian Library, Oxford; Clerk of the Records, House of Lords; Edinburgh University Library; Glasgow University Archives and Business Records Centre; National Museum of Labour History; Scottish Conservative and Unionist Party; Special Collections Department, Glasgow University Library; Stirling Constituency Labour Party; United Services Museum.

We have made all efforts to obtain necessary permission with reference to copyright material; however, we apologise should there be any omissions in this respect.

'A Coronach in Stone'

E. W. McFarland

Scotland laments the glorious, England mourns the dead.
The noble Scottish National War Memorial typifies this
characteristic of the race, as the silence on Armistice Day
is symbolic of the English temperament. When the Englishman bows his head on Armistice day, the Scot lifts up
his voice. England has made an etherial monument of her
backwardness, Scotland has mobilised all the resources of
her national art into a visible monument. Scotland needs
sorrow for her art to be manifest ... the Scot watches the
cloud shadows chase over the hills and mourns dead
chieftains.[1]

THE CONTROVERSIAL WORK OF RAISING a Scottish National War
Memorial in Edinburgh Castle had begun during the last year of
the Great War and was finally brought to completion with its formal
opening on 14 July 1927. Monument building in this case, as in most
societies, was an act of love and remembrance, fulfilling the need to
give dignity in death, while assuring the living that their loved ones
had not died in vain. The scale of Scotland's war losses demanded no
less. In 1921 the official estimate of the war dead stood at 74,000, but
unofficial claims of 110,000 or more went on to fuel nationalist propaganda in a later generation.[2] On the memorial tablets of the Scottish
infantry regiments in the National Memorial could be read 85,548 names
alone. The greatest losses had been suffered by the Royal Scots: 583
officers and 10,630 men in its 35 battalions; the Gordon Highlanders
had lost 9,000 from its 21 battalions; the Black Watch had suffered
most of the Highland regiments with 10,000 killed.[3] Becker, in his
account of the French at war, has written of the 'abstract quality' of so
many conscripts' deaths.[4] But many of Scotland's war dead were not
conscripts. In their own minds, they were 'civic soldiers' – men like the
'Writer-Fighters', an unlikely band of Dundee journalists who enlisted

[handwritten annotation in top margin: "Scots born / Scots parents / served Scottish Reg."]

in the autumn 1914 and for whom, after the discipline of the newspaper office, army training was 'a great lark'.[5] In the public mind, despite their temporary military status, they remained civilians whose death on the battlefield was 'unfair'.[6]

Yet the National Memorial represented more than a simple commemoration of the fallen. Scotland's sacrifice was such, it proclaimed, that her lament too must stand out in proud relief. Just as Scots from every corner of the world contributed to the 'casket of memories', the Memorial's trustees declared that the nation's losses transcended national boundaries. Still holding fast to her sense of imperial mission, Scotland claimed her own. The Roll of Honour would include those who were of Scots birth or born of Scots parents or had served in Scottish regiments, whether home or dominion-based. The sense of collective loss which had long found voice in the poetry corners of Scotland's local newspapers was thus given physical expression:

> Some may return tae their hames in Auld Scotland,
> Others return tae their hames o'er the sea;
> But mony brave hearts are now gone forever,
> And ne'er return tae their ain countries.[7]

In a decade when Scottish national identity was coming under increasing threat from economic and political dislocation, the monument builders also felt compelled to restate the characteristics of the race which had served Scotland well in war. It was a blend of romanticism and practicality which, they trusted, in peacetime would mark Scotland out from her powerful neighbour. While England's cenotaph was the 'crystal deposit of a passing, if splendid, emotion', 'designed in an evening by Sir Edwin Lutyens and set up hurriedly in lath and plaster', it was characteristic of the genius of Scotland and her Celtic strain that she alone among the British kingdoms, 'set surely and unhurriedly about the solemn task of creating a national memorial to her Hundred Thousand Dead'.[8]

Searching for inspiration, artist and architects turned consciously to Scotland's martial past and not to a cynical present. The Memorial was to be a 'coronach in stone' crowning the Castle Rock, Scotland's ancient fortress. War was to be neither glorified nor condemned, but in the pillared arcades of the Hall of Honour the Scottish regiments each had their own memorial, most decorated with their historic colours and battle honours. In death at least, the Saturday afternoon soldiers of the territorial battalions and the volunteers of Kitchener's Armies were to be granted a place in the line of spiritual succession which stretched from Quatre Bras and Inkerman. They had died for the crowning glory which Lord Rosebery had set before them in October 1914: 'a world-wide British influence which shall be a guarantee of liberty and peace'.[9] The slaughter of modern war had changed nothing. Scotland remembered her shattered battalions as modern crusaders.

In addressing Scotland's experience of the Great War, the current volume, like the monument builders, cannot escape the themes of distinctiveness and change. As we pass the eightieth anniversary of the Armistice, we reach a point when the war is slipping from living memory and yet is still firmly rooted in an emotionally-charged complex of images and popular mythology. Historians have made their own contribution here. Indeed, in historiographical terms, the Great War was remarkable for the speed at which it was written into formal 'history'. As Hynes suggests, it was not only in stone that war monuments were raised: massive serial treatments appeared as the fighting unfolded, including John Buchan's twenty-four volume history for the Edinburgh-based publisher, Nelson.[10] These were directed at a popular public who were disorientated by the new scale and intensity of the conflict and who needed to be reassured that this was a campaign which could be captured in conventionally heroic words and pictures. As Buchan could still write after Gallipoli: '"Joy of battle" is a phrase too lightly used ... the Happy Warrior fights not because he has much to hate, but because he has much to love.'[11] Even the evocative post-war histories of Scottish territorial and volunteer battalions can be read as expressions of traditional martial pride, albeit suffused with an acute sense of loss.[12]

In extending our understanding of the Great War, professional historians from the early 1980s have increasingly challenged our preconceptions, both heroic and anti-heroic. In a useful bibliographical essay, Ian Beckett examines the paradigms set by studies such as Jay Winter's, *The Great War and the British People* (London, 1986) and Beckett and Keith Simpson's edited collection, *A Nation in Arms: A Social Study of the British Army in the First World War* (Manchester 1985).[13] The thrust of much work over the last decade has been to continue reconciling the separation between military and social history, leading to a sharper awareness of the social underpinnings of what had in the past, been viewed as exclusively 'operational issues'. This scholarship is stylishly incorporated, for example, in DeGroot's recent survey of British society at war and in the sweeping, *Facing Armageddon* collection.[14]

It is unfortunate, if understandable, that Scottish experience is seldom disaggregated in these British and international overviews. Indeed, Scottish historians themselves have been slow to give concentrated attention to the impact of the Great War, beyond its implications for labour relations on 'Red Clydeside'.[15] There are limited exceptions. Harvie, for example, has offered a broader than usual focus on the economic and political consequences of war in his analysis of twentieth century Scottish history, while Brown has examined the impact of war on the Scottish Presbyterian churches.[16] Individual studies of the Scottish military tradition stand out, such as Baynes' examination of the role of morale in the conduct of the 2nd Scottish Rifles at the battle of Neuve Chapelle in 1915.[17] Similarly, Spiers has mastered an impressive range of personal diaries and memoirs in his review of the Scottish soldier's wartime experience, focusing on the role of comradeship and officer leadership, and on the construction of a positive self image through the symbolism of kilt and bagpipes.[18] These accounts are complemented by the individual testimonies of Great War combatants and war resisters from a variety of traditions assembled in Ian Macdougall's *Voices from War* (Edinburgh, 1995). More general works also contain useful material on the Great War experience. Challenging popular accounts in which Scottish soldiering has a timeless quality, Wood's *Scottish Soldier*, for example, adopts a critical perspective on the myth-making and invention of tradition which has surrounded Scottish regiments, while Henderson's study of the Highland soldier offers a detailed social and domestic history of a century of everyday military life.[19]

Against this background, the essays in the present collection focus scholarly attention across a variety of topics from wartime industrial production to anti-German riots. The picture they present is not of an experience which was dramatically different in kind from elsewhere: economic dislocation, the hardships of trench warfare and spiritual uncertainty were characteristic across a range of combatant nations. Yet the way in which this experience was handled in cultural terms and its impact on Scotland's economy and society were bound to be distinctive. This was partly the result of the unique configuration of Scottish civil society and domestic politics, but also reflected Scotland's place in the British imperial system and the role that popular empire loyalty and its associated military tradition had played in shaping her national identity in the decades before the war.[20]

The contributors have also addressed the question of how far Scotland was transformed by her experience of war. Academic shorthand has often shared the tendency of contemporaries to view the Great War as a gulf, separating 'the world of sunshine and laughter, of beauty and courage' from that of economic depression and class politics.[21] In these essays, a more complex picture emerges where disruptions and new departures must be disentangled from war's familiar capacity to act as a forcing house on pre-existing points of vulnerability. Nor was a desire for change inevitable. At the close of a war fought to defend 'the great principles of humanity' which were believed to underpin Scotland's imperial mission, for some the pressing need was to restore tradition and continuity whether in the 'purity' of Scottish regiments or the piety of Scottish womanhood.[22]

The first three essays consider the effects of the Great War on the economic and political life of Scotland. In his analysis, Clive Lee suggests that the lights did not 'go out' for the Scottish economy in August 1914. Admittedly, despite the chivalric and pastoral illusions which coloured the views of some early participants, this was the first total war of industrialised powers.[23] As a disproportionately large and heavily specialised sector of the British and imperial economy, Scotland was bound to play a key role in producing the materials of war and in providing indirect support through the mobilisation of the home front. While the war clearly enhanced Scotland's productive capacity, the long term nature of its economic effects is more difficult to determine. Before the war, Scotland had an economy which was already quietly declining in competitiveness. The social gains and technological advances which resulted from the war were, it seems, more liable to reversal than the inherent industrial weaknesses which it exacerbated and the new penalities it imposed in terms of accumulated debt and trade disruption. The war, argues Lee, did not cause Scotland's subsequent industrial woes, but the consequent restructuring of international trade and finance represented ominous blows for a struggling open economy.

In a companion chapter, I. G. C. Hutchison analyses the extent to which the Great War redrafted the political map of Scotland. One casualty of war-time politics was the proud colossus of the Liberal Party in Scotland. Far from 'business as usual', for the Liberals, war left a legacy of crisis and schism which failed to dissipate. In contrast, the Unionists were heartened and unified by this supreme test of national purpose. Their enhanced reputation as defenders of patriotism and property was to find its political reward in the ideologically-polarised climate of post-war Scotland. The status and unity of their opponents in the Labour camp had also benefited from the demands of war, although a triumphalist surge in the wake of victory ensured that wartime labour unrest was not immediately translated into concrete political gains in 1918.

In his essay, William Kenefick examines the case study of the Independent Labour Party and the Great War. Whereas elsewhere in Britain the party suffered for its anti-war stance, in Scotland its membership more than trebled by 1918. This, he argues, was not simply due to its campaigning on social issues in communities and workplaces, but also represented an electoral dividend for the consistent opposition to war and conscription which featured in its 'Home Front Offensive'. Drawing on the columns of *Forward*, the essay enters into the 'conceptual thicket' surrounding consciencious objection.[24] A picture emerges both of the intense individuality of anti-war protest, even within the context of an organised party campaign, and of the practical overlap between the religious and secular well-springs of dissent. Clearly, in Scotland the left did not simply jettison internationalist and anti-militarist perspectives on the outbreak of war. On the contrary, Kenefick argues, these years saw the consolidation of an ethical and political outlook on which future generations of Scottish socialists could draw.

While 5,000 turned out to support a peace demonstration in Glasgow in August 1914, this was untypical of the Scottish mood. Scotland produced 320,589 recruits during the months of voluntary enlistment from August 1914 to December 1915 – the highest proportion of enlistments in the United Kingdom.[25] During the first ten weeks of hostilities, Glasgow alone raised 30,000 men, or the equivalent of every able-bodied male from nineteen to twenty-four years of age.[26] The rhetoric of recruiting drew heavily on traditional concepts of Scottish martial prowess as evidenced in regimental records of 'service and gallantry second to none in the annals of our Empire'.[27]

As Ewen Cameron and Iain Robertson suggest in their chapter, this tradition was more than the British regimental spirit writ large. It drew heavily on the military identity of the Highlands, a romantic image which had developed in tandem with the massive expansion in military recruiting from the region from the late eighteenth century. The symbols of Highland heroism proved both durable and effective and the recruiters in 1914, especially when themselves members of traditional landowning families, were able to play on a powerful complex of local identities and national loyalites. The romantic spirit was carried on into the opening stages of the conflict and even non-Scots were drawn in. As the Yorkshireman, Linton Andrews commented of the 4th Black Watch: 'We were more like a Highland chieftain and his faithful followers that an ordinary battalion'.[28] Following demobilisation, the thoughts of many surviviors turned to land settlement. In enlisting, Highlanders had expected not only glory, but their traditional reward for military service in the form of a croft or the enlargement of existing holdings. However, the war had raised expectations without solving the fundamental problem of land hunger. The post-war Highlands were thus to witness a new and distinct phase of land protest which drew on the rhetoric of ancient loyalties and broken promises.

With Ian Wood's chapter, the focus shifts to the lowland regiments. Wood reminds us that the Scottish military elites did not always welcome their temporary new recruits with open arms – however they may have later glorified their exploits. While happy for the Scottish public to identify with the Scottish regiments, they were less certain of the affect that 'socially undesirable elements', or a civilian ethos, might exercise on traditional military mystique. 'Dilution', it would seem, was not only an issue for Scottish trade unions. Wood's study traces the tragic journey of the territorial battalions of the Royal Scots, from the drill halls of Edinburgh and Leith to the deadly ravines of Gallipoli. The spirit of amateurism and improvisation which DeGroot identifies as charac- terising much of Britain's military effort was to have a high cost on 28 June 1915, as inexperienced territorials launched an unsupported frontal attack on entrenched Turkish postitions.[29]

If Gallipoli represented the 'blooding' of Scotland's territorial battalions, for the New Army volunteers, this came at Loos in September 1915 – a battle which Terraine has termed 'the true beginning of the martyrdom of the British army'.[30] Two Scottish volunteer Divisions, the 9th and 15th, were committed to the attack: the 9th lost almost 3,000 men killed and missing from 25 to 28 September, while the 15th lost over 3,000 in a single day.[31] What the *Glasgow Herald* had initially hailed as 'A Great Advance' and 'The Triumph of the New Army' was soon to fill its columns with massive casualty lists, featuring 'many well-known Scots names', as 'the Price of Victory'.[32] In his essay, Gordon Urquhart directs our attention to this 'Scottish battle' of the Great War. While Culloden has entered national mythology, Loos, with its myriad of personal tragedies, was perhaps too immediate and painful to achieve 'mythic status', and was instead destined to pass out of collective memory. This is the battle which forms the climax of Ian Hay's *First Hundred Thousand*. Urquhart considers this resolutely cheerful war novel with its realistic dialogue as a 'letter home'. In the same spirit as the Scottish war artist, Muirhead Bone, translated the alien landscape of war into familiar artistic forms, Hay not only humanised Scottish martial virtues, but helped render the new lives (and perhaps deaths) of loved ones who had volunteered comprehensible to friends and relatives.[33] The novel, Urquhart suggests, stands at a junction point for Scottish literature, created by the destructive reality of the Great War. After 1918 Scottish writing begins to slip the shelter of empire and 're-enters history' on its own account.

The final two essays return to the home front and examine wartime journalism and the contribution of war to the shaping of gendered piety. Strange bedfellows at first glance, both the Scottish press and the Scottish churches were cornerstones of national identity during the Great War period and beyond. Catriona Macdonald's essay examines the role of the press in relation to Scotland's unique pattern of anti-German riots. Total war, she argues, collapsed the boundaries between the battlefield and the domestic sphere, implying that participation could no longer be defined in terms of direct combat experience. In this novel situation the newspaper had a crucial mediating role, encouraging ident-ification with an imagined national community, while shaping the sense of loss of local communities. What emerged from the narrativisation of the war was an identifiably Scottish war effort, just as the press itself was distinctly Scottish in terms of ownership and readership. The vision of the Empire's struggle as a Scottish campaign required nationhood to be defined against a range of 'others' – including German immigrants. How this group were percieved locally depended on a complex interplay of discourses, economic, generational and geographic. Yet, even here the press fed on Scottish political sensibilities, framing Scotland's war experience within a distinctive Scottish Liberal Imperialism which took longer to transfer war guilt from nations to peoples.

Like the moblisation of public opinion, the impact of the Great War on religious culture has remained an under-researched area. Callum Brown's essay extends our understanding with a discussion of how the different male and female experiences of war were reflected in distinct discourses of piety. Like their British counterparts, Scottish churchmen looked to the war for a national spiritual awakening. In the event, the male 'home heathen' was to survive the transition to the battlefield. Not all Scottish soldiers found, like Douglas Haig, a new spiritual uplift and sense of purpose in Presbyterianism.[34] Despite an elemental spirituality shading into trench fatalism, the traditional military capacity for drink, blasphemy and fornication co-existed with a continuing alienation from institutional religion. While war confirmed Victorian male stereotypes, it created a crisis for the parallel discourse of female piety, as the moral and sexual conduct of women on the home front shocked church missions. The result was a last gasp campaign of evangelical revival, particularly directed at young females, which helped rally Scottish church member-ship in the inter-war decades.

The Great War was an event which touched every aspect of life in Scotland. The present collection does not claim to provide a definitive statement on such a vast subject area, but is instead intended to open up new lines of research. These can benefit from the incredibly rich and largely untapped reserves of primary source material on the experience of war. Indeed, many obvious questions, such as the popular dynamics behind voluntary enlistment, remain unresolved. Why did the Scots fight? What was the balance between national, imperial and personal loyalties? How far did John Buchan's 'trumpet call of national need' sustain Scottish society during four years of total war? [35] Finally, what of the aftermath?

Armistice Day, 11 November 1918 produced a range of reactions. In Glasgow, factors despaired as tenants burned fixtures and fittings in a desperate show of joy and relief.[36] In Flanders, one Scottish battalion, just withdrawn from the trenches, 'felt they had bourne the weight of the pain and the strife and were in no condition for such mafficking'. For them,

> The silence was almost unearthly and it was difficult to realise that the conditions under which we had existed for so long had ceased to be. With nerves dulled to withstand sorrow, the men could hardly appreciate joy – and the day was spent in rest and conjecture as to whether this was indeed the end, or only a respite.[37]

In the post-war world, many Scots were to share their hesitant vision.

Notes

1. Sir Lawrence Weaver, *The Scottish National War Memorial* (London, 1927).
2. D. Duff, *Scotland's War Losses* (Glasgow, 1947), pp. 35–46.
3. Weaver, *Scottish National War Memorial*, p. 15; Using a broad definition, S. Wood suggests that as many as 147,000 'with a claim to be Scots' were lost, that is, allowing for expatriates, one in four of Scotland's males between 19 and 49 who enlisted: *The Scottish Soldier* (Manchester, 1987), p. 88.
4. J. Becker, *The Great War and the French People* (Leamington Spa, 1985), p. 116.
5. *The Baillie*, 1 Sept. 1915; W. L. Andrews, *Haunting Years: The Commentaries of a War Territorial* (London, 1929), pp. 19–20.
6. D. Winter, *Death's Men* (London, 1978), p. 204.
7. *Western Supplement*, 30 Oct. 1915.
8. Weaver, *Scottish National War Memorial*, p. 9. For a more sympathetic treatment of Lutyen's 'expression of existential truth' see J. Winter, *Sites of Memory, Sites of Mourning: The Great War in European Cultural History* (Cambridge, 1995), pp. 102–5.
9. J. Buchan, *Nelson's History of the War* (London, 1915–19), vol. i, p. 8.
10. S. Hynes, *A War Imagined* (London, 1990), p. 47; for examples of popular illustrations of the war see Newman Flower (ed.), *The History of the Great War* (London, 1915).
11. Buchan, *Nelson's History*, vol. xii, p. 144.
12. Of particular interest is *The Fifth Battalion Cameronians (Scottish Rifles) 1914–19* (Glasgow, 1936). The '5th SR' was Glasgow's premier territorial unit and had Lord Kelvin, Henry Campbell-Bannerman, and Andrew Bonar Law among its

ex-members. (Thanks to David Donald for this reference.) For other examples of the genre, see also J. W. Arthur and I. S. Munro (eds), *Seventeenth Highland Light Infantry (Glasgow Chamber of Commerce Battalion) Record of War Service 1914–1918* (Glasgow, 1920); T. Chalmers, *A Saga of Scotland: The History of the 16th Battalion Highland Light Infantry* (Glasgow, 1930), and by the same author, *An Epic of Glasgow: History of the 15th Battalion. The Highland Light Infantry (City of Glasgow Regiment)* (Glasgow, 1934).

13. H. Cecil and P. Liddell (eds), *Facing Armageddon: The First World War Experienced* (London, 1996), pp. 981–5. For a bibiographical overview see also B. Bond, *The First World War and British Military History* (Oxford, 1991).

14. G. J. DeGroot, *Blighty. British Society in the Era of the Great War* (London, 1996); Cecil and Liddell, *Facing Armageddon*.

15. J. Foster, 'Red Clyde, Red Scotland' in I. Donnachie and C. Whatley (eds), *The Manufacture of Scottish History* (Edinburgh, 1992), pp. 106–24.

16. C. Harvie, *No Gods and Precious Few Heroes: Scotland 1914–1980* (Edinburgh, 1981), pp. 1–34; S. J. Brown '"A solemn purification by fire": responses to the Great War in the Scottish presbyterian churches 1914–19', *Journal of Ecclesiastical History*, xlv (1994), pp. 82–104.

17. J. Baynes, *Morale: A Study of Men and Courage: the Second Scottish Rifles at Neuve Chapelle 1915* (London,1967).

18. E. Spiers 'The Scottish soldier at war', in Cecil and Liddell, *Facing Armageddon*, pp. 314–35.

19. Wood, *Scottish Soldier*; D. Henderson, *Highland Soldier: A Social Study of the Highland Regiments 1820–1920* (Edinburgh, 1989).

20. R. J. Finlay, 'The rise and fall of popular imperialism in Scotland 1850–1950', *Scottish Geographical Magazine*, cxiii (1997), pp. 13–27.

21. Arthur and Munro, *Seventeenth Highland Light Infantry*, p. 77.

22. As Douglas Haig commented, while unveiling the Cameronians' memorial in Glasgow in 1924: 'If our Lowland Scottish regiments are to preserve their old-time character and renown, they must be recruited here ... among men of our own kin': H. C. Wylly, *A Short History of the Cameronians (Scottish Rifles) 1689–1924* (Aldershot, 1924), p. 51.

23. P. Fussell, *The Great War and Modern Memory* (New York, 1977).

24. K. Robbins, 'The British experience of conscientious objection', in Cecil and Liddell, *Facing Armageddon*, pp. 691–706.

25. Wood, *Scottish Soldier*, p. 87.

26. *Glasgow Herald*, 15 Oct. 1914 , 5 Dec. 1915.

27. Arthur and Munro, *Seventeenth Highland Light Infantry*, p. 19.

28. Andrews, *Haunting Years*, p. 249.

29. DeGroot, *Blighty*, p. 30.

30. J. Terraine, *Douglas Haig: The Educated Soldier* (London, 1990), p. 154.

31. Buchan, *Nelson's History*, vol. x, pp. 166–203.

32. *Glasgow Herald* 27, 30 Sept., 4 Oct. 1915.

33. *The Western Front: Drawings by Muirhead Bone*, Part 1 (London, 1916).

34. G. J. DeGroot, '"We are safe whatever happens" – Douglas Haig, the Reverend George Duncan, and the conduct of war', in N. Macdougall (ed.), *Scotland and War AD 79–1918* (Edinburgh, 1991), pp. 193–211.

35. Buchan, *Nelson's History*, vol. viii, p. 137.

36. Glasgow University Business Archives, Minutes of the Property Owners and Factors' Association Glasgow Ltd, UGD 342/1/10, 24 Dec. 1918.

37. *Fifth Battalion Cameronians*, p. 169.

CHAPTER ONE

The Scottish Economy
and the First World War

Clive H. Lee

THE GREAT WAR was the first major conflict of the modern era in which the destructive potential of modern technology was frighteningly demonstrated. Its cost in terms of human suffering, the annihilation of property and financial expense far exceeded previous wars and provided a warning for the future which was little noticed. Economic historians have generally stressed the Great War as an economic turning point, elevating the importance of the emerging United States and diminishing that of the United Kingdom and Germany in economic pre-eminence and financial strength. The destruction and dislocation in Europe, the collapse of the Austrian and Russian empires, and the economic depression which persisted through most of the interwar years, all contributed to this. The world economy was reshaped under American hegemony and new economic powers, such as the Soviet Union and Japan, emerged to challenge the pre-eminence of Europe. For many historians 1914 marks the end of the European century in the history of the world economy and inaugurates the American century.

The direct economic effects of war are easy to identify. The productive process is redirected away from normal peacetime activity, designed to satisfy the demands of consumers, to the pursuit of war. Armaments and all the necessary supportive production and manpower take pride of place and secure first option on the use of resources. This obviously produces dislocation and shortages in the short term and waste in the long term. The conduct of war wreaks destruction on the land and property of the territories over which it is waged, on the individuals engaged in armed conflict, and on the products of war, as ships are sunk, guns destroyed, and shells exploded. Beyond these immediate effects lie less obvious costs. War is expensive and must be financed. Government borrowing, increased taxation, and the commandeering of manufacturing and transport without recompense are all means to satisfy this need. Even victory comes at a high cost. Bogart's estimates for the

First World War suggested that the main belligerents, the United Kingdom and Germany, together bore the brunt of the cost and very nearly the same share of the bill for that conflict.[1]

Modern war involves the harnessing of economic power to sustain military effort. This takes two obvious forms. The first involves the production of the means of waging war such as armaments, munitions, warships, tanks, and even uniforms. The second involves the support of the main war effort, especially through transport networks and the provision of essential supplies of food. This need extends, of course, to the domestic population who do not take part in the military engagements but whose labour provides the equipment essential for that effort. Thus Scotland played a major role in the productive underpinning of the British effort in the Great War.

Military production

The immediate demands of war boost production while largely ignoring the usual constraints of cost and the need to use resources efficiently. The west of Scotland played an important part in military production. The Clyde contained 90% of Scottish shipbuilding and marine engineering activity in 1914 and provided an ideal location, secure from the attentions of the German navy. The three main naval dockyards on the Clyde came under Admiralty control on the outbreak of war and this was extended to the rest of the industry under the Munitions of War Act 1915. Between 1914 and 1918 the indicated horse power (ihp) of naval vessels built on the Clyde reached 5.9 million, a total tonnage of 816,984.[2] The majority of these vessels were destroyers, however, the constant struggle to replace tonnage of merchant shipping lost at sea meant that this branch of the industry could not be neglected. In the first submarine campaign, between February 1915 and November 1916, 2.25 million gross tons of shipping were lost and, in an eight month period in 1917, a further submarine campaign destroyed 2.5 million tons of British shipping. This concentrated activity on the shipbuilding programme for the merchant fleet by late 1916. In sum, the Clyde mercantile output reached 1,556,877 tons and 1.7 million ihp during the Great War.[3]

The growth of activity in Scottish shipyards had an immediate impact on steel production. Scottish steel ingot and castings production rose from 1.23 million to 2.24 million tons.[4] Even before the war, Scottish steel manufacturers, such as William Beardmore & Co, had been closely linked to the armaments industry. The threat of war actually saved Beardmore's from liquidation through Admiralty orders secured from 1910 onwards. Employment at the Parkhead Ordnance Works rose by almost 50% and by 8,000 jobs in the war, and the value of output rose from £1.9 million to £7.1 million.[5] During the war, Beardmore's also produced aircraft and aero-engines and light armour plating for tanks.

The Great War generated considerable activity in Scotland's heavy industries, especially in the Glasgow and Lanarkshire areas. Apart from the increases in production and employment, there were some technological gains, for example, in shipbuilding where standardisation created substantial simplification in the production process. The programme of standardised production for merchant vessels was imposed by the Ministry of Shipping in face of objections by the shipbuilders. Furthermore, wartime pressure to increase the speed of construction led to the introduction of pneumatic and electrical tools, and yard reorganisation brought further productivity gains. There were similar advances in munitions manufacture, again under central control introduced by the Munitions of War Act. Work on shells involved heavy manual labour and use of automatic or semi-automatic machinery. The massive demand for shells encourged the introduction of standardisation and the importation of American machinery. By 1917, the engineering industry of the Clyde 'had been virtually revolutionised by the introduction throughout of automatic machinery and the adoption of mass production.'[6]

Many of these advances were, however, temporary. The influence of trade unions ensured that traditional practices were largely restored when hostilities ended, reinforced by the effects of recession. The policy of standardising merchant ships was immediately reversed when state control ended. Other inherent weaknesses were exacerbated by the war, notably in steel manufacture. The industry had a major historical weakness in the highly unusual division between iron and steel production in Scotland. In the late nineteenth century Scottish iron production had remained specialised at the level of pig iron production, and the manufacturers integrated backwards to form a self-contained sector based on iron, coal and their by-products. The original initiative for steel manufacture in Scotland came from shipbuilding. The malleable iron producers adjusted to steel production by using local ore, supplemented by imports and scrap. The growth of steel manufacturing capacity was thus not accompanied by growth in basic pig iron production. Iron manufacture suffered from a declining resource base. During the war years, Scottish output of iron ore declined, despite the conscription of German prisoners of war as miners to work at such unlikely excavation sites as Raasay.

However, until 1916 Scottish pig iron production, supplemented by imports from England and the run down of existing stocks, was sufficient to supply the industry. But Scottish steel producers relied increasingly upon imported iron ore, principally from Spain and North Africa. The import of iron ore into the western ports, mainly Glasgow, was fairly steady between 1914 and 1918 at an average 1.56 million tons per annum. This brought other difficulties, through the high exchange rate and shortage of shipping tonnage, until the government took control of chartering in 1917. These problems were compounded by a shortage of labour and wagons at the docks.

The Great War, therefore, had an obvious impact on heavy industry in the west of Scotland. Its significance has been much debated by historians. Payne has been inclined to attribute to the war a substantial and deleterious effect on Scottish industry, arguing that pre-existing structural and locational weaknesses in iron and steel were exacerbated by policies adopted to meet wartime demands. The iron and steel industry emerged from the war even more divided than hitherto. Expectation of a shipping boom and fear of steel shortages at the end of the war led to a scramble amongst shipbuilders to buy steel plant. Within two years of the end of hostilities, almost all the steel-making capacity was in the hands of shipbuilders and they descended into the recession together.[7] Tolliday, however, has offered a more critical assessment, at least of Scottish steel, stressing the inherent weaknesses in Scottish industry, such as fragmentation, which were endemic prior to 1914.[8]

Perhaps the most obvious effect of the war was to increase productive capacity. David Colville & Sons took over Clydebridge Steel Company and Glengarnock Iron & Steel Company in 1916 and established new plant.[9] In the war years the company increased production by 250% and increased its share of Scottish production from 24 to 46%. While steel productive capacity increased, ownership became more concentrated and the lack of integration in the whole productive chain was reinforced. Manufacturing capacity also increased in other countries which, in peace, would be competitors. The war caused the loss of 30% of the world mercantile tonnage so that shipbuilders had high expectations of replacement orders to make good these losses. But world shipbuilding capacity doubled between 1914 and 1920, the post-war boom was short-lived and, in Scotland, the industry remained wedded to its highly conservative working practices. Inherent historical weaknesses, the effects of war, and the state of the international market in the 1920s brought little lasting advantage to Scottish heavy industry.

Feeding the Home Front

The provision of food under wartime conditions was an immediate and major problem for the British war effort. More than any other economy, in the later decades of the nineteenth century, Britain had adjusted to the opportunities for specialisation within the international economy. As a result there was a marked fall in self-sufficiency in agricultural production and an increasing proportion of the nation's food was imported. When war broke out, national productive capacity was sufficient to feed the population for a weekend, from Friday evening to Monday morning, while Germany could feed its population for six to seven days each week. Contemporary estimates of calorific requirements suggested that each individual required about one million calories per annum. Further calculations based on data for 1909–1913 indicated that the average British citizen consumed 9% more calories per annum than the million required. But only 34% of this intake was derived from home soil.[10] This deficit in self-sufficiency became a major concern for military strategists on both sides. Britain was, of course, largely excluded from European food supplies during the war, so the Atlantic trade became an essential lifeline. It is hardly surprising that the submarine campaign in the Atlantic, designed to disrupt such supplies, became a major element in Germany's military strategy.

The major aim of British war policy was to maximise the level of self-sufficiency in food provision. By 1917 the effectiveness of submarine attacks in the Atlantic had induced the transfer of three million acres of land from pasture to arable cultivation. This was not a policy to which Scotland was well suited to contribute. Much of the best arable land lay in southern England, and it was there that the main conversions to pasture had taken place. Between 1888 and the outbreak of war, there was a 25% reduction in arable cultivation in England and Wales compared to a 10% reduction in Scotland. By contrast, Scottish production was oriented towards root vegetables, providing winter food for cattle and sheep, and rotation grasses. Scotland had a far higher acreage of mountain and heath land for grazing than other parts of Britain and a much greater concentration on sheep farming.[11]

Nevertheless, the war made a very significant impact on Scottish farming. The most obvious effect was the need to maximise the production of food and to adjust the distribution of food produced to compensate for supplies lost through trade dislocation. The disruption of trade meant some loss of exports and, more significantly, loss of imports which deprived Scottish farmers of important inputs such as feed and fertiliser. Scottish food imports changed during the war, primarily as a consequence of the loss of east coast trade passing through Leith and the eastern ports and its partial replacement by west coast trade passing through Glasgow. Imports of oats, barley, oatmeal, eggs and butter all fell but wheatmeal and flour, from North America, increased markedly. The army added to demand in providing a voracious appetite for horses, hay and food, while threatening supplies through the recruitment of rural labour. By July 1918 the Board of Agriculture estimated that 36.5% of Scottish farm workers had joined the army. This had an obvious effect on efficiency as young and fit men were drafted.

But the most obvious product of increased demand was inflation. Although aggregate farm wages rose by 150% between 1914 and 1920, prices also rose, with the result that for much of the earlier part of the war workers suffered falling real incomes. Wage inflation also favoured single men whose contracts were determined every six months rather than annually. As a consequence, the wage of a single ploughman in Aberdeenshire doubled in the course of the war. The demand for wool pushed up the price of sheep. In this way, wages for shepherds doubled in the course of the war, while the stock fell to 6.4 million sheep in 1919 compared to the 7.0 million averaged in earlier years. While prices were fixed by the government for purchases made by the War Office, the farming lobby protested when it thought that the prices set were too low. The year 1918 was just such a case, even though the price for sheep was fixed at 60% above the 1914 price. An upper limit was set on the price of milk in 1917, and meat rationing was introduced late in the war. However, farmers appear to have enjoyed considerable prosperity. The rapid rise in prices, especially in the earlier years of the war before controls were introduced, allowed substantial profits to be realised.[12]

Scottish agriculture responded to the incentives of inflation-boosted demand, supplemented with government support and exhortation, by producing the required increase in output. The acreage of arable land in Scotland increased by almost 5% during the war. Increased cultivation was brought about by breaking up grass land and shortening rotation, and by increased ploughing. Wheat acreage rose only slightly during the war, although there was an increase in yield of 11.4% between 1915 and 1918. The main increase in Scottish agricultural production, however, was in oats, with acreage growing by over 25% and yield by over 40%. Barley production also increased, replacing lost imports from Europe, as did potato production late in the war.[13] While the principal

Scottish agricultural crop was oats for porridge and stock feed, the main Scottish agricultural effort was devoted to the production of meat and dairy produce. Labour productivity gains were achieved as the employment of male agricultural labour fell during war from 107,000 in July 1914 to a low point of 89,000 in November 1918. But only in the final year did the shortage of labour become acute enough to threaten production. This put much more onus on the efforts of women workers in agriculture, whose numbers remained constant at 22,000, and upon the juveniles and older men not liable for military service.

The war also helped the land settlement scheme which had been established originally by the Small Landholders (Scotland) Act 1911 under the auspices of the newly created Board of Agriculture. By the end of 1914 the Board had settled 434 new holdings and extended 239 existing holdings mainly in the Highlands. The scheme was initially accorded a low priority in the war, but became linked to the programme for the resettlement of servicemen. In 1916 the Board was charged to consider a scheme for soldiers stimulated by the free gift of 12,000 acres in Sutherland by the Duke. By the end of 1918 the Board had created 6,471 new holdings and enlarged 4,254, but it still had 10,000 applications outstanding.[14] Legislation passed between 1916 and 1919, however, gave the Board power to acquire land for small holdings. Price inflation helped those already established on the land but created problems for those starting cultivation because of the high cost of equipment. Even so, by 1921 applications exceeded 18,000, mainly from Highland counties. In sum, between 1912 and 1923 a total of 2,275 new holdings were created of which 1,507 went to ex-servicemen. These were unofficially augmented by land raids in the Hebrides and the colonisation of Raasay.[15]

Fishing

The sea was an important theatre of war and the conflict had an immediate and disruptive effect on Scottish fishing which was both an important source of food and a significant export industry. Before the war, almost half the herring catch was exported, principally to Germany and Russia. This trade was rapidly curtailed. An even more dramatic effect was the sudden disappearance, on the outbreak of war, of the German trawler fleet of thirty-two vessels which had established Aberdeen as its base for fishing in Icelandic waters and whose loss severely disrupted fish curing in the city. Yet apart from being a source of food, the sea represented an important strategic battleground, in particular the sea lanes between the North Sea and the Atlantic around the northern coast of Scotland. The threat of enemy vessels and mines in these waters remained significant throughout the war. Nor was it an idle threat. Fifteen drifters were sunk off Shetland in a single night in 1915 and throughout the course of the war, 89 Scottish boats were sunk while fishing – an aggregate loss of 10,500 tons.

The fishing industry was involved in the war in two different ways, in the provision of food as part of the drive towards self-sufficiency and directly as part of the war at sea. The Admiralty chartered many seaworthy vessels, often including the entire crew, and arranged for the storage of fishing gear. Only the smaller and older craft were left to continue fishing. Most of the vessels adopted by the Navy were involved in coastal patrols or minesweeping in both home and foreign waters. In the early weeks of the war such vessels often had limited protection, usually two rifles and a few rounds of special ammunition for sinking mines. By the end of the war they had guns, depth charges, bomb throwers, mine and submarine sweeps, radio and hydrophones. A survey taken in April 1917 showed 1,143 Scottish fishing vessels in Admiralty service, principally from the north east ports: Aberdeen (247), Buckie (171), Findhorn (135), Peterhead (115), Fraserburgh (102) and Banff (91). Also, as in the case of other occupations, many fishermen enlisted. When conscription was introduced, a special section was established for fishermen, the Royal Naval Volunteer Reserve, which freed them from army service and allowed them to continue fishing until they were required by the Navy. A survey taken in April 1917 showed that out of an estimated 50,623 men normally engaged in fishing, including ancillary workers such as fishcurers, fishmongers, boat builders and coopers, 21,780 were engaged in their normal business activity, 11,570 were serving with the army or navy, and 12,214 were in Admiralty service on mine sweepers or patrol vessels.[16]

The pursuit of fishing was thus hampered by the loss of boats and men to military service and by the threat of enemy action. Initially the government prohibited all fishing, but this restriction was gradually relaxed and the regulations which effectively applied throughout the war were introduced at the end of 1914. From Kinnaird Head northwards to Lerwick and on the entire west coast, fishing was restricted to local boats according to permits issued by the Fishery Board. The North Sea coast was open to fishing, although restrictions were placed on fishing in the approaches to the Firth of Forth in 1915. The diminished fleet inevitably brought a change in the pattern of fishing. In 1914 there were 313 steam trawlers fishing from Scottish ports: Aberdeen which accounted for 60% of white fish landings had 233, Granton had 49 and

Dundee had 31. Many of these had disappeared into naval service by the end of that year. By 1918 the fleet had been reduced to 92 vessels, 67 working from Aberdeen and the rest from Dundee and Granton. Not surprisingly, the size of the annual catch fell. The quantity of white fish landed in Scotland fell from 3.0 million cwts in 1914 to a low of 1.0 million cwts in 1917 before recovering slightly in 1918 and then strongly in 1919. Shortages and inflation, however, increased the value of the catch so that it rose every year throughout the war. The price of fish rose to such levels that the government placed it under restriction in 1918. The war also shifted the main activity of the herring fishery from the east to the west coast. In 1917 and 1918 the combined catch landed at Stornoway, Loch Carron, Skye and Fort William exceeded the total catch of the east coast. In total, herring landings fell from 4.5 million cwts in 1914 to 0.75 million in 1915 before recovering to about 2.0 million in each of the next three years, while the value of the catch followed a similar pattern.[17] Conventional fishing was supplemented by line fishing in inshore waters and off Shetland, although eventually it was restricted by a shortage of mussels for bait.

At the end of the war, 1,140 steam and 100 motor powered fishing vessels were decommissioned by the Admiralty, which also offered compensation for boats in a deteriorated condition and loans for fishing gear and for the replacement of small craft. During the war the Admiralty had built vessels to replace lost tonnage and these vessels were now available for disposal to some of the 250,000 Scottish fishermen who were demobilised. The fishing industry was optimistic at the end of the war, but there were reasons for anxiety. Admiralty shipbuilding had greatly increased the size of the fleet, and inflation had increased the cost of gear, fuel, and wages. Possibly worse was the collapse of the eastern market for herring as a result of persisting revolutionary chaos in Russia and the Baltic, which had been, with Germany, the main overseas market before 1914.

Managing manpower

Together with production, wartime reallocation of economic resources implies the redistribution of employment. This is most apparent in the draft of manpower into military service. The related effect is the replacement of those lost by additional workers who are new to the labour force, as well as the redistribution of remaining workers to fulfil the new productive requirements of war.

There remains considerable uncertainty about the precise number of casualties sustained in the First World War. The estimates of British and Irish dead range from 550,000 to 1,184,000. Winter's estimate of 768,000, derived from the 1921 Census of Population, is a little higher than the most plausible of earlier calculations made by Dearle, which gave a figure of 729,000, or the best estimate based on military records which gives a figure of 722,785.[18] These estimates suggest a figure for Scotland's dead within the range of 70,000 to 78,000. The Census of Population for Scotland in 1921 estimated the war dead at 74,000.[19] Winter's estimates for all British and Irish combatants suggests that, of those who served, 11.8% were killed, 27.3% were wounded and 2.7% were captured, giving a total casualty rate of 41.7%.[20] It seems unlikely that the relative distribution of Scottish casualties would be very different from this. The problems of estimation are, however, very great. Reported casualties were often intentionally misleading to maintain morale or confuse the enemy, some estimates include deaths occurring after the cessation of hostilities in November 1918 as the result of wounds sustained in battle, while others count only those who died before the Armistice. The substantial loss of life in the 1918–1919 influenza epidemic adds further complications. In addition, Britain sustained 15,000 fatalities in fishing and merchant vessels which do not appear in the records as war casualties.[21]

The figures for enlistments are more reliable than the estimates of casualties. During the Great War 585,171 Scots served in the Regular Army and the Territorial Army, 72,219 in the Royal Navy and Allied Services, and 32,845 in the Royal Flying Corps and Royal Air Force, making a total of 690,235 men.[22] Volunteers comprised 26.9% of Scottish men aged 15–49 in 1911, slightly higher than the rate for England and Wales at 24.2%. The conscription rate was much lower for Scotland – 14.6% as compared to 22.1%. This reflected the concentration of reserved occupations and munitions work. As a result, the percentage of Scots serving, as a proportion of males aged 15–49, reached 41.4%, compared to 46.2% for England and Wales.

The uncertainty of the aggregate figures make it even more difficult to estimate the age distribution of the casualties, a task which is necessary if the demographic impact of the war is to be assessed. There are occasional records. The combined Roll of Honour for the districts of Paisley, Arbroath and Shetland suggested that about 72% of the dead were under thirty and only 14% over 35, a pattern which was very similar to a statistical simulation based on Prudential life tables.[23] Further there is statistical support for the traditional belief that officers were more likely to be casualties than their men. This is reflected in the Roll of Honour of the Scottish universities. While the overall death rate was 11.8% of those who served, the percentage of graduates and undergraduates of Scottish universities who did not survive were as follows: Aberdeen 12.5; Edinburgh 15.0; Glasgow 16.7; Royal Technical College, Glasgow 19.0; and St Andrews 12.8.[24]

The impact of war on the population and its age distribution is difficult to estimate with great clarity, given the uncertainty which surrounds the estimates of the number of casualties. The main trends are, however, fairly clear. As indicated in Table 1, Scotland had demographic problems prior to the war, in that economic deprivation saw a substantial outflow of migrants, exceeding a quarter of a million people in the first decade of the twentieth century. Migration in the decade of the war fell only slightly below that level. In addition, the enumerators of the Census estimated that Scots in the armed forces suffered 74,000 deaths abroad in the war. Consequently, the net gain of males was substantially reduced, falling from 5.9% of the male population in 1911 to 1.7% in 1921. Female additions also fell, from 6.3 to 3.3% without sustaining military casualties. The consequence of these changes was to effect a marked change in the age distribution of the population of Scotland. There were two aspects to this, comprising a fall in births during the war – so that the proportion of children under fifteen years of age was much lower in 1921 than it had been in 1901 – and a loss of young men in the conflict. As a result, the 1921 male population was far more heavily weighted to those over thirty years of age than had been the case twenty years earlier. Even so, it can be argued that the demographic effects of the First World War were not great. In Scotland, migration muted the effect of military casualties on the population distribution, since migration, like war, affects the young proportionately more than the older generations. War may simply have made migration less necessary.[25] This is supported by the fact that the probability of female marriage showed little change between the 1911 and 1921 censuses. The high levels of unemployment actually recorded in the 1920s would have been even greater had more men survived the conflict.

War has an obvious and immediate impact on the level and structure of employment. The mobilisation of a substantial part of the male labour force soon caused shortages in the labour market. In the eighteen months following the outbreak of hostilities, 29.4% of British workers had volunteered for military service, including over 40% of professional men and those engaged in finance and commerce.[26] Scotland lost the equivalent of 46.8% of the male workforce recorded in 1911, and 41.4% of those aged between 15 and 49 years, to military service in the course of the war. In addition to this massive diversion of manpower for direct participation in the war, the economy generated an increased demand for labour for the wide range of activities needed to support and supply the military effort. The burden necessarily fell upon males too young or too old to fight, those in reserved occupations, and upon women workers. Not surprisingly, the latter group increased from 593,210 in 1911 to 638,575 a decade later, although by then the female labour force was already contracting in response to the restoration of peace and economic recession.

The long run pattern of the main sectors of male employment in Scotland is indicated in Figure 1. In some industries, notably shipbuilding and the iron, steel and engineering trades, there was a clear upward surge in employment in the war decade. In agriculture, the long-term pattern of contraction was temporarily halted, while in the service sector the long-run expansionary trend was reversed. The same pattern can be seen in sharper relief in employment changes between 1911 and 1921 which clearly reflected the diversion of manpower from services, construction and some industries towards engineering, shipbuilding and the armed forces. The long term pattern for female employment is clear but a little more complex, as shown in Figure 2. There was a temporary shift towards military and manufacturing employment and a temporary decline in some service industries. There was also some acceleration of trends already in progress, notably the decline in employment in textiles and clothing manufacture, and the growth in employment in the food and drink trades and, especially, in distribution. In the war decade there were substantial transfers of working women into distribution and military activities. For women, it appears the impact of the war was just as important in fostering the long-term and large-scale growth in employment in distributive services as in the short-term and highly visible draft into munitions work.

Even so, one of the most contentious aspects of wartime employment change was the 'dilution' of the labour force, as semi-skilled and unskilled workers, often women, replaced skilled men who were on military service. Board of Trade figures for Great Britain showed an increase in female employment from 2.18 million to 2.97 million in the four years following July 1914. Of these new jobs for women 704,000 were replacements for male workers and many of which were in the engineering and munitions industries.[27] Industrial dilution was primarily a process by which men were replaced by women. Typically, in the first stage a substantial number of new workers were recruited on the bottom rungs of the work hierarchy, while the later phase comprised an upgrading of all workers throughout the labour hierarchy. Given the substantial number of workers enlisting for military service, the efforts of skilled men, who were at a premium, became concentrated on the most difficult and specialised elements in the manufacturing process.

The process of dilution was especially marked in munitions manufacture which was strongly represented in the west of Scotland. The number of women employed in munitions in Scotland rose to 31,500 by October 1918, with the vast majority employed in the industrial west.[28] In munitions manufacture the distinction between skilled and unskilled was strongly marked prior to the war. But the pressure of demand and the shortage of labour led the government to take the initiative in forcing dilution and increasing the mechanisation of production. The Shells and Fuses Agreement 1915 introduced single purpose and mainly automatic machines, or the adaptation of existing machines for repetitive processes. These were mainly operated by women. The Treasury Agreement of the same year allowed the substitution of semi-skilled for fully skilled workers using turret and capstan lathes. The Dilution Scheme, also introduced in that year, upgraded workers to higher levels of technical competence. Furthermore, cost constraints were relaxed in order to maximise production, so that productive efficiency was less important than it would have been under peacetime competitive conditions. There was a further round of upgrading in 1917 when there was a skilled manpower shortage, again as a consequence of additional demands for military recruitment.

The dilution programme was not popular with the trade unions who remained suspicious of its long-term implications. The Clyde Dilution Commission was established at the beginning of 1916 to negotiate local agreements. There was industrial unrest on Clydeside, notably a strike at the Parkhead Works in March 1916 concerning obstacles placed by Beardmore's against the efforts of the shop stewards to organise women workers. This spread to other firms and delayed the completion of a howitzer gun needed at the front. In response, the government suppressed the dispute and 'deported' to other parts of Scotland several of the perceived ringleaders who remained in internal exile for over a year.[29] Despite the apprehension of the trade unions, all agreements expressly indicated that dilution should persist only during the war and did not warrant 'any employer making such arrangements in the shops as will effect a permanent restriction of employment of any trade in favour of semi-skilled men or female labour.'[30] Employment in the engineering and munitions industries rose by over 500,000 during the war, drawing in many semi-skilled workers. Consequently, by the end of the war there had been a vast increase in the supply of workers with some knowledge of machine processing work and a large contingent of semi-skilled women workers. There was also a substantial increase in trade union membership during the war especially amongst semi-skilled men and women workers. In the course of the war, the National Federation of Women Workers increased its membership from 10,000 to 50,000, and there were over 60,000 women in the National Federation of General Workers by 1918.[31] Women were still paid much less than men, although the war narrowed the gap in pay differentials between skilled and unskilled workers. Even so, at the end of the war there was an immediate and effective restoration of traditional working practices.

As men volunteered or were conscripted, women drawn into employment in traditionally 'male' activities faced difficulties in their new jobs. There was opposition from the male staff to the employment of women on the Aberdeen Tramways. The President of the Aberdeen Trades Council declared they were a danger to the public (on the trams) and that to employ them on Sundays was to lower the dignity of the city. The first woman conductor in Aberdeen started work in August 1915, and women were employed as drivers from the beginning of 1917. By 1917–18, the period of maximum employment, there were 150 women, principally conductors, compared to 229 men, although there were only five female drivers. By 1919–20, female employment had fallen to eleven, nearly all of whom were office staff and and no conductors remained.[32]

Trade dislocation

The impact of war on any economy obviously extends beyond the immediate requirements of military provision. There are indirect costs involved in the loss of peacetime activities, as industries are subject to loss and/or distortion in their production and trading activities. There are usually additional distortions in that inflation generates winners and losers in income redistribution, as does the uneven increase in incomes. Furthermore, there is a direct cost in that warfare, especially in the modern world, is highly expensive and must be financed.

Like the rest of the United Kingdom, the Scottish economy in the early twentieth century depended heavily on international trade, especially for bulk products which were transported at much lower cost by sea than by land. The war effected a major disruption to that trade. The gross tonnage of seagoing merchant vessels lost in the war reached almost 15.4 million, of which Great Britain alone sustained almost 8.9 million tons, or 57.8% of the world total.[33] The east coast ports, facing

Germany across the North Sea, were more severely affected than those in the west which were relatively well protected from the threat of the German navy. Scottish coal production in the east was hit by the loss of export markets. In 1913 the main export markets for Scottish coal had been Germany, Denmark and Sweden, followed by Italy, France and Russia. The great bulk of this was shipped from east coast ports. Scottish coal exports as a whole fell from 10.4 million tons in 1913 to 2.6 million tons by 1919, and the main burden fell on the east coast.[34] While domestic demand rose slightly in the war, it was insufficient to compensate for the loss of exports so that total output fell.

The nature of hostilities gave a great advantage to west coast ports, especially Glasgow. Jute imports were landed there during hostilities instead of making the now hazardous journey round the northern coast to Dundee. Similarly, coal from Fife and the Lothians was shipped from Glasgow rather than from Leith. Even so, the volume of goods passing through the port of Glasgow fell from 10.4 million tons in 1913 to 6.9 million tons by 1919. The volume of foreign imports remained steady but coastwise imports fell as did all exports. Nevertheless, trade remained extremely important for war supplies. The value of imports of arms and munitions into Scotland rose from £6,598 in 1916 to £3.7 million in 1917 and £10 million in 1918.[35]

The disruption to normal economic activities caused by trade dislocation abroad was compounded by inflation at home. War marks a sudden and extreme redistribution of activities and resource allocation. As a result, some shortages will almost invariably occur. This generates price inflation. Both wholesale and retail prices grew during the first three years of the war at a fairly constant rate. The imposition of price controls and the provision of subsidies checked inflation from the summer of 1917 until the Armistice. When the controls were removed, and especially after May 1919, prices rose again. The growth of wage rates lagged behind prices but earnings, when they were determined by piece rates or overtime, grew more rapidly. There were two main reasons for this: the shortage of labour under wartime conditions and improved technology. In fact, unemployment fell during the war from 3.3% in 1914 to less than 1% during the war, before rising to 2.4% in 1919.[36] This led to difficulties in the munitions industry, where piece rate workers could earn more that their skilled supervisors who were paid by a time rate, although these skilled workers were awarded a bonus of 12.5% in 1917.[37] Even so, during the war the main gains in earnings were achieved by semi-skilled and unskilled workers. Bricklayers did less well than their labourers, as did engineers relative to their labourers.

This trend towards wage equalisation was not the result of policy but an unforeseen effect of the practice adopted in the earlier years of the war of giving flat rate increases to allow wages to keep up with the rise in the price of essential goods. On the other hand, many white collar workers secured little if any increase in pay during the entire period of the war. The greatest gain in living standards was probably secured through the reduction in the working week in 1919. This large reduction was proposed by an industrial conference held by representatives of employers and employees which recommended a statutory forty-eight hour working week. As a result, the hours of time-workers in many industries were reduced without any change in the weekly wage. Generally, although not universally, piece rates were raised, so that the same weekly income could be obtained by working the reduced hours. The reductions affected 6.4 million workers and marked an average cut in the working week by 6.5 hours or about 10%.[38]

The effects of wartime needs and priorities had widely divergent effects on established industries. Some were able to continue with little adjustment. The North British Locomotive Company of Glasgow, for example, diverted part of its productive activity to the production of shells and sea mines. But it continued to manufacture locomotives, a total of 1,412 in the war years, almost half of which were for military use, principally in France. The rest were exported as commercial sales to India, China, Australia and South America. The main hazard to normal working for this firm was a shortage of steel. Other industries actually gained from the disruption of normal trade. Chemicals had been previously imported from Germany on a substantial scale, but during the war some producers were able to develop substitutes for those imports, aided by government investment for scientific research. Consequently there was a large increase in the production of paraffin wax and candles, lubricating greases, mineral oils, sulphate of ammonia and sulphuric acid. Some manufactures benefited from government intervention. Prior to 1914, half the sugar consumed in Britain was processed from beet imported from Austria and Germany. In the war, a Commission on Sugar Supplies was established by the government as the sole importing agent, buying extensively in Cuba, Mauritius, Java and South America. The Commission also took control of sugar refineries, supplying them with raw sugar, but controlling prices and profits. Before the war, Greenock handled about 4.7 million cwts of sugar per annum. There was a slump early in the war, so that unrefined sugar imports were only 3.1 million cwts in 1915, but by 1917 and 1918 imports exceeded 4.8 million cwts despite rationing.[39]

But for many industries and companies the war was a massive and malign disturbance to their normal activities. Some were adversely affected by the supply of raw materials. The main source of yarn for the fancy flannel trade of the west of Scotland was Belgium. Woollen production was further hampered by War Office controls which involved the purchase of the entire wool clip and a claim to 70% of the output. This generated considerable price inflation. Cotton remained free of such restrictions until the shortage of shipping tonnage led to the imposition of restrictions in 1917. Scottish producers adjusted as well as possible to these changes, taking advantage of the government demand for army blankets and flannel shirts. By 1919, however, the export of textiles from Glasgow had fallen to 57% of its 1913 level for cotton piece goods and to 62% for woollen goods. For others, problems were simply postponed. In the chemical industry export markets were lost, partly as a consequence of government restrictions, while high wages, a shorter working week, and expensive raw materials represented major cost problems at the end of the war.

The experience of the jute industry demonstrates almost the full range of wartime effects. It was heavily concentrated in Dundee, and was entirely dependent on international trade for its raw material. When the industry worked at full capacity it occupied 25% of male and 67% of female workers in Dundee. Yet jute depended on the hazardous supply of a raw material, the cultivation of which was heavily concentrated in the Ganges delta and subject to frequent fluctuations in the size of the annual crop. The industry in Dundee thus depended entirely on international trade for its raw material. Furthermore, in 1913, 54% of its output was exported, principally to the United States, Argentina and Germany. During the war, government purchases of sandbags soon forced prices to a high level. This, in turn, induced an unsuccessful eleven week strike in 1916 for higher wages. Further massive price increases in 1917 brought government intervention through price controls. Demand was further increased by the effective removal of competition from Calcutta by the government, which commandeered shipping and prohibited the export of jute goods from India to the United Kingdom. Also, demand accumulated from customers who had been pushed out of the market by government purchases. The food industry in particular was in great difficulty because of the shortage of bags and sacks essential for distribution. Further government intervention in 1918 saw the introduction of a priority grading system for purchases and controls on exports.[40] The removal of restrictions at the end of the war was expected to reduce prices. Hessian cloth per ton had increased between 1916 and 1919 from £25 to £45, although the Calcutta price had remained at £15.[41] Both Dundee jute companies, and those owned by Scots but based in Calcutta, made large profits in the war, and the Dundee workers enjoyed higher wages. But prices collapsed after the war and the removal of trade restrictions reopened the threat of competition from Calcutta in world markets.

In war all efforts are geared towards military victory. Little attention is paid to the replacement of ageing machinery or the refurbishment of the economic infrastructure. Assets tend to be run down or even worked to destruction. The deficit in capital replacement and maintenance is a normal legacy of war. In the coal mines, there was a shortage of timber for pit props and a shortage of wagons and trucks both within the pits and on the railways. The easiest seams were worked out – efficient operation was not a serious consideration. Coal cutting machinery improved productivity but the fall in the use of mechanical conveyer belts offset that gain. The railways suffered from a lack of investment and a shortage of wagons which caused major problems for the coal industry. The individual operation of separate companies was highly inefficient. A scheme was introduced in 1917 to rationalise the transport of coal so that it would travel the minimum distance necessary. One Scottish railway company, comparing its experience in October 1917 with that in October 1916, estimated that the changes could save 2.6 miles per ton equivalent to 2.67 million ton miles and 334,450 wagon miles per month.[42] In Aberdeen the routine replacement of track and cars on the tramway system was postponed. By 1920, over 70% of the trams were over 17 years old (a 15 year life span had originally been assumed) and the service had seriously deteriorated because there were insufficient trams fit for service.

Paying for the war

Wars are always costly. The First World War demonstrated how expensive a war with modern technology could be, although it was a lesson which was soon forgotten. As Figure 3 indicates, government spending escalated rapidly during the war and soon outstripped revenues. The state of balance in the national accounts soon changed to a massive deficit and, while the long run state of balance was restored after the conclusion of the war, an accumulated debt remained.

The greater part of the funds to pay for the war were raised by government borrowing. Thereafter, the balance was raised by taxation which increased almost sevenfold between 1913–14 and 1918–19. There was a substantial change in the pattern of revenue raised: property taxation grew modestly and became a rapidly falling share of revenue. Similarly, Customs and Excise revenue, which had been the major source of taxation at the beginning of the war, diminished in importance. The principal growth in taxation fell on incomes, including supertax and excess profits tax, which together grew from 24.2% of total revenue on the eve of the war to 64.9% in 1918–19. Income tax also impinged upon more citizens as the exemption rate fell from an annual income of £160 before the war to £130 in 1915–16, and as inflation increased money incomes. Supertax, however, applied only to incomes in excess of £2,000 per annum.

The relative poverty of Scotland, compared to England and Wales although not Ireland, meant that Scotland made a relatively lower contribution in taxation. In the years immediately preceding the war, the Scottish contribution to the net receipts of the Inland Revenue averaged only 80% of the contribution of England and Wales in per capita terms. This share increased during the conflict, but the Scottish per capita taxation revenue for the period 1911–12 to 1919–20 averaged 86% of that for England and Wales.[43] Scotland paid less per head under most of the categories of taxation. In 1919–20, for example, Scotland's per capita share of taxation, expressed as a proportion of the revenue obtained from England and Wales, was particularly low with regard to property taxes: 55% for Stamp Duties, 39% for Land Tax, and 57% for Inhabited House Duty. With regard to income tax, which accounted for 44% of Scottish taxation in that financial year, the ratio to England and Wales was close to the aggregate figure of 86%. Scotland did, however, pay rather more in Excess Profits Duty because of the importance of munitions production in Scotland. This form of taxation accounted for 46% of the total Scottish contribution in 1919–20. In that year it was at almost the same level as for England and Wales, but in the previous three financial years it had been markedly higher. Excess Profits Duty comprised a charge on the excess of the actual profit rate realised over a standard or normal rate of profit. Two definitions were formulated to define the standard rate of profit. One used a standard which was normally the average profit realised in any two of the three years before the war. The other used a percentage standard represented by a share of the capital employed in the business before the war, usually between 6 and 11%. The Munitions Levy, which was important in Scotland, applied only to firms controlled by the government. This entailed a charge on the excess profits above a defined retainable amount, plus special allowances for exceptional circumstances.[44] It was the increased payment through Excess Profits Duty by Scottish companies which primarily explains the convergence in per capita taxation between Scotland and the rest of Britain during the war.

The number of people liable to income tax in the United Kingdom in 1913–14 was 1.2 million and this figure rose to 1.5 million in 1915–16 when the exemption rate was lowered. Tax liability was further increased by inflation, so that by 1919–20 there were 6.8 million taxpayers.[45] Supertax payers were far fewer, numbering only 77,000 by 1920–21, compared to 14,000 in 1913–14. The sum of Scottish income liable to taxation increased from £83 million in 1913–14 to £267 million by 1919–20. The total liability of Scots to taxation per capita was still lower than that for England and Wales, remaining stable at about 77% of that rate for most of the war years. But there was convergence towards the close of the war and the Scottish rate reached 93% of that for England and Wales in 1919–20. Throughout, relatively low Scottish incomes provide the most obvious explanation for the disparity.

Bogart estimated the cost of the Great War at $186.3 billion net, of which Britain with $35.3 billion (19.0%) and Germany with $37.8 billion (20.3%) bore the major burden. This estimate included only the direct outlays made by the belligerents. If additional costs such as the destruction of property, loss of production and trade, and depreciation of capital are included, the cost increased to $370 billion. The full real cost is even harder to estimate since it should include the ruination of lives caused by gassing, trench fever, tuberculosis and other maladies suffered by those returned as 'wounded'. The loss of life was greater than in all nineteenth-century wars combined, which Bogart estimated at 4.4 million people, 2.1 million of whom died in the Napoleonic Wars. In contrast, the known dead in the First World War reached almost ten million plus three million presumed dead, and a further 20 million wounded. Great Britain sustained 8.1% of the known dead and 9.8% of the seriously wounded.[46]

Consequences

Recent analyses have suggested that the impact of the Great War on the British economy as a whole was seriously deleterious. Statistical analysis suggests that the First World War marked a major structural discontinuity, more significant than either the return to the gold standard in 1925 or the worldwide depression which followed the collapse of the American stock market in 1929. Critically, the excess demand of the war period produced a massive overvaluation of sterling, estimated at over

30% in the immediate post-war years. When normal trade was resumed in the 1920s, the massively weakened position of British manufacturers in export markets became apparent.[47] Other countries not involved directly in the conflict, took advantage of the war to expand their trade and production and to infiltrate markets vacated by the belligerent nations. Between 1913 and 1922, the number of power looms in India and Japan increased from 120,000 to 200,000. Steel production in Japan, China, India and Australia grew from 360,000 tons in 1913 to 858,000 tons a decade later.[48] British exports of cotton piece goods fell during and after the war, while those of Japan increased markedly, replacing them in Asian markets.

Another strand of the same argument reinforces the malign effect of wartime disruption. The effect of controls and shortages generated an accumulation of unsatisfied demand, as well as an accumulation of forced savings. Private consumption fell by 7.7% amongst civilians during war and by 15.8% when military personnel are included. As might be expected, compared to pre-war consumption, there was a decline in spending on alcoholic drink by £232 million, on food by £101 million and on clothing by £165 million. Lack of spending opportunities generated the growth of small savings accounts in War Savings certificates, in Trustee Savings Bank accounts and in Post Office accounts, and most of these funds were drawn on to support the national debt. Broadberry argues that this accumulation of spending power underpinned the substantial cut in hours worked in 1919–20. The reduction in hours of work was not matched by a cut in money wages and this, together with the effect of a fall in prices, increased the real wage.[49] The fall in prices was reinforced by the fact that the pound remained overvalued after the war by as much as 17%, and government attempts to return to the high pre-war exchange parity forced prices downward. This combination of events seriously weakened British industrial competitiveness. It was augmented by financial weakness resulting from the cost of the war. The First World War was paid for principally by borrowing, both at home and abroad, particularly in the United States. In 1914 the British national debt had been £650 million, and much of that had been accumulated in the Napoleonic Wars over a century earlier. By 1920, the debt had risen to £7,828 million.[50]

These consequences of the war, in accumulated debt and loss of international competitiveness, were just as influential in Scotland as they were in other parts of Britain. The war certainly shifted the balance of international trade against Scottish shipbuilders by increasing worldwide capacity, and against textile manufacturers by enabling competitors to establish themselves in Asian markets and especially in India. But the war also demonstrated the fragility of the Scottish heavy industry base, with the separation of iron from steel manufacture and the growing need for imported raw materials. The war exacerbated a situation which was already a source of industrial weakness, accelerating the decline rather than causing it. Scottish heavy industry faced great difficulties in the 1920s, as it had also done in the 1900s. In the case of Scottish industry, it seems probable that the discontinuity identified by Greasley and Oxley was not caused by the war. Rather, they were coincident and related events, augmenting and distorting their separate influences.

Many of the changes induced by the war were temporary, in the readjustment of agricultural production, in the decline of coal mining in the Lothians and Fife, and in the boom in the jute industry. The loss of manpower through injury and death represented a host of personal and family tragedies. But given the high unemployment of the 1920s, this cannot be regarded as a source of significant economic difficulties. Wages did eventually improve and hours of work fell as a result of the war, but it was lack of work which provided the spectre overshadowing the following decade. The progress of women in the workplace was accelerated, but immediately and extensively eroded by the subsequent recession. The war did, however, demonstrate work capabilities which had hitherto not been widely accepted.

There are few benefits from war of any kind. This is true of the economy. The few positive changes in work practice which wartime conditions allowed, such as more flexible working, increased mechanisation and the relaxation of demarcation conventions, which might have increased competitiveness had they continued, were swept away swiftly after the war as recession took hold. The economic effects of the war were primarily to restructure international trade and finance, and to undermine the stability of the era which preceded it. As an open trading economy, Scotland was fully exposed to the harsh effects of those changes in the 1920s. In 1919 Scotland was a vulnerable economy with many inherent weaknesses, as evidenced by widespread poverty, outdated technology and a limited capability to succeed in international competition. But all these same characteristics had been present in 1913, on the eve of the Great War.

Table 1. *Components of population change in Scotland*

	Male 1901–11	Male 1911–21	Female 1901–11	Female 1911–21
Natural increase	285,299	229,324	257,544	204,856
Loss by migration	−150,215	−116,521	−103,827	−122,066
Loss by war deaths	0	−74,000	0	0
Net gain	135,084	38,803	153,717	82,790

Source: Census of Scotland 1921, vol. ii, p. vi (HMSO, Edinburgh)

Figure 1. *Scottish Male Employment by Major Sectors, 1901–1931*

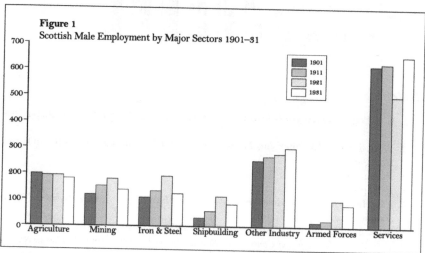

Figure 2. *Scottish Female Employment by Major Sectors, 1901–1931*

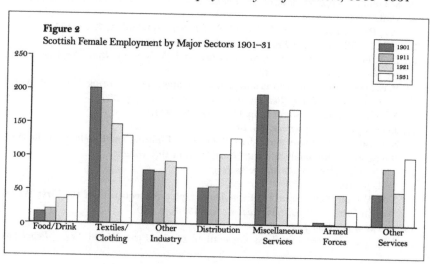

Figure 3. *Uk Government Income and Expenditure 1911/12 – 1920/21*

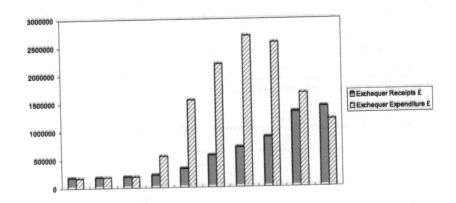

Notes

1. E. L. Bogart, *Direct and Indirect Costs of the Great World War* (Oxford, 1919), pp. 267–74.
2. W. R. Scott. and J. Cunnison, *The Industries of the Clyde Valley during the War* (Oxford, 1924), p. 77.
3. *Ibid.*, pp. 81, 84.
4. *Ibid.*, p. 64.
5. J. R. Hume and M. S. Moss, *Beardmore: The History of a Scottish Industrial Giant* (London, 1979), pp. 118, 142.
6. Scott and Cunnison, *Industries of the Clyde Valley*, p. 102.
7. P. L. Payne, *Growth and Contraction: Scottish Industry c.1860–1990. Studies in Scottish Economic and Social History*, vol. 2 (Glasgow, 1992), pp. 27–8.
8. S. Tolliday, *Business, Banking and Politics: The Case of British Steel 1918–1939* (Harvard, 1987), p. 85.
9. P. L. Payne, *Colvilles and the Scottish Steel Industry* (Oxford, 1979), p. 127.
10. T. H. Middleton, *Food Production in War* (Oxford, 1923), pp. 90–1.
11. D. T. Jones, J. F. Duncan, H. M. Conacher, and W. R. Scott, *Rural Scotland During the War* (Oxford, 1926), p. 133.
12. P. E. Dewey, 'British farm profits and government policy during the First World War', *Economic History Review*, 2nd ser., xxxvii (1984), p. 386.
13. Middleton, *Food Production*, pp. 112, 154, 192, 241.
14. Jones *et al.*, *Rural Scotland*, pp. 16, 203, 242–5.
15. See also E. A. Cameron and I. J. M. Robertson, 'Fighting and bleeding for the land: the Scottish Highlands and the Great War' in this volume.
16. Jones *et al.*, *Rural Scotland*, pp. 84–5.
17. *Ibid.*, p. 119.
18. J. M. Winter, 'Some aspects of the demographic consequences of the First World War in Britain', *Population Studies*, xxx (1976), p. 540.
19. *Census of Scotland 1921*.
20. J. M. Winter, 'Britain's 'Lost Generation' of the First World War', *Population*

Studies, xxxi (1971) p. 451; N. B. Dearle, *Labour Costs of the World War to Great Britain 1914–1922* (New Haven, Conn. 1940).

21. *Ibid.*, p. 451.
22. *Ibid.*, p. 450.
23. Winter, 'Some aspects', p. 549.
24. Winter, 'Lost Generation', p. 462.
25. D. Baines, 'Population, migration and regional development 1870–1939', in R. Floud and D. McCoskey (eds), *The Economic History of Britain since 1700: Volume Two 1860–1939* (Cambridge, 1994), p. 46.
26. Winter, 'Lost Generation', p. 454.
27. G. D. H. Cole, *Trade Unionism and Munitions* (Oxford, 1923), p. 186.
28. Scott and Cunnison, *Industries of the Clyde Valley*, p. 98.
29. Cole, *Trade Unionism*, pp. 126–7.
30. Quoting the Shells and Fuses Agreement, *ibid.*, pp. 67–8.
31. Cole, *Trade Unionism*, p. 204.
32. M. J. R. Mitchell, 'Municipal Transport in Aberdeen 1898–1975' (University of Aberdeen, Ph.D. thesis, 1993), pp. 71–4.
33. Bogart, *Direct and Indirect Costs*, p. 289.
34. Scott and Cunnison, *Industries of the Clyde Valley*, p. 196.
35. *Ibid.*, p. 62.
36. F. W. Hirst, *The Consequences of the War to Great Britain* (Oxford, 1934), p. 282.
37. A. L. Bowley, *Prices and Wages in the United Kingdom 1914–1920* (Oxford, 1921), p. 99.
38. *Ibid.*, p. 101.
39. Scott and Cunnison, *Industries of the Clyde Valley*, p. 123.
40. Jones *et al.*, *Rural Scotland*, p. 284.
41. *Ibid.*, p. 288.
42. Scott and Cunnison, *Industries of the Clyde Valley*, p. 37.
43. *Report of the Commissioners of H.M. Inland Revenue, 1920.* (Cd 1083), pp. 7, 89.
44. *Ibid.*, pp. 86–8.
45. Hirst, *Consequences of the War*, p. 195.
46. Bogart, *Direct and Indirect Costs*, pp. 267–74.
47. D. Greasley and L. Oxley, 'Discontinuities in competitiveness: the impact of the First World War on British industry', *Economic History Review*, 2nd ser., xlix (1996), pp. 93, 98.
48. Hirst, *Consequences of the War*, p. 267.
49. S. N. Broadberry, 'The emergence of mass unemployment: explaining macroeconomic trends in Britain during the Trans-World War I period', *Economic History Review*, 2nd ser., xlii (1990), pp. 271, 273.
50. Hirst, *Consequences of the War*, p. 251.

CHAPTER TWO

The Impact of the First World War on Scottish Politics

I. G. C. Hutchison

FOR MOST OF the decade before the Great War, the Liberal Party seemed in a virtually impregnable position. Both in terms of its own strength and in the weakness of the two opposition parties, the Liberals were better placed than in Britain as a whole. The party had won 58 of the 70 Scottish seats in the December 1910 election, against 212 out of 489 in England and Wales. Labour, with 3 MPs, had under-performed compared to 39 wins in England and Wales, while the Unionists, with a mere 10 seats, lagged far behind the party's tally of 238 south of the border.

Politics on the eve

The strength of Liberalism lay in part in the continuing pull of certain traditional party issues which were more prevalent than elsewhere in Britain, and in part in the advocacy of the New Liberal programme. Temperance reformers, for example, were a significant coalition in Scotland, embracing many Independent Labour Party (ILP) and Labour supporters, as well as religious evangelicals. Similarly, the land question was a particularly potent local issue. As the Labour Party acknowledged in an enquiry held in 1911: 'the Land Question in Scotland dominates everything else. Scotland has stood by the Liberal Government so solidly because it hates the House of Lords and the landlords'.[1]

Lloyd George's 1914 land campaign accordingly drew a strong response in Scotland.[2] While the issue was popular among traditional Liberals because of its historical association with the Highland Clearances and the struggles of the Free Church, it also reached social reformers through the concept of the taxation of land values. The 'Single Tax' was widely seen as the best device to finance social reform, without resorting to tariff reform or higher income taxes. The Scottish wing of the progressive alliance was further buttressed by the Dundee election victory in 1908 of Winston Churchill, a vociferous proponent of the New Liberalism. Forward-looking Liberals were urging the case for the minimum wage, nationalisation of the mines, state afforestation and poor law reform. Even on the housing question – later to be a vital source of support for Labour – the social radicals offered policies which promised to tackle the crisis, mainly by applying the land-tax principle to urban areas.[3]

The face of the party was also adapting to the times. Since the 1906 election, the advent of younger, socially-engaged MPs had given the party an image of energy and contemporaneity, contrasting favourably with its rather jaded and elderly appearance in the later 1890s and early 1900s. There seemed to be fewer of the older type of solid local businessmen, small lairds and pillars of the Dissenting churches in Liberal ranks. In their stead were articulate and forceful individuals, notably advocates, barristers, journalists and teachers. At the parliamentary level, for example, Arthur Ponsonby, J. W. Gulland, A. MacCallum Scott, J. W. Pratt and J. M. Hogge were the leading lights in this process of re-invigoration.

Grass-roots organisation remained equally healthy. The Young Scots – a ginger group formed in the difficult years of the Boer War – were active in many parts of the country, especially in industrial-urban areas, and continued to produce policy statements which promoted radical ideas as an alternative to socialism. In particular, the movement's espousal of Scottish Home Rule made it attractive to a broad section of opinion. In 1910 the Young Scots had a membership total of 2,500 – about the same as the Scottish membership of the ILP.[4] Constituency organisation, which had frequently atrophied under the old guard, was shaken up by joint pressure from a revivified central office and the impetus of new MPs. Ponsonby, for example, built up the Stirling Burghs party, long neglected in the days of Campbell-Bannerman's personal popularity, while in Bridgeton MacCallum Scott attracted new young office-bearers to combat the challenge of Labour. The number of subscribers to the party stayed buoyant, and there was little evidence of the propaganda war being lost by the Liberals in the immediate pre-war years.[5]

A combination of factors left the Tories struggling to win the affection of voters in Scotland. The noisy resistance to the Scottish Land Bills, and the accompanying formation of the Scottish Landowners' Federation – mainly spearheaded by prominent Tories like Buccleuch – damaged the perception of the party in the years of heightened interest in the land question.

Tariff reform was similarly a greater drawback in Scotland than in England. Scottish agriculture, much less dependent on arable cultivation, was less affected by foreign competition. Hence many landowners opposed protectionism. The Scottish manufacturing sector, in comparison to England, was more geared to international markets and accordingly viewed tariff reform with grave unease. The heavy industries opposed the trend of Unionist policy from 1903: the two Tory representatives in parliament of this interest, J. G. A. Baird and J. M. Denny, came out on the side of free trade, and defections to the Liberals in 1906 were rife.[6]

As late as the end of 1912, George Younger, a strong protectionist, warned his party leader that tariff reform was the stumbling-block to advances in Scotland:

> One and all of them [Unionists] ... are in a considerable state of anxiety with regard to the party's position upon the question of food taxes in connection with any scheme of Imperial Preference, and they are insistent that their chances and prospects may be blighted if any positive determination to tax grain in any shape or form is attached to our scheme of preference. We have all had experience during the last three elections of the difficulties caused by our supposed attachment to this policy ... so long as it is possible to misrepresent the position and to flood the constituencies once again with lying posters of one kind and another, we cannot, I am afraid, hope that the undoubted disaffection towards the Government is strong enough to carry the [fifteen or sixteen] seats we must win in Scotland if we are to have a working majority ... The position in Scotland is an extremely critical one from the Scottish point of view.[7]

The plight of the party was intensified by the failure of the familiar stand-by policy – opposition to Irish Home Rule – to generate much momentum. This had proven spectacularly successful in mobilising support for the party in the 1880s and 1890s. But during the Third Home Rule Bill crisis, interest in Scotland was only modest, both in comparison with past protests and with elsewhere in the United Kingdom. When the Irish Unionists took their case to Merseyside, they were feted and attracted vast crowds, numbering perhaps 150,000; yet in Glasgow they could only attract a mere 8,000.[8] In the run of by-elections leading up to the outbreak of war, it is revealing that neither Liberal nor Tory post-mortems put much stress on the impact of opposition to Irish Home Rule as an influence on the results.

The Unionists also suffered from a degree of defective organisation. Liberal Unionists had remained distinct from the Conservatives in Scotland, whereas in England virtual full integration had been achieved quite quickly after 1886. The merger carried through in 1911 was only achieved amid considerable bitterness on the side of the Liberal Unionists, who claimed to have a different style and political culture to the Tories. Squabbles over the right to nominate candidates added to the gulf, while the tariff reform controversy served to remind Liberal Unionists of their identity and historic roots. Without real fusion, either at the central or local level, Unionist organisation often displayed an uncertain quality. The three years before the start of the war were occupied in devising new administrative structures and integrating personnel from the two camps into one unit, a task not everywhere completed by August 1914.[9]

Labour's failure to make inroads in Scotland was perplexing, not least to the party itself. Scotland had, after all, produced the two main leaders of the party, Keir Hardie and Ramsay MacDonald, and the impetus to form a separate party had originated with the Scottish Labour Party, established in 1888. The formation of the Labour Representation Committee (LRC) in 1900 was preceded by some months by its Scottish equivalent, the Scottish Workers Representation Committee (SWRC). The subsequent retardation in Scotland owed much to a potent mix of institutional, organisational and ideological factors.

The institutional framework in Scotland was weaker than in England in crucial respects. Trade union membership was proportionately lower in the former before the war. Many of the Scottish unions were small, localised outfits with little wider vision or 'clout'. Few of the unions took to political organisation in a whole-hearted manner. The miners – potentially the most important body – were either organisationally inept or politically indifferent for almost the entire pre-war period. Hardie, a miners' agent himself, bewailed the miners' unco-ordinated efforts to mobilise the vote:

If he were asked to explain why all the miners' candidates in Scotland were defeated [in 1906], he would say that it lay at the door of the Miners' Federation. They refused to spend money beforehand on the constituencies which they were to fight.[10]

It was only immediately before war began that signs of serious registration work in the coalfields could be detected. Even then it was confined to a smattering of seats – mainly some districts in West Fife and certain parts of Lanarkshire.[11]

The SWRC, although launched ahead of the LRC, turned out to be a highly defective organisation. It was under-funded and badly administered. Candidates were rarely found in time; propaganda material was not properly prepared or distributed; constituency parties were left to fend for themselves.[12] It was absorbed into the Labour Party in 1908, after the strategies of the two at by-elections came into conflict.[13] As a consequence, the development of a proper organisation was much delayed in Scotland. It was not until 1912, for instance, that a city-wide Labour Party was established in Glasgow.

Despite the early interest in ILP socialism shown in Scotland before 1914, only limited and sporadic progress was made in spreading these ideas across a wide spectrum of the working class. Total membership of the ILP was proportionately smaller than in other industrial areas of Britain – notably South Wales – and many branches had only a short life, opening and closing within a few years.[14] Looking back from the vantage point of the 1920s, a prominent activist reflected on the state of the pre-war ILP: 'The record of the Glasgow ILP Executive is a struggle with adversity. The party did not seem to make headway.' [15] The bulk of the ILP's support seems to have been drawn from the lower middle class, such as clerks, and skilled workers, with little penetration into the rest of the working class.[16] In addition, the Irish nationalists pursued a tactical policy, oscillating between Labour and the Liberals as electoral circumstances dictated, so leaving Labour unable to count on the wholehearted support of a sizeable portion of its potential constituency.

There was little electoral evidence in the last years of peace that the prevailing political disposition was liable to radical alteration. In particular, any forward march by Labour, necessarily at the expense of the Liberals, was hesitant at best. Labour came nowhere near winning any of the by-elections it fought. In three instances, Labour wounded the Liberals by taking enough votes to let the Unionists win, albeit by wafer-thin margins. In two of these seats, however, there were signs that the miners were distancing themselves from the Liberals. In Midlothian and South Lanarkshire the creditable performance of Labour was seen to be almost exclusively derived from the mining vote. But there were other seats where a more negative picture was presented. In North-East Lanarkshire, the party's share of the poll in 1911 (16.3%) was significantly lower than in previous by-elections fought in 1901 (21.7%) and 1904 (27.9%). Elsewhere Labour did not consider conditions to be propitious for a fight. This occurred at Kilmarnock, a constituency with a substantial mining vote. Even more striking was the decision not to contest Govan in 1911. Govan was the only Clydeside seat to go to Labour in 1918, yet at this earlier juncture the local ILP believed that there was no ground for expecting a decent performance. There was likewise no Labour intervention in the two solid working-class Glasgow seats of St Rollox and Tradeston, while the mining constituency of West Lothian – adjacent to Midlothian – was not fought in November 1913. All three seats were won by Labour in 1922. Labour's plans for fighting the next general election, had war not broken out, were distinctly modest in Scotland.

Similarly, the Unionists were not making dramatic gains: most of their victories depended on Labour splitting the anti-Tory vote. Where there was a straight fight with a Liberal, the latter held off the Unionist challenge in all but one out of nine contests.[17] Elsewhere, while bigger swings were recorded, the Liberals remained fairly unassailable.

Wartime politics

The splits induced within the Liberal Party by the war were deep and widespread in Scotland. Schisms began with the declaration of war, with Arthur Ponsonby immediately opposing Britain's involvement. The introduction of the Conscription Bill further heightened divisions within Scottish Liberalism. For example, J. H. Whitehouse, MP for Mid-Lanark-shire, was prominent on the Anti-Conscription Committee from the outset.[18] The accession of Lloyd George to the premiership in 1916 sharpened the crisis for the party in Scotland. In part, this was because Asquith, as a Scottish MP, had a particular pull on many of the party faithful. On the other hand, Churchill, who along with Lloyd George was a major proponent of Coalition government, also sat for a Scottish seat. He likewise inspired affection among many in Scotland, notably the younger radical adherents, one of whom, MacCallum Scott, was his parliamentary private secretary for most of the war.

Perhaps the most destructive feature in the long-term was the rift in the radical camp, whose pre-war vigour had helped the party face the challenge posed by Labour. J. W. Pratt and J. W. Greig, both progressive Liberals, followed Lloyd George. Others of the pre-war advanced Liberals stayed with Asquith. On the more Whiggish side, most became Asquithians, including the Dumfriesshire MP, Percy Molteno, a South African gold millionaire who had been hostile to the pre-war social reform legislation. However, moderate Liberal backers of the 1916 Coalition included two influential newspaper owners: Sir Henry Dalziel, MP for Kirkcaldy, and R. L. Harmsworth, MP for Caithness. The former was one of a trio of leaders of the Liberal War Committee, advocating the fight à l'outrance.[19]

Moreover, the unity of the Asquithian group was never firm, and a number of early supporters grew restive. Two of the most significant in this category were W. M. R. Pringle and J. M. Hogge. Although both tended to end up in the lobbies on the Asquithian side, it was really faute de mieux, rather than a positive endorsement.[20] Pringle, initially behind the war, grew increasingly unhappy with policy, and by late 1915 had adopted a distinctly critical stance. He declared the formation of the Coalition 'fatal to Liberalism' and 'disastrous to the country'; opposed breaches of free trade; and attacked the prosecution of members of the Clyde Workers' Committee (CWC).[21]

The disunity at Westminster had repercussions at constituency level, where two trends were apparent, both undermining Liberal strength. On the one hand, anti-war MPs ran into conflict with local supporters, and on the other, loss of morale spread through the ranks. Ponsonby's experiences give the most graphic instance of the former factor. His consistent outspoken criticism of the commitment to war soon produced a counter-reaction among his constituency activists. He was strongly urged by the association office bearers to moderate his outbursts, or, better still, stifle them entirely, on the grounds that the overwhelming feeling, even among former pro-Boers, was behind the war. Ponsonby spurned such cautious counsel and relations deteriorated sharply over the next two years.[22] Finally, at the end of 1916, the Liberal executive resolved that Ponsonby 'no longer commands their confidence and that they will be unable to recommend him as Liberal Candidate at the next election.'[23]

Two other examples may be cited. Like Ponsonby, Pringle's views led him into collision with his local activists. In December 1915, he was warned that there was little prospect of his being accepted as the party standard-bearer in a post-war election: 'I am afraid your chances at an election would be very small indeed, as we could not get men who would work for your return.'[24] Indeed, Pringle switched seats in 1918, running for Glasgow St Rollox. In January 1916, the Military Conscription Bill had been supported by the Aberdeen South constituency council, with only two dissenting votes. The sitting MP, G. B. Esslemont, asked whether he would support the government after this resolution, adamantly refused: 'I have no hesitation in saying that I won't.' A year later he announced his resignation, on the advice of his doctor.[25]

A major consequence of these tensions among MPs was to make the rank and file supporters – and, still more, voters – demoralised and disaffected, as one victim of the 1918 annihilation of Liberal candidates reported to his party leader.[26] So acute was the friction in the Stirling Burghs seat that in October 1916 the Liberal agent intimated his resignation and complete withdrawal from politics, adding that the party secretary was doing likewise.[27]

After peace returned, revivifying Liberal Party organisation proved extremely difficult. For example, in Stirling Burghs – solidly Liberal before 1914 – it was not until after the 1922 election that the local association was re-activated. A repeated problem after 1918 was the absence of new, young members. In 1920 the Aberdeen Liberals addressed the problem despairingly:

> The President then dealt with the matter of the older members of the association and indicated that there seemed to be a general feeling that younger men should be permitted and encouraged to take a more pre-eminent part in the management and work of the Association.[28]

The degree of progress made may be gauged from a report a couple of years later that the chairman of the Aberdeen South association wanted to stand down as his 'defective hearing' was impeding his efficiency in the chair.[29]

At the Scottish Liberal Association (SLA) headquarters, the consequences were apparent: funding dropped heavily and this forced reduced levels of activity. A calculation made in 1920 reckoned that 25% of subscription money was lost in the war years, with between 600 and 700 subscribers withdrawing because of 'sectional feeling.'[30] This paralysis at the centre left constituencies to manage as best they could with scant central support. In the run-up to the 1918 General Election, the SLA secretary left local parties to organise their own literature and canvass cards, providing special advice if needed.[31] As a result, influencing change in the constituencies was impeded. Efforts to merge men's and women's sections, initiated in mid-1917, had been implemented in barely one half of the seats by the autumn of 1918.[32]

Constituency associations also struggled to function while starved of finance. It was stated that at the end of 1916 the Stirling Liberals had received no subscriptions for three years.[33] On the day war ended, Aberdeen Liberals were informed that their committee: 'came to the conclusion that unless additional subscriptions were obtained, it would be impossible meantime to appoint Organisers'. Eighteen months later, the financial problems remained unsolved.[34]

The problems facing the Asquithian Liberals were underlined when many officially pro-Liberal newspapers backed Lloyd George. Perhaps the greatest loss in circulation terms was the long-standing Liberal organ, the Glasgow *Daily Record*. Owned by Harmsworth, the *Daily Record* consistently and unhesitatingly promoted the goals and polices of the Coalition government, while it simultaneously deplored the opposition of the Asquithians. The Maurice Debate was described as 'pin pricks, poison darts' hurled by embittered critics of Lloyd George, and Asquith's participation was regretted.[35] In the 1918 General Election, the paper pressed the case for Coalition candidates, assuring wavering Liberals that they had no grounds to fear a Coalition victory.[36] One heavily defeated Glasgow candidate in 1918 ascribed the 'press boycott' as the first reason for the party's setback in the city.[37]

Disaffection and despair at the stasis in the party's policy under Asquith induced a number of left-leaning Liberals to move out of the party and into Labour in the early post-war period. Ponsonby was one of this group. In his local battle with the Liberal Party, he was drawn closer to the ILP, who were among his staunchest supporters. In 1918 he ran in Dunfermline as an Independent, but with the organisation for his campaign supplied by individual ILPers and other socialists. He then joined Labour, becoming a Cabinet Minister in 1929. J. Dundas White was another MP who switched to Labour. John L. Kinloch, identified before the war with Lloyd George's land campaigns, and subsequently amanuensis to the radical M.P. Josiah Wedgwood, switched to the ILP and stood as a Labour candidate in subsequent elections.

At the grass-roots, similar movement occurred. MacCallum Scott recorded in early 1921 that his constituency secretary 'is very restive and out of sympathy with Liberalism ... he is really drifting steadily away from Liberalism into the Labour camp.' The next day he remarked on the changing position of William Hill, whom he described as 'the best specimen I have struck of the Liberal workman.' Even this stalwart was 'getting uneasy' at the post-war economy, so that 'he would be half-inclined to welcome my joining the Labour Party'.[38] Many in the Young Scots seem to have done the same: the Rev. James Barr, a United Free Church (UFC) clergyman who opposed the war, joined Labour and eventually sat in parliament for that party. R. E. Muirhead, the leading Home Ruler, and Daniel Stevenson, a wealthy businessman, were more inclined to Labour than to the Liberal Party after 1918.

A further weakening of Liberal support came with the alienation of the Irish nationalist community in Scotland. Before 1914, they had tended to use their parliamentary votes to promote the goal of Irish self-government. In most instances this meant supporting the Liberals, more especially in the period from the January 1910 election, when a hung parliament handed the fate of the Liberal administration to the Irish nationalists. This infuriated Labour, which had previously detected signs of the Irish vote moving in their direction. The party's poor showing in several by-elections between 1910 and 1914 was blamed on the lack of Irish nationalist support.

Initially, Irish nationalist opinion in Scotland endorsed the war: enlistments were as high as among native Scots; the organ of the community, the *Glasgow Observer*, approved of full participation in the war; and six Glasgow Irish Roman Catholics were awarded the Victoria Cross. But the aftermath of the 1916 Easter Rising produced a more critical approach towards the Liberals. The execution of the leaders of the rising, along with the introduction of conscription to Ireland in the closing stages of the war, meant that many in the Irish community were alienated from the Liberals, since Asquith and Lloyd George were the premiers responsible for the injuries done to Ireland.[39]

Labour were the major beneficiaries of the Irish hostility to the Liberals. Labour had championed the cause of Irish self-government long before 1916 and now seemed to be the only British party consistently supporting this demand. In the 1918 election, the *Glasgow Observer* urged its readers to support Labour candidates. Indeed, ten Roman Catholics stood for Labour and the nationalist political machine endorsed forty-seven candidates, of whom thirty were Labour. In some seats, local nationalist parties defied central instructions to vote Liberal, instead supporting Labour. The loss of Irish nationalist backing was the more serious because the Fourth Reform Act of 1918 almost certainly greatly increased their electoral power.[40]

For the Conservatives, the war was a welcome reprieve. Instead of the futile pre-war thrashing around for policies on which to mount a strong anti-Liberal attack, a natural Tory issue was now to the fore. Unlike the Liberals, or Labour, the Tories were wholeheartedly and unanimously in favour of the war. The party's greatest electoral advance in Scotland had occurred in the 1900 General Election, contested under the shadow of the Boer War. For most of the Great War opinion in Scotland was strongly committed to the cause. This naturally boosted the Tories. Many of their regular party workers were prominent in administering the war effort – a factor which enhanced their credibility. In Edinburgh, Unionist officials worked in Lord Derby's recruiting campaign and on behalf of the Red Cross and the Edinburgh offices of the Scottish Unionist Association were turned over for this purpose. In

Glasgow, Tory staff were also active in recruiting work, with the Western Council's premises used as a centre for administering the campaign.[41]

Yet partisan political work was not completely abandoned for the duration of the hostilities. The Scottish Conservative Club continued its pre-war bankrolling of needy constituencies. In 1915, its Political Committee, learning that 'in view of the War, many Associations were finding themselves in grave financial difficulty and in many cases had no funds to keep the Political organisation going', donated £315. Early in 1918, it was reported to the Annual General Meeting of the club that numerous grants had been given to local parties, since 'it [was] of the utmost importance that local organisations shall be maintained in a state of efficiency and ready for any emergency.' The club extended its assistance beyond cash, and in 1916 the Political Committee discussed 'formulating a scheme to encourage members to assist the Whip's Office in the work of organisation, canvassing and speaking.'[42] In late 1915, MacCallum Scott felt that the Unionists were displacing the Liberals in his Bridgeton seat by dint of their prominence in recruiting work. His agent told him this was because the Tories had more money than the Liberals to spend on this type of work.[43]

In the 1918 election, a very conspicuous difference between the Tories and the other two parties was that the former put up many candidates with military titles. Of Conservative candidates, 46% had a military prefix; for all Liberals, Coalition and Independent, the respective statistics are 10% and 6%; for Labour 0%. In Fife East, the heroism of the Tory candidate in the war was one factor in unseating Asquith. Walter Elliot, elected for Lanark, had been awarded the Military Cross in 1917.

Although the Unionist party machine was not active during the war, it was never as decimated by disaffection and apathy as the Liberals. The Unionist press never swerved from full backing of the war, so that little stress was placed on ordinary supporters. With the return of peace, the Tories were able to mobilise their organisation speedily across most of the country. This placed them in a very superior position vis-à-vis the Liberals, whether pro- or anti-Coalition. Faced with an implacable foe on the left, and with internal disarray, many Liberals opted to back the Tories. In Stirlingshire West – staunchly Liberal before the war – the Unionists could not restrain themselves from gloating as their erstwhile conquerors sought an accommodation to withstand the challenge of Labour.

During the war, the Tories were able to establish a clearer image as the party representing important Scottish qualities. The view of the war as a heroic military undertaking meant that the officer class was highly esteemed – at least for a time in the immediate post war years. The close social integration of the military with the landowning classes may also have been highly useful to the Tories. Field-Marshal Haig, a member of a Lowland landowning family, was a close kinsman of Col. A. B. Haig, the Conservatives' Chief Agent in Scotland in the Edwardian era. The rehabilitation of the landowning class, which was greatly assisted by the war, patently helped the Tories.[44]

The business community, sorely divided by the Tories' espousal of protectionism in the decade before the war, pulled together unstintingly during the conflict. With very few exceptions, they seemed to be on the side of vigorous prosecution of the war. Sir William Beardmore, for example, was part of a syndicate of millionaires who donated lavishly to support a campaign to press the government to adopt an aggressive approach.[45] The division in the Liberal camp undoubtedly accelerated the movement of capital to the Tories. Similarly, the rise of Labour, linked to the impression of a militant, highly unionised and class-conscious proletariat in Lowland Scotland, could hardly fail to boost the shift to Toryism. In this way, by the end of the war, it was almost axiomatic that most employers, particularly those in manufacturing and trade, would identify with the Unionists.

Of the Unionist MPs returned in 1918, it is surely indicative that eleven were businessmen, against nine landowners and military men, nine lawyers, and three other professionals. This was the first time the representation from business was larger than land or law. Several of the business MPs represented large industrial concerns, notably T. S. Adair (manager of Beardmore's ordinance factory), D. H. MacDonald (chairman of the Motherwell-based Brandon Bridge Building Co.) and R. W. F. R Nelson (chairman of the Wagon Repair Co.).

A further bonus was the virtually solid endorsement of the war bestowed by the Presbyterian churches.[46] Hardly any significant churchmen came out against the war, and after its conclusion, few were to show the central Christian attribute of forgiveness, calling instead for punitive treatment of vanquished Germany. The Church of Scotland – always more Tory-inclined than the Presbyterian dissenting churches – was zealously involved: over 200 of its clergymen volunteered for service chaplainships. Several leading UFC figures also threw themselves into pro-war propaganda. Aberdeen University's Principal, George Adam Smith was a striking instance, making several transatlantic trips to raise support in the United States. Indeed, the long-standing umbilical tie between Presbyterian dissent and the Liberal Party was seriously weakened during the war and never subsequently recovered.

Historiographically, the topic of war-time politics which has received the greatest attention has been the unrest in the Glasgow region. In 1915–16, the demands of the workers in the munitions factories on the Clyde became ever more militant. Their resistance to the introduction of new management and workplace procedures resulted in strike action, and the ultimate arrest and removal from the Clyde area of the shop-steward leaders of the campaign. For some historians, a near-revolutionary moment occurred, only to be stemmed by vigorous state action and disunity among the local socialist leadership. For others, an industrial dispute was badly handled on several sides and got out of control, until the government stepped in and isolated the revolutionary elements in the CWC from those who were simply pursuing an industrial grievance.[47]

Along with this surge of protest on the shop-floor came a campaign waged in the streets and closes of Glasgow. The opposition to rapidly spiralling increases in housing costs was most impressively manifested in the rent strike movement. This agitation was led by women, while the factory unrest involved mostly men. It was highly successful: the government intervened to freeze rental levels at the levels set in August 1914.

These episodes had a range of political consequences. First was the greater strength of socialism. The shop stewards' movement was led by ardent socialists who used the crises to illuminate the socialist critique of capitalism at every opportunity. The gains of business from war production were contrasted with the sacrifices experienced by the working class in a highly pertinent manner. Coercive measures adopted by the government further reinforced the socialist conception of the repressive nature of capitalism. It is revealing that many in the ILP shifted markedly to the left under the influence of the events on the Clyde: most notably James Maxton, who was jailed for his part in these incidents.

Equally, the rent issue politicised many women in a socialist direction. The housing question united the working-class in two important ways. Firstly, while the CWC's campaign involved an implicit distancing of the skilled from the unskilled, as evidenced in the resistance to dilution, the rents crisis had a more broadly-based impact. Secondly, it transcended sectarian barriers, with Protestant and Catholic districts acting in concert. Labour and the ILP received a boost, as housing reform – a major pre-war Labour policy plank – now came to the fore. The Liberals were discredited as offering no viable alternative to state intervention.[48] The saliency of housing in Scottish politics was highlighted by surveys of regional opinion carried out by the Unionists during the 1918 election.

In Scotland, the leading domestic issue was housing, but in Lancashire, Yorkshire and South Wales, pensions were a priority. Of these other three areas, only Wales identified housing as a topic of importance, and then it came last out of four.[49]

It is perhaps too easy to assume that the unrest on Clydeside resulted in direct and tangible political gains for Labour. The immediate electoral benefits were limited: only one new Labour seat was won in the Glasgow area in 1918 – admittedly that of Govan, the epicentre of the Clyde's industrial militancy. Moreover, the critical response found in parts of Glasgow was not replicated elsewhere. Indeed, gains for Labour logged in the 1918 General Election were more frequently located in areas of non-militancy.

It is well to remember that the war was immensely popular among the working class for most of its duration. Scottish miners were such enthusiastic volunteers for military service – a higher proportion enlisting than in any other coalfield area – that labour direction was designed to keep them at work in the mines. It is probably correct to say that the majority of organised labour was pro-war. Only two of nineteen ILP councillors on Glasgow Corporation came out against the struggle. J. O'Connor Kessack, a leading ILPer, vice-president of the Scottish Trades Union Congress (STUC), and the narrow loser as Labour candidate in Glasgow Camlachie in 1910, was killed on military service. The three Scottish Labour MPs supported the war effort throughout: none, for instance, voted against the Conscription Bill.

Many areas outwith Glasgow, and industries not involved in engineering and ancillary war production crafts, were not swept up into socialist politics. The bulk of the miners' unions were little stirred from their initial stances, at least if their choice of candidates in 1918 is an indicator. James Brown, leader of the Ayrshire miners and staunch supporter of the war, carried the South Ayrshire seat in 1918 for Labour. At a trade union rally held during the war, Duncan Graham, the victor at Hamilton in 1918, had torn up a denunciation of the war by Ramsay Macdonald to loud applause.

The Stirling Trades Council was fairly hostile to the anti-war socialist element. The decision to affiliate a local branch of the Union for Democratic Control (UDC) was vigorously resisted by the Stirling miners' representatives. The miners withdrew from the council for the rest of the war rather than be contaminated by contact with the UDC delegates. The council received several requests for the CWC for assistance, both moral and practical, at flashpoints in the war. Invariably the Stirling trade unionists refused to act.[50] Aberdeen Trades Council was also pro-war and disinclined to help out the Clydeside socialists.[51] Yet Aberdeen North was one of the handful of seats won by Labour in 1918.

The war was important in creating a sense of unity across working-class institutions, which permitted the tensions between the pro- and anti-war camps to be contained, whereas Liberal disunity turned out to be beyond successful remedy. The position of the Co-operative movement was highly influential for the emergence of a more cohesive Labour identity. In 1918, 9.6% of the English population were members of co-operatives, but in Scotland the figure, at 13.5%, was half as high again. The Scottish movement had a particularly lively social and educational wing, based on the Men's and Women's Guilds. The presence of the Scottish co-operators at the founding of the SWRC in 1900 was different from England, where no official co-operative representatives were present. After this initial interest, however, the Scottish co-operators rather withdrew from political involvement before 1914.

During the war a change occurred, as the movement felt itself discriminated against in the allocation of food supplies. In the localities, such as Dunfermline and Paisley, links were forged with the broader labour movement to protect working class interests.[52] Nationally, too, closer relations developed. In 1917 the Scottish Co-operative and Labour Council was formed, bringing together the Labour Party, the Scottish co-operative organisations and the STUC. The council was initiated by the Scottish Co-operative Union, and its long-term objective was 'ultimately realising a Co-operative Commonwealth.'[53] By 1918 a separate Co-operative Party existed, and it fought a number of Scottish seats, but always in alliance with Labour: in Glasgow, for instance, there was joint selection of candidates with the city trades and labour council.[54] The Liberals especially were alarmed at the adhesion of the co-operators to Labour, but found it well-nigh impossible to reverse the social and political sea-change triggered by war. Aberdeen Liberals tried to mobilise Liberal co-operators to stop the Northern Co-operative Society from siding with Labour, but not very successfully.[55]

In many instances, it was a shared response to the exigencies of the war, rather than an outright opposition to the war itself, which fostered unity in working-class movements and which ultimately assisted Labour. Rising prices, shortages of food supplies, housing problems, injustices to ex-servicemen and their dependants – particularly involving pensions and allowances – all acted to broaden and deepen support for Labour. In Paisley, for example, it was these issues rather than rent strikes and workshop militancy which mobilised working class opinion. A local Workers' War Emergency Committee brought co-operators, unions, friendly societies and the Labour Party into concerted action: some £4,000 was spent pursuing 2,700 individual grievance cases. In Stirling, where militancy was not at a premium, 'rents, trade conditions and wages' were on the agenda from the outset of war. Later food prices, pensions and allowances were raised by the council.[56] As a careful study of Edinburgh indicates, the war also showed that there were matters which were beyond the power of trade union action alone to remedy. At the same time, ideological differences were subordinated by the trades council to the over-riding need for unity of organisation as the key to further progress.[57] Labour was, of course, the main beneficiary of this approach.

For many in the labour movement, the war also gave them unprecedented access to political and governmental agencies which enhanced their status and made them anxious to preserve this role after war. Stirling Trades Council, for example, was invited to choose representatives to serve on the local pensions and food committees, and in Edinburgh the same process of inclusion applied.[58]

The aftermath

The immediate test of the war's political impact came with the General Election held in December 1918. The outcome of this election was a decisive advance for the Conservatives, a massive rout for the Liberals and a serious setback for Labour. The Coalition Unionists held twenty-eight seats; Coalition Liberals, twenty-four; Coalition Labour, one; Coalition National Democratic Party, one; the Asquithians, eight; and Labour, six. In addition, there were two un-couponed Unionists and one Independent Labour MP. In a move symbolic of the shifting political complexion of Scotland, Bonar Law returned north, after twelve years sitting for a London seat.

The rout of the Asquithian Liberals was, from the perspective of the pre-war position, remarkable. The Scottish secretary in 1914, MacKinnon Wood, lost his deposit. H. J. Tennant, his successor, came a bad third, just saving his deposit. The defeat of Asquith himself in the seat he had represented for over thirty years was symbolic of the disintegration of the party. Asquith suffered from being identified with a negative approach to the war and from his pre-war resistance to female enfranchisement. Many other sitting MPs, often with a better record of commitment to their constituency than Asquith, were swept away. W. M. R. Pringle, who had tried to defend the Clyde shop stewards in parliament, lost his deposit – a fate which befell seven Liberal candidates, but only one

Labour and no Unionist. The Liberals' policy, as advocated by Asquith, seemed out of date: free trade and the Irish question were less pressing than other issues such as the peace terms and economic and social reconstruction, on which the Liberals seemed quiet.

The prospects of the Liberals were reduced by the redistribution which accompanied the mass enfranchisement of the Fourth Reform Act. Constituencies were now required to be much more closely equal in numbers. The result was the suppression of thirteen constituencies, of which six were less populous counties and seven, small burghs. Eleven of these had normally been held by the Liberals before 1914. The constituencies thus liberated were assigned to urban industrial regions previously under-represented: Glasgow, for example, acquired eight additional seats to its existing seven. The number of constituencies in the northern and southern regions of Scotland fell from sixteen to ten.[59] Thus the traditional bases of Liberal support were squeezed, while Labour's prospective hinterland was enlarged.

Yet, while the party seemed pulverised, particularly in Lowland urban-industrial seats, there were interesting cross-currents. For instance, in some constituencies in this group, Asquithian Liberals staved off defeat: Collins at Greenock, MacCallum at Paisley and Wedgwood Benn at Leith are three cases in point. Indeed, Benn regained a seat lost in a by-election held in 1914 under the impact of Labour intervention. Moreover, once the immediate peacetime pro-Coalition mood wore off, the Liberals began to recoup lost territory – Asquith's former seat, East Fife, reverted to the Liberals in 1922 and remained Liberal for the rest of the inter-war period.

The major organisational influence assisting the forward movement of the Tories was the electoral pact struck between them and Lloyd George's Liberals. The allocation of the 'coupon' to approved candidates was decisive in settling who was likely to win seats. Since the Unionists had been exceptionally weak in Scotland before the war, the distribution of the coupon on exceptionally favourable terms to their candidates was a brilliant coup. Bonar Law himself admitted that his party had been generously dealt with in Scotland, while from the Lloyd George perspective, his Scottish manager, Sir William Sutherland, confessed that 'Scottish seats were badly handled'.[60] The Tories were thereby established as the main anti-socialist party in Scotland at a point where class and ideological boundaries were shaping political allegiances. The Liberals had been thrust to the periphery – a position from which they would struggle to reassert their pre-war pre-eminence in the new, tense, political context.

It is ironic that one of the grounds for so many Tories being 'couponed' was the strength of Scottish Asquithian Liberalism, both in the parliamentary party and in the local party organisations: only twenty-two of the fifty-four Liberal MPs in 1918 were regarded by the Lloyd George camp as sympathetic.[61] The Coalition Liberals were doubly caught: they had to cede the larger share of candidatures to the Tories: thirty-five Unionists and twenty-seven Liberals ran under the Coalition colours. Yet in Scotland the share of seats fought by Coalition Liberals was twice as great as in England (43% to 22%). This meant that the Liberals had to take a prominent part in the campaign, thus exacerbating the tension with Independent Liberals.

On the whole, the war-time coalition survived the transition to peace-time conditions. Some Unionists protested vociferously at being expected to stand down for Liberals. This tended to occur when the latter had a reputation before 1914 of being identified with the social radical wing. MacCallum Scott in Bridgeton and J. W. Pratt in Cathcart, for example, both encountered reluctance from local Tories to fall in behind them on the election campaign.[62] Liberals, too, were reluctant to accept the permanence of the war-time political truce: Alexander Shaw and Mac-Callum Scott stressed that their attachment to the Coalition would survive only as long as Liberal principles were pursued. At the grass-roots level, the Aberdeen Liberals took a similar line. Implicit in these statements was the threat to secede if protectionism was pushed by the Tories.[63]

For Labour, the results were disappointing. Most notably, the turmoil on the Clyde did not translate into seats: only Govan was won, although John Wheatley narrowly missed victory at Shettleston, losing by seventy-four votes. If anything, the major breakthroughs came in mining seats (Ayrshire South, Hamilton) and in the eastern urban areas (Aberdeen North, Edinburgh Central). This has been interpreted as a sign that, while the Liberals were too weak to win many constituencies in the west, they still retained sufficient support to deny Labour an early post-war success. It was not until 1922 that the collapse of Liberalism was secured in the industrial Lowland west, thus opening the way for Labour.[64]

Moreover, the marked lack of socialist fervour in all except one of the MPs – Neil MacLean of Govan – may underline the argument of Tanner, namely, that much of the support for Labour at this election came for specific, instrumental reasons. In a number of industries, workers were attracted to the concept of state intervention, not for ideological motives, but because they had found the government's role in wartime highly beneficial to the interests of the labour force in their industry. In some cases this meant better wages, superior working conditions and the imposition of higher standards of safety at work and welfare facilities. Tanner sees these arguments as applying with particular force in railway, mining and engineering centres.[65] This perception is underscored at the local level by Holford in his study of Edinburgh. Here he found the case for public ownership of the railway system much enhanced among employees during the war. Willie Graham's capture of Edinburgh Central was grounded in the large number of railway workers resident in the area which included the two great termini, Caledonian and Waverley stations.[66] Similar factors would seem to apply in Aberdeen North, where a large railway vote was based on the Kittybrewster depot and where there was also a considerable engineering presence.[67]

Labour's prospects had seemed promising and a skilful strategy was put in place to maximise gains. The Fourth Reform Act should have been very helpful to the party. The redistribution element certainly appeared highly propitious. The virtually full male adult enfranchisement created by the bill again offered only sustenance. While in some parts of the country, for instance Haddingtonshire (East Lothian), it is probable that the new voters were fairly similar in social composition to the existing ones: in the more urban-industrial parts the pattern was probably different. Smyth's analysis of Glasgow voters has established that the vast bulk of those voteless before 1918 were drawn from the working class. Even among representatives to the Glasgow Trades Council in 1911, only 55% were entered on both the 1910–11 and 1911–12 registers, with markedly higher rates of disfranchisement found among the less skilled trades.[68] The 1918 measures swept away the technical and socio-economic obstacles to full adult male enfranchisement. Yet Labour could not attract the bulk of these voters until 1922 at the earliest.

Again, the granting of the vote to a large number of women did not yield the dividends Labour anticipated from the radicalising of working class women over rents and other social issues. Labour also tried to woo the Catholic vote – still primarily Irish – by adopting a very emollient stance towards the rights of the Catholic church to retain control of its schools while the state bore the cost. This was a more open expression of support than the other two parties were perceived to offer. In the north, Labour forged an alliance with the Highland Land League and left the latter to fight Highland seats, where, it was calculated, overtly socialistic labels would be off-putting, but a focus on the land question might rekindle the pre-war radical spirit. These assumptions were pretty well all unfulfilled in 1918.

It would seem that the General Election campaign, fought essentially in a triumphalist euphoria in the wake of the Armistice, counteracted socialist influences. So it would appear not unreasonable to conclude that the mainsprings of Labours' 1922 performance were rooted in the post-war years, rather than in the wartime experiences on Clydeside.[69]

Conclusion

The impact of the Great War is not only to be traced in the fortunes of the main Scottish parties. In the longer term, war-time experiences also encouraged two more general features of the post-war political landscape. Scotland in the 1920s and 1930s was firstly characterised by an increasing corporatist trend. On the one hand, the high degree of state involvement in directing economic activity in Scotland during the war encouraged a reappraisal of the traditional anti-statist standpoint of the business community. This movement was spearheaded by figures such as Lord Weir who had themselves been prominent in directing production for the war effort.[70] Similarly, the trade unions also appreciated the positive consequences of state involvement, and under the leadership of William Elger, Secretary of the STUC, strove to perpetuate the set-up in the post-war era.

Finally, the war and its aftermath may also have contributed to the shaping of Scotland's sense of identity. This was a complex process. The Versailles peace settlement, enshrining the principle of the rights of small nations to self-determination, carried political weight, as evidenced in the inclusion of Scottish Home rule in the policy platforms of both the Labour and Liberal parties in the post-war years.[71] Yet the experience of war seems also to have reinforced the identification of some Scots with the United Kingdom and the Empire. This was a spirit which found expression not only in Scottish public life, with its formal Armistice Day and Empire Day commemorations, but also in the countless personal pilgrimages made to local cenotaphs in the decades following the Great War.[72]

Notes

1. Manchester, National Museum of Labour History [NMLH], Labour Party MSS, National Executive Committee Minutes, 'Report on Scottish Conference', 5 Aug. 1911.
2. I. Packer, 'The land issue and the future of Scottish Liberalism in 1914', *Scottish Historical Review*, lxxv (1996), pp. 52–71.

3. I. G. C. Hutchison, *A Political History of Scotland, 1832–1924* (Edinburgh, 1986), pp. 240–5.
4. *Glasgow Herald,* 11 Apr. 1910; 6 May 1912.
5. Hutchison, *Political History,* pp. 230–4.
6. *Ibid.,* pp. 218–21; A. Sykes, *Tariff Reform in British Politics, 1903–13* (London, 1979).
7. House of Lords Record Office [HLRO], Bonar Law MSS, BL27/4/7, G. Younger to A. B. Law, 6 Nov. 1912.
8. T. Gallagher, *Glasgow. The Uneasy Peace* (Manchester, 1987), p. 82.
9. D. Urwin, 'The development of Conservative Party organisation in Scotland until 1912', *Scottish Historical Review,* xliv (1965), pp. 89–111; Hutchison, *Political History,* pp. 221–7.
10. *Ayr Advertiser,* 1 Feb. 1906.
11. W. H. Fraser, 'The Labour Party in Scotland', in K. D. Brown (ed.), *The First Labour Party, 1900–14* (London, 1985), pp. 52–9.
12. *Ibid.,* pp. 40–55; Hutchison, *Political History,* pp. 256–7.
13. Fraser, 'Labour Party', pp. 49–52; Hutchison, *Political History,* pp. 249–53.
14. J. Smith, 'Taking the leadership of the labour movement: the ILP in Glasgow, 1906–14', in A. MacKinlay and R. J. Morris (eds), *The ILP on Clydeside, 1893–1932* (Manchester, 1991), pp. 56–82; J. J. Smyth, 'Labour and Socialism in Glasgow, 1880–1914: the Electoral Challenge prior to Democracy' (Edinburgh University Ph.D. thesis, 1987), pp. 57–147; Hutchison, *Political History,* pp. 245–9.
15. W. M. Haddow, *Socialism in Scotland: its rise and progress* (Glasgow, n.d.), pp. 49–51.
16. Smyth, 'Labour and Socialism', pp. 94–101.
17. This was North Ayrshire, where the swing was a mere 2.1%.
18. J. Turner, *British Politics and the Great War. Coalition and Conflict, 1915–1918* (London, 1992), pp. 77, 80–1.
19. *Ibid.,* pp. 77, 132.
20. *Ibid.,* pp. 145n., 186–7, 217, 256–7.
21. HLRO, Pringle MSS, Hist. Coll. 226/II/26, 24, W. M. R. Pringle to J. Rabone (copies), 19, 11 Dec. 1915.
22. See Oxford, Bodleian Library [BL], Ponsonby MSS, MS Eng. Hist. c. 660–5 *passim.*
23. *Ibid.,* MS Eng. Hist. c. 665, D. Gorrie to A. Ponsonby, 26 Dec. 1916; J. S. Henderson to A. Ponsonby, 27 Dec. 1916.
24. HLRO, Pringle MSS, Hist. Coll. 226/II/23, Rabone to Pringle, 6 Dec. 1915.
25. Aberdeen University Archives [AUA], Aberdeen Liberal Association MSS, MS 2472, Minute Book, 21 Jan. 1916; 26 Feb. 1917.
26. BL, Asquith MSS, 33, W. M. R. Pringle to H. H. Asquith, 29 Dec. 1918.
27. BL, Ponsonby MSS, MS Eng. Hist. c. 665, W. Donaldson to A. Ponsonby, 13 Oct. 1916. It seems, however, that the secretary, J. S. Henderson, was still in office two months later.
28. AUA, Aberdeen Liberal Association MSS, MS 2472, Minute Book, 23 Mar. 1920.
29. *Ibid.,* 4 Apr. 1922.
30. Edinburgh University Library [EUL], Scottish Liberal Association MSS, Minute Book, 30 Apr. 1920.
31. *Ibid.,* 11 Nov. 1918.
32. *Ibid.,* 23 Jul., 5,19 Oct. 1917; 19 Sept. 1918.
33. BL, Ponsonby MSS, MS Eng. Hist. c. 665, W. Robertson to A. Ponsonby, 18 Dec. 1917 [recte 1916].
34. AUA, Aberdeen Lib. Ass. MSS, MS 2472, Minute Book, 11 Nov. 1918; 23 Mar., 13 Apr., 25 May 1920.
35. *Daily Record,* 5, 9 Dec. 1916; 9, 10 May 1918.

36. *Ibid.*, 23, 25 Nov., 28 Dec. 1918.
37. BL, Asquith MSS, 33, W. M. R. Pringle to H. H. Asquith, 29 Dec. 1918.
38. Glasgow University Library [GUL], MacCallum Scott MSS, MS 1465/12, Diary, 29, 30 Jan. 1921.
39. Letter from Liberal party agent, Kilmarnock Burghs, to A. Shaw, cited in Turner, *British Politics*, pp. 213n, 225.
40. See Gallagher, *Glasgow. The Uneasy Peace*, pp. 86–90; I. Patterson, 'The Impact of the Irish Revolution on the Irish Community in Scotland, 1916–23' (Strathclyde University M. Litt. thesis, 1990), pp. 218–54, 267–302.
41. National Library of Scotland [NLS], Scottish Conservative and Unionist Association MSS, Acc. 10424/45, Scottish Unionist Association Central Council Minute Book, 26 Jan. 1917.
42. Scottish Record Office [SRO], Scottish Conservative Club MSS, GD 309/45, Political Committee Minute Book, 27 Oct. 1915; 12 Jan. 1916; 20 Feb. 1918.
43. GUL, MacCallum Scott MSS, MS 1465/6, Diary, 19 Jul., 30 Oct. 1915.
44. For a discussion of this general process, see I. G. C. Hutchison, 'The nobility and politics in Scotland, c. 1880–1939', in T. M. Devine (ed.), *Scottish Elites* (Edinburgh, 1994), pp. 144–6.
45. Turner, *British Politics*, p. 115.
46. See S. J. Brown '"A solemn purification by fire": responses to the Great War in the Scottish presbyterian churches 1914–19', *Journal of Ecclesiastical History*, xlv (1994), pp. 82–104.
47. J. Melling, 'Whatever happened to Red Clydeside?', *International Review of Social History*, xxxv (1990), pp. 3–32; also T. Brotherstone, 'Does Red Clydeside really matter any more?', in R. Duncan and A. MacIvor (eds), *Militant Workers* (Edinburgh, 1992), pp. 52–80.
48. See J. Melling, *Rent Strikes!* (Edinburgh, 1983), pp. 59–111.
49. HLRO, Bonar Law MSS, BL 45/95/2, G. Younger to A. B. Law, 3, 6 Dec. 1918.
50. Stirling Council Archives [SCA], Stirling and Falkirk Labour Party MSS, Stirling Trades and Labour Council Minute Book, 1 Sept., 27 Oct. 1915; 12 Jan., 22 Mar. 1916; 10, 24 Jan., 28 Nov., 5 Dec. 1917.
51. C. Phipps, 'Aberdeen Trades Council and Politics, 1900–39. The Development of a Local Labour Party' (Aberdeen University M.Litt. thesis, 1980), pp. 94–100.
52. NMLH, Labour Party MSS, Scottish Advisory Council Minutes, 23 Sept., 4 Oct. 1914 (for Dunfermline); C. M. M. MacDonald, 'The Radical Thread: Political Change in Scotland, Paisley Politics, 1885–1924' (Strathclyde University Ph.D. thesis, 1996), pp. 181–92.
53. NMLH, Labour Party MSS, Scottish Advisory Council Minutes, 17 Mar., 11 Aug., 8 Oct. 1917.
54. Glasgow, Mitchell Library, Glasgow Trades and Labour Council MSS, Minute Book, 1 Oct. 1918.
55. AUA, Aberdeen Liberal Association MSS, MS 2472, Minute Book, 26 Feb., 20 Mar., 5 Jun. 1918.
56. SCA, Stirling and Falkirk Labour Party MSS, Stirling Trades and Labour Council Minute Book, 11, 25 Nov. 1914; 20 Jan. 1915; 1 Nov. 1916; 7 Feb., 8 Aug. 1917.
57. J. Holford, *Reshaping Labour. Organisation, Work and Politics – Edinburgh in the Great War and After* (London, 1988), pp. 63–233.
58. SCA, Stirling and Falkirk Labour Party MSS, Stirling Trades and Labour Council Minute Book, 7 Feb., 8 Aug. 1917; Holford, *Reshaping Labour*, pp. 151–4.
59. M. C. Dyer, *Capable Citizens and Improvident Democrats. The Scottish Electoral System, 1884–1929* (Aberdeen, 1996), pp. 118–21.

60. HLRO, Bonar Law MSS, BL 95/4, A. M. Shaw to A. B. Law, 5 Dec. 1918; Lloyd George MSS, LG F22/1/33, W. Sutherland to D. Lloyd George, n.d. [May 1920].

61. HLRO, Lloyd George MSS, LG F21/2/28, F. E. Guest to D. Lloyd George, 20 Jul. 1918.

62. Hutchison, *Political History*, pp. 312–13 for examples.

63. *Ibid.*, p. 312.

64. Turner, *British Politics*, pp. 404–31. Impressive statistical analysis lies behind this argument, but it should be noted that his regional division of Scotland is a trifle eccentric. Stirlingshire is included in the eastern region, although it is at its nearest only a dozen miles from Glasgow. West Lothian, which is to the east of Stirlingshire, however, is allocated to the western region. Quite bafflingly, three Aberdeenshire seats are placed in the Highland grouping, but Moray and Nairn and Banffshire are not. Social designations are also questionable: it is not certain that the bulk of the residents in Glasgow Cathcart, Hillhead and Pollok would care to be described as 'working-class'. West Renfrewshire, embracing Port Glasgow and Johnstone, is hardly a mainly rural seat. In addition, several Lanarkshire seats are completely omitted from the listing of constituencies on pp. 478–9.

65. D. Tanner, *Political Change and the Labour Party, 1900–18* (Cambridge, 1990), chap. 13.

66. Holford, *Reshaping Labour*, pp. 63–99.

67. Phipps, 'Aberdeen Trades Council', chaps 4–5.

68. Smyth, 'Labour and Socialism', chap. 6, esp. pp. 271–4.

69. Turner, *British Politics*, pp. 420–5.

70. See K. Middlemas, *Politics in Industrial Society* (London, 1979). Although, as Turner suggests, employers in some areas such as shipbuilding were more anxious to cast off government intervention.

71. See R. J. Finlay, '"For or Against?"' Scottish Nationalists and the British Empire, 1918–39', *Scottish Historical Review*, lxxi (1992), pp. 184–206.

72. J. Mitchell suggests a similar shift towards 'Britishness' in the aftermath of World War Two: 'Scotland in the Union, 1945–95: The Changing Nature of the Union State', in T. M. Devine and R. J. Finlay (eds), *Scotland in the Twentieth Century* (Edinburgh, 1996), pp. 87–97.

CHAPTER THREE

War Resisters and Anti-Conscription in Scotland: an ILP Perspective

William Kenefick

BEFORE 4 AUGUST 1914, the average British citizen thought little about the liberty and freedom implicit in the living-out of his day-to-day life. Such a citizen had no need to carry an identity card and required neither passport to travel abroad nor permission to leave the country. He enjoyed one other important freedom:

> Unlike the countries of the European continent, the state did not require its citizens to perform military service ... [he] could enlist, if he chose, in the regular army, the navy, or the territorials. He could also ignore, if he chose, the demands of national defence.[1]

All this was to change after Britain went to war. For perhaps the first time, the people of Britain became 'active citizens', expected to place personal wants and wishes below the needs of the state.

From the moment hostilities broke out, the Independent Labour Party (ILP) and its membership argued that the war had no 'just cause' and throughout the conflict they held consistently to this position. As the party's main propaganda organ, *Forward*, proclaimed in August 1914 that the war was being fought to satisfy the lust for industrial profit on the one hand, and the desire to promote the rise of the British military state on the other. 'The Alliance between Holy Russia, Cut-Throat Servia, Protestant Britain, Heathen Japan, and Catholic France', was evidence enough, it was reported, to show the duplicitous and self-serving actions of British diplomacy in the run-up to the crisis.[2]

As war hysteria reached fever pitch, the government was urged to take all necessary action to ensure a British victory. The state rapidly took control of the railways, impounded enemy ships, interned aliens and mobilised the territorials. Against this background, many in the ILP feared the inevitable growth in state power should the war continue. Already, political propaganda and social and economic coercion followed in the wake of the government's war recruitment campaign, typified in

immediate calls to introduce conscription. On this last issue the ILP
was determined: if compulsory military service were introduced it would
lead inexorably to the militarisation of civil and industrial society. Should
the state procure such powers, the ILP warned, the result would be
'the negation of all law', the denial of the right of conscience and the
curtailment of individual freedoms.[3]

The No-Conscription Fellowship (NCF), formed in November 1914 –
some fourteen months before compulsory military service was introduced
– was also prominent in the anti-war campaign. It was this organisation,
claims Hayes, which 'bore the brunt of the struggle against conscription'.[4]
He also points out that three out of every four Conscientious Objectors
(COs) were political objectors, many of whom 'owed their primary al-
legiance to the ILP.'[5] In the long-term, he suggests, the NCF was to
win the argument against British militarism: 'International Socialism
had failed on the outbreak of war, but British war resisters had provided
a stirring tradition for the second and third generations of Socialists to
follow.'[6]

The Military Service Acts of January and May 1916, which first
imposed conscription, provided for the full exemption of COs on moral,
religious and political grounds, but many COs still found themselves in
prison over the exercise of conscience. Indeed, five months after the
war had ended *Forward* was continuing to campaign for the release of
men who remained in prison because of their conscientious beliefs. This
situation prompted W. J. Chamberlain to write in March 1919, that these
men were 'victims of the most scandalous persecution since the sixteenth
century.'[7]

To date there has been no comprehensive account of the Scottish war
resisters of 1914–18. Nor indeed has there been an adequate exposition
of the role of the ILP in the anti-war movement in Scotland. As noted
by William Marwick, the principal works dealing with war resistance
essentially concentrate on the issue surrounding conscientious objection
and conscription. J. W. Graham, *Conscription and Conscience* (1922), Denis
Hayes, *Conscription Conflict* (1948), and John Rae, *Conscience and Politics*
(1970), all consider anti-war sentiment, but make 'few and slight references to Scotland.'[8] Indeed, Marwick's own contribution does little to
rectify this, although he does attempt to highlight the main influences
on Scottish war resisters and conscientious objectors. Yet he says little
about the role of the ILP as one of the principal political organisations
which not only opposed conscription, but also warned of its inevitable
imposition in the course of what it viewed as Britain's capitalist war.[9]

It seemed certain that when the war broke out the ILP would suffer considerably because of their anti-war stand. Yet by the time the war had come to an end, the number of ILP branches in Scotland had more than doubled and actual membership had more than trebled.[10] In contrast, elsewhere in Britain the ILP never fully recovered from the losses sustained in terms of branches and members during the war years.[11] Why then, given the great support for the war effort generally in Scotland, was the ILP so successful? Focussing largely on the regular news reports and editorial articles drawn from the columns of *Forward* and reports of ILP activites in the wider Scottish press, this chapter seeks to shed some light on the period, by considering in greater detail the role of Scottish war resisters and the ILP in the 'anti-war' movement in Scotland. It also gives particular consideration to the political objections raised over the question of conscription and 'conscientious objection'. Is the explanation for the ILP's success largely confined to its 'exploitation of welfare issues', or did the party's opposition to the war also play a significant role?[12] Despite the clamour for war in Scotland and the vitriolic attacks on the ILP and its membership, the party remained true to its anti-war position. Through the columns of *Forward*, it gave the people of Scotland at least the opportunity to consider a critique of the war at a time when few dissenting voices were to be heard.

Scotland and war hysteria

It has never been in doubt that the Scots responded in great numbers to the call to arms at the onset of war in 1914. As the *Daily Record* was to report, within two days of war being declared, and over the very first weekend of war, six thousand men 'from all classes' enlisted in Glasgow alone, almost fighting with each other to push through the doors of the recruiting offices.[13] By December 1914, 25% of the male labour force of western Scotland had already signed up.[14] The Scottish press also took great pride in the early reports of Scottish enlistment. As the *Dundee Advertiser* reported in November 1914: 'All honour to the lads who have put Scotland in the front this time ... We must not let the sons of the Rose or the Leek or the Shamrock get in front of the proud Thistle.'[15]

In attempting to understand the high levels of enlistment, Harvie suggests, 'it is difficult to assign precise motives, but the fear of unemployment was probably as great as patriotic enthusiasm and solidarity with 'Brave Little Belgium.'[16] He notes, for example, that in the Lothian coalfields, where the overseas market for coal had already collapsed because of the war, 36% of miners had volunteered. By contrast, in the

Ayrshire coalfields, where trade had not been so adversely effected, only 20% of miners signed up. But while economic considerations held back recruitment in some areas, 'following one's pals' remained a powerful component in the decision to join-up, as was the general expectation of a short war.[17] Even when it became clear that the war would not be over by Christmas and that the loss of life would be greater than first estimated, few argued for a peaceful settlement to end the hostilities between Britain and Germany. By late August 1914, the *Glasgow Herald* proudly proclaimed its editorial position on the issue: 'Germany is the criminal. Let Germany pay the penalty.'[18]

Such anti-German sentiments were prevalent throughout British society, and were often at their most vociferous within the ranks of the labour and trade union movement. While not all of its members were 'Hun-hating jingoistic super-patriots' who, like Ben Tillett, 'wished to have the Germans eliminated from civilisation', most were, nevertheless, convinced that the war was justified and that it was necessary to defeat Germany at all costs.[19] Despite the resolution passed by the Second Socialist International at Basle in 1912, declaring its members' opposition to war, no action of that type was ever taken and few suggested that it should. As Nan Milton has argued, the Second International had failed its first test, and 'failed dismally.' Writing of the life and times of her father, a British Socialist Party (BSP) leader, John MacLean, she stressed:

> In Britain the socialist movement as a whole responded 'gallantly' to the Liberal government's appeal to protect "poor little Belgium" and to "fight for democracy" against the threatening Prussian despotism. The TUC, the co-operative movement and the Labour Party unreservedly gave their services in the cause of the allies, the TUC promising complete industrial peace for the duration of the war ...[20]

Milton also asserted that the ILP, despite taking a 'fairly strong pacifist line' on the war, still tended to sit on the fence on the major issues. To that end, she suggests, the ILP retreated from the public gaze into the intimacy of local halls 'where they could reach nobody but the converted.'

Milton's censures aside, the ILP's strong 'anti-war' line was clearly and consistently evident in the weekly columns of *Forward.* In contrast, the BSP organ, *Justice*, was being used by her father's former colleagues, Robert Blatchford and H. M. Hyndman, 'for both blatant and subtle war propaganda.'[21] Moreover, as she herself notes, many members of the BSP in Scotland, and in Glasgow, rejected Maclean and remained loyal to Hyndman, resulting in a definite split in the ranks of the BSP, something that did not happen in the ILP's case.

It cannot be denied, however, that the cause of socialism was initially set back because of the war. The *Glasgow Herald*, which before 1914 had published many articles and reports warning of the evils of socialism, by August was claiming with some justification, 'Scratch a Socialist and find a patriot'.²² *Forward*, unhappy with such sentiment, attempted to play down the working class zeal for war, by arguing that socialists too were patriots, not because they supported war, but rather because they opposed it. They did not want war, they wanted peace, and a new land to defend: 'not that of the capitalist, but one which all shared equally.'²³ There was also practical support for peace. The Glasgow ILP, with the assistance of the BSP under John MacLean, and the Peace Society, helped to organise a peace demonstration in Glasgow within a week of the war being declared.²⁴ *Forward* reported: 'the gathering was cosmopolitan in character and included doctors and dock workers and rebels of every possible brand from the mild peace advocates to the wildest of revolutionaries'.²⁵

The meeting heard various speakers pronounce that 'the war was simply the outcome of Capitalism, Militarism and Secret Diplomacy', and also agreed a resolution calling for the government to sue for a peaceful settlement to the war. There were similar meetings organised across Scotland. But generally, unless noted in the columns of *Forward* or those of the *Labour Leader*, they were given little coverage.

Although over 5,000 turned out for the Glasgow Peace demonstration, these were a dedicated minority of Scots. The ILP and *Forward* continued to oppose the war, but this position immediately lost them considerable support, particularly in the industrial areas where they had previously been gaining ground. When the war broke out the ILP had ninety-six branches, but many branches were to collapse, with membership slumping to 3,000.²⁶ The ILP also suffered because it openly opposed the Labour Party's support for the war and that party's decision to become actively involved in the government's recruitment campaign.

Already by February 1915, some ILPers were beginning to detect a change in attitude. Willie Stewart, Scottish organiser of the ILP, was to write that they had been caught in the full glare of public interest because they had come out so openly against the Labour Party. This strategy had been necessary, he claimed, in order to preserve the ILP as 'a socialist organisation'. He suggested that now the crisis had passed, the work of Socialism could be revived and their efforts in the fight against the war renewed. But Stewart urged caution. He asked, 'would the people listen?':

> With our hospitals filled with broken men, with bereaved families in every street ... in every village and hamlet, how can we expect people to listen to the arguments about the rights and wrongs of war? We shall be misunderstood and will only increase the mental pain ... We must be tender and considerate to the feelings of our fellow workers, however hot our wrath against the war-makers ...[27]

He concluded that things had already improved for the party since the early days of the war, and that in time they would get their message across if they adopted such a strategy, not least when war-weariness set in. The ILP's experience of the next four years was to prove him correct.

The anti-war movement and the shadow of conscription

By September 1914, the columns of *Forward* were regularly reporting on the rift between the ILP and the Labour Party over the latter's decision to back Lord Kitchener's recruitment campaign. The National Administration Council of the ILP quickly mobilised its own campaign and advised its members not to take part in any proposed recruiting campaign, but to stand firm. The words of Rudyard Kipling's *If* were invoked to aid *Forward* readers' resolve, but the central theme of the paper's message was to, 'Remain true to the goals of International Socialism and in all conscience remain firm in its opposition to war'.[28] This was echoed by the Rev. James Barr, a leading Scottish war resister and ex-president of the Peace Society. In what would prove to be the first *Forward* article to tackle the question of conscience, set against the prevailing pro-war mood of the nation, he asked:

> What is a man ... if he cannot abandon himself to the natural rage, and identify himself to the full with the popular passion, if he does not "cry havoc, and let slip the dogs of war," if, above all, he hints that there may be just something to be said for the other side, and that the whole war might someway have been avoided, he is at once set down as an unpatriotic, cranky, and absolutely impossible man in a time of war ...[29]

But who did the war benefit and who gained from waging war?

> no one but the British, American, French and German industrialists, financed by British, French and German banks ... [and] if Britain

and Germany can federate to sell implements of destruction, can they not unite together in a bond of eternal peace?

Barr clearly articulated the moral and political objections to war, illustrating how the two strands could be seen to be part of one over-arching philosophy. This was in essence the philisophical and ideological position adopted by the ILP before the war and was to be developed and extended during the conflict.

By the end of October, it was being reported throughout the press and announced from every recruitment platform, that the numbers enlist-ing were falling slightly. It now seemed, proclaimed the editors of *Forward*, that 'The Cannon fodder ... was rather backward in coming forward.'[30] Such reporting incurred the anger of one reader, who, writing in that same edition under the lofty pseudonym 'Deep thinker from Larkhall', had no doubt who was to blame for the falling off in recruitment levels: 'Lanarkshire miners have got the fighting spirit implanted within their breasts. If that has been diminished to a great extent, it is vastly due to bastard Socialism and the deficencies of Christian teaching'. So there we have it, replied the editor, 'Christian teaching results in fighting spirit.' There was a serious side to this issue. Even a slight fall in recruitment meant that the topic of conscription was raised once again. In reality, recruitment levels were initially relatively stable, but by the end of January 1915, the recruitment rate had fallen from 300,000 to around 120,000 per month.[31] Requiring to balance both military and civil needs, the government was not, for the moment, particularly per-turbed about falling recruitment levels, but to conscriptionists and supporters of compulsory military service, such news was a godsend.

If the matter had been left to much of the Scottish press, the decision to introduce compulsory military service would have been a foregone conclusion. The *Glasgow Herald* ran a leading article in December 1914 which put the question of conscription to its readership with the com-ment: 'Is it Unfair?'[32] It would seem that they had already decided in favour of the matter some weeks earlier, when it was reported that they made no apologies for stating that if voluntarism did not work, then conscription, or something approaching conscription, was the only alter-native.[33] The *Daily Record*, ran similar articles, including one under the headline: 'Should our boy go to war'. In this issue they invited two parents to put their views on the matter and suggested that somehow these issues were being debated seriously. Nothing could have been further from the truth. The 'boy' in question was left in no doubt that it was his duty to enlist.[34]

In the meantime, the Labour Party had swung determinedly towards the pro-war position, albeit still contending that conscription was not an option. Their support of the war effort was noted in a letter printed in *Forward*, sent by a regular contributor who wrote under the pseudonym, 'Rob Roy':

> We are not discussing whether we should be at war or not. We are in it ... [and] to get well through, to avoid Belgian risks [sic], we require sufficient soldiers. The Labour Party accepted responsibility for finding them, and its members have courageously played their part. If they hadn't, if they had adopted the attitude of some socialists, would conscription not already be upon us? Has not the slow, sure commonsense of the Labour Party washed-up better than the theories of its critics? [35]

The ILP recognised that this was aimed principally at themselves and the sentiments expressed in the letter were considered 'quite disingenuous' in tone. The editors of *Forward* argued that the main aim of the letter was to place the Labour Party in the right and 'some socialists' in the wrong. The editorial itself went on at some length, raking over many old coals, but the main argument was clearly put: 'that there was no evidence to suggest that the recruiting energies of the Labour Party [had] saved the country from conscription.' [36] Restating their anti-war position, they argued that unlike the Labour Party, they would never deviate from that line: 'The Anti-War Socialists will fight against Conscription if ever it is proposed. The Labour Party has given away their right to do so, and, on their present line of action, should not desire to do so!' Acting almost as a postscript, a further short but prophetic letter was published in the same edition of *Forward*. Under the heading 'The Question of Conscription', it suggested that, 'it might be as well for us who refuse to take the part of a combatant in the present war to form ourselves into a body to consider the matter.' [37]

At this point, the anti-conscription movement was more or less still at an embryonic stage of development in Scotland. In November 1914, Fenner Brockway wrote to the *Labour Leader*, inviting young men to form an organisation 'suggesting joint action for mutual help and encouragement.' The No-Conscription Fellowship (NCF) was formed as a result. [38] Believing that it was only a matter of time before compulsory military service was introduced, the aim of the NCF was to create an organisation to offer support, guidance and direction for those men who would refuse military service if it were imposed by the state. [39]

According to Rae, 'this fusion of idealism with the promise of active resistance attracted young men with a variety of religious and political views.' The BSP, for example, produced many COs, as did the Socialist Labour Party (SLP), the Socialist Party of Great Britain and the Industrial Workers of the World.[40] Yet it was the young men of the ILP who were to provide the active initiative and leadership of the organisation.[41] Indeed, after conscription was finally introduced in January, 1916 it has been estimated that 'almost seventy percent of conscientious objection cases involved ILP members.'[42]

In January 1915, Bruce Glasier, a leading ILP member, was sent north to gauge how the ILP's pacifist position was being received by the wider Scottish public. He made the following observations:

> My mission has been somewhat in the nature of that of an Apostle among the Primitive Churches in Pagan Rome. For the present the ILP Branches are almost as sharply isolated from the surrounding population as were the Christian communities of Ephesus, Galicia, and Corinth in Apostolic days. Though not under any formal interdict as a seditious organisation, the ILP is nonetheless regarded with grave suspicion as a pestilentially pacifist faction, as a damper of the war enthusiasm of the nation, and a noxious shrub in the glowing flowerbed of British patriotism ...[43]

Despite this situation, he noted that the branches were bearing up well, although membership had fallen off slightly. He praised the Dundee, Leith and Glasgow branches in particular, for holding regular lectures and propaganda meetings in their areas. All in all, the situation was very encouraging:

> The unanimity and steadfastness of the Branches in their adhesion to International principles, and the opposition to Militarism in all its forms, amidst the thunderstorm of war passion that has swept the country and the civilised world, must be reckoned one of the most distinctive and memorable events in the life of the ILP and the history of the Socialist movement. I can remember no occasion during the twenty-one years existence of the ILP where such virtual complete unity has been displayed in its ranks on any question critically affecting the party or the nation ...[44]

Glasier then went on to suggest that the anti-war feeling in Scotland 'was more energetic and aggressive than in English Branches'. He attributed this attitude, 'to the keener dialectical habit of the Scottish mind, and partly to the courageous and brilliant Red Flag propaganda of *Forward*'. He concluded:

I have never felt more reassured of the spirit and power of the ILP than now in beholding the Scottish branches bearing the banners of their Socialist faith unfalteringly against the almost universal crash of religion and politics ...[45]

For Glasier at least, the anti-war position of the ILP in Scotland was holding well against the 'super-patriotism' so evident throughout the rest of Scottish society.

Not only were there major ideological differences between the ILP and other political groups, not least the Labour Party, but on the issue of morality and the war there were often serious divergencies in opinion between the ILP and various religious bodies in Scotland. The Glasgow Study Group, a Christian pacifist group, was particularly influential in promoting the pacifist position, but in the case of the large denominations, ecclesiastical support for the war was evident and more typical.[46] This found voice, for example, in the Bishop of Edinburgh's *Quarterly Letter* in 1914, and in the Very Rev. Sir George Adam Smith's Address as Moderator of the Church of Scotland in 1916 which he used to denounce COs.[47] It was for this reason, perhaps, that *Forward* was particularly anxious to give full coverage to pacifist clergymen, such as the Rev. Malcolm MacCallum, who gave a warning to his congregation: 'Beware of the Churches as presently organised for this war was neither God's war nor a Holy War! It was a war of sinful men ... between misguided brothers.'[48]

It was sentiments such as these which were to add a further spiritual and moral resonance to the ILP's essentially political anti-war message.

Exploiting wartime discontent

Opposition to war and the pursuit of peace was still the main aim of the ILP, but, as James Maxton had argued, 'the war also brought with it new opportunities to proclaim the socialist message.'[49] Concerns over the rising cost of food, fuel and housing; the militaristic invasions of civil rights and liberty; and threats of compulsion and conscription, were the type of issues the ILP were to exploit to their benefit. It was because of such issues that Willie Stewart felt sure that 1915 would become 'memorable for other things than the war.'[50]

One topic that was to absorb the attentions of the ILP was the concern over the issue of wartime evictions – particularly those of the families of men in military service. *Forward* reported cases from Kilsyth to Sutherland. The Sutherland estate, for example, was proposing to evict crofters in the parish of Clyne in order to extend the Brora Golf course. While the crofters were serving at the the front, the petition was already before the Scottish Land Court.[51]

That the ILP's tactics were a cause of great concern to many in Scotland was evident in the reaction of the country's press to the party's annual conference in April 1915.[52] The *Edinburgh Evening Dispatch* castigated ILP delegates as 'enemies of their country', while the *Sutherland Echo* was particularly vitriolic and only had one regret: 'that there [were] no legal powers for seizing such men, putting them under the grimmest of drill sergeants for severe and rapid training, and hurrying them to the hottest place at the front.' More perceptively, the *Aberdeen Evening Express* reported that, 'when the backwash of the war began to perturb the nation', more people would have sympathy with the ILP line.[53]

By May and June, such criticisms were put to one side as relations with the Labour Party sunk to an all time low following Arthur Henderson's decision to join the new Coalition Ministry. Underlying this concern was the issue of conscription. As Willie Stewart put it: 'Are they joining the Government, as they started their recruitment campaign, to save the country from conscription?' Stewart went on to note that the Labour Party now sided with Tariff Reformers, anti-Home Rulers, imperialists and Conscriptionists: 'reason enough for not joining the government,' concluded Stewart.[54] By early June 1915, it was clear that the issue of military and industrial conscription was to be used to assist in the ILP's anti-war propaganda campaign.[55]

Conscription becomes a reality

Despite the National Registration Act of June 1915, recruitment levels fell to around 80,000 per month before the end of January 1916.[56] The Military Service Act which followed in the same month imposed conscription upon single men aged eighteen to forty-one, with exemption clauses covering those in ill-health, engaged in work of national importance, or acting as sole breadwinner with dependents. It also maintained the right of individuals to refuse military service on conscientious grounds. These cases were to be heard by a local tribunal in each district which could grant exemptions on a temporary, conditional, or absolute basis. Problems in the operation of the Act meant that by March 1916, out of the 193,891 men called up, 57,416 did not appear and as a result, notes Hayes, the conscriptionists then turned their attentions to married men, extending the Military Service Act in May 1916.[57]

Over a year before, W. C. Anderson MP, in an address to the National

Council of the ILP, warned that conscription would lead to the 'militarisation of the whole working class' and maintained that the organised workers had been 'emphatic in their declarations against it'.[58] Political opposition to conscription had indeed been growing and, as Anderson suggested, the trade union movement came out against it. Not a single delegate spoke in favour of it at the TUC conference in 1915 which unanimously rejected any policy of forced service.[59] By January 1916, the Scottish Trade Union Congress passed an anti-conscription resolution by sixty-six votes to forty-six, and the Glasgow Labour Party and the Scottish Labour Conference also rejected conscription.[60] But once conscription became law, workers were left with two choices: to oppose it, or accept the democratic decision and the will of Parliament. Many joined campaigns to repeal the Military Service Act, and in September 1917 the TUC passed a unanimous resolution against both military and industrial conscription. A later Labour Party conference in January 1918 also demanded the absolute withdrawal of the Military Service Acts.[61]

In the meantime, the ILP and the NCF were growing in strength, and in the early months of 1915 the Glasgow Branch of the NCF was formed. The founding meeting had been organised by the BSP and was widely advertised in both the *Labour Leader* and *Forward*.[62] By the first anniversary of the war, the NCF had expanded and set-up branches in various locations around the country, often paralleling the network of ILP branches. A branch of the NCF was set up in Dundee, for example, following a large ILP meeting there in November 1915.[63] Indeed, Dundee became an ILP and NCF stronghold in Scotland: Willie Stewart was to report sometime later that not only was the ILP gaining in strength there, but the town 'was fair hotchin with conscientious objectors'.[64] There were also comrades from one town in Fife, reported *Forward*, who had fifty men waiting to register and follow the ILP line.[65]

By the end of 1915, the ILP had begun its own register for COs and claimed to speak for 10,000 men in Scotland.[66] Some trade unions were also organising Non-Conscription registers, including the Gasworkers Union of Scotland, the Shop Assistants Union, the Glasgow branch of the Workers' Union, the Leith Dockers, the Central Iron Moulders, and Clydebank Trades Council.[67] Moreover, Aberdeen, Dundee and Kirkintilloch Labour Representation Committees intimated that they too would help organise registers if the support of the Scottish Labour Party was forthcoming. The best organised district was Glasgow, where the ILP set in motion a series of demonstrations and meetings on the topics of conscription and freedom of speech. In December 1915, 7,000 people were reported to have turned out for a 'Free Speech and No Conscription

Demonstration', addressed by a host of well-known speakers including John Maclean, Emmanuel Shinwell, Mrs Helen Crawfurd and Willie Gallacher.[68] In short, the ILP had fought hard, along with the NCF, the BSP and other groups such as the Union of Democratic Control, to ensure that conscription was not introduced, but once it had been imposed they worked tirelessly for its repeal.[69]

By this time, *Forward* and the *Labour Leader* were running regular reports on the treatment of conscientious objectors both at the tribunals and at the hands of the military. One typical report noted the case of a man who claimed exemption because he had a crippled brother and mother to look after. He was given a temporary exemption of three months despite having four brothers already at the front. In contrast, a riding instructor was given six months exemption because he trained horses used by officers on their return from France.[70] The Master of the Berwickshire Fox Hounds likewise claimed exemption for one of his huntsmen. In the process he drew the attention of the tribunal to a War Office letter stating the desirability of keeping a large number of light animals suitable for the army: on this occasion a complete exemption was given.[71]

Forward's new feature, 'Round the Tribunals', reported on what was appearing in the columns of other papers around the country. One report noted in the *Glasgow Herald* was the case of a dowager marchioness who claimed exemption for her chauffeur, aged twenty-eight, because he was 'indispensable' in running her to her 'war work' at the hospital.[72]

By contrast, in that same edition of *Forward*, James Maxton gave an example of how he filled in his exemption application form in preparation for his appearance before the tribunals. He had stated simply:

I am a Socialist and a member of a Socialist organisation. As such I have worked to establish a better system of society, which would make for the peace and brotherhood of peoples of all lands. To take part in a war would be for me a desertion of these ideals, and I must therefore decline to take part.[73]

Willie Stewart similarly pleaded to tribunal members to 'do no outrage to the one supreme product of human growth and development – the human conscience'.[74] Such sentiments apparently fell on deaf ears in Scotland. Here, these bodies seem to have displayed 'a particular vindictiveness', as illustrated in the selection of the cases noted by *Forward.*[75] One account in the *Highland News* noted the words of the local tribunal upon hearing the case of a religious objector who claimed absolute exemption because he could obey only the Lord. The Chairman dismissed his claim saying: 'You are the most awful pack that ever walked this earth. To think that you would not stand up and defend our women and children from the ravages of the Germans. Is this Christianity? It is acting with the devil in the place of Christ.' [76] In other instances it seemed as if the 'good tribunes' simply toyed with those who came before them. Mr Spence, of the Dundee local tribunal, heard the case of a draper's assistant claiming exemption on religious grounds. When asked what his religion was, he replied 'spiritualist.' On hearing this, Mr Spence concluded, 'you are the very man for the front. You might come in contact with a few of them there.' His case was dismissed. [77] Another tribunal member, on hearing the statement that Christ told us to love our enemies, replied, 'we can love our enemies and kill them at the same time.' [78]

Despite outbursts of ridicule and verbal abuse, the Scottish tribunals were not always consistent in their deliberations. In one instance, for example twenty-one ILP COs were given exemption on political grounds. [79] Decisions often depended on where the tribunal met and how many cases they had to hear. One of the reasons that the Glasgow tribunals were seen to be harsher than others was perhaps due to the fact that they simply heard so many cases. Rae noted that the City of Glasgow local tribunal heard more cases in the month of July 1916 than the majority of tribunals disposed of in six years in the Second World War. [80] It may also have been the case that political COs were treated more harshly than others, for as *Forward* reported in April 1916, most COs in Glasgow were ILPers. [81]

Whatever the outcome, there is little doubt that these public gatherings provided the ILP with an opportunity to carry out some political propaganda on the issue of the war. Rae, using evidence gathered from the Glasgow tribunals, noted:

> In industrial areas, with strong socialist loyalties, an ILP applicant would be accompanied by a vociferous group of supporters. Tribunal members were interrupted and jeered, and it was commonplace for *The Red Flag* to be sung at the hearing ... [82]

In response to their treatment as 'renegades', some attempted to marry the political and moral arguments against conscription. The ILPer, William Leslie, appeared before the Elgin local tribunal during July 1916 and applied for 'absolute exemption' on conscientious grounds:

> ... according to his religious and moral beliefs he could take no part in the slaughter of his fellow-creatures. His religion was socialism, and he believed in the law laid down by Christ in the

Immortal Sermon on the Mount. He asked for absolute exemption from military service, even non-combatant service, because he would not relieve someone to do what he was not prepared to do himself...

In response to questioning, he stated that 'no righteousness could be gained by armed force', and admitted to being a member of the ILP and the NCF. He was quite willing to undertake work of national importance, he claimed, but not under military discipline. The Military representative dissented from his application and Leslie's case was rejected.[83] Leslie appealed against the decision and in August his appeal was sustained on condition that he joined the Friends Ambulance Unit within twenty-one days. This he refused to do and he was later arrested and jailed.[84]

Harvie argues that while the ILP were particularly militant on the issue of conscription, the Scots ILPers were 'a more subversive, less principled bunch, [who] usually avoided the martyrdom of prison.'[85] Leslie's admission that he would accept work of national importance, but not under military supervision, was an example of this response. Similarly, James Maxton was given an exemption, on condition that he found himself work of national importance. While he found this difficult, Maxton eventually found employment in a small shipyard which was not directly involved in war work. Maxton had by then spent some considerable time in prison for breach of the Defence of the Realm Act in 1915. Prison may have attracted publicity, but precluded him from his socialist agitation. He was to recollect these times in the book, *We Did Not Fight* (1935):

> I appreciated and understood the attitude of my friends who absolutely declined to do anything, and suffer continuous imprisonment over the whole war period, but it did not suit my philosophy, which demanded active carrying on of the class struggle, nor did it suit my temperament to be cribbed, cabined and confined when the urge within me was to be out trying to influence my fellows to use the opportunities presented by war conditions for the purpose of social revolution ...[86]

With war weariness setting in and more trouble brewing over the issue of industrial conscription, this pragmatism was soon to be rewarded. From 1916 onwards, the ILP were again beginning to attract listeners. Even well-known COs were being given a hearing, where before they were shouted down, and more importantly, after early 1917, ILP membership was rising.[87] By this point, more and more ILP members were also being brought before the tribunals and more cases for exemption on conscientious grounds were being rejected.[88] Not all were treated harshly, but those who did choose prison also accepted that their sentence often entailed hard labour.

The mainstream press were all too happy to publish tribunal proceedings, especially when COs were dealt severe sentences, and particularly if they were being re-arrested and imprisoned for the same offence. There were several cases where the tribunals and the military authorities acted unlawfully. One such case concerned an Edinburgh ILP member. A High Court decision found that he had been illegally detained for some four months. What surprised *Forward* was that it was not reported anywhere other than in their columns: only his initial arrest had been reported elsewhere.[89] The most severe cases occurred where the military had become involved with COs. Arthur Marwick uncovered one case where thirty-four men, who were deemed to have enlisted in the 'Non-Combatant Corps', were smuggled into France, and there 'the sentence of death was read.'[90] Had it not been for the NCF hearing of their plight, they would have been shot; instead, their sentence was commuted to ten years penal servitude.[91] As a result of such cases and consequent public pressure, after May 1916 it was decreed that the military had to turn COs over to the civil authorities if they refused to obey military orders.

As the war progressed, the ILP tended to leave practical CO issues increasingly to the National Council of the NCF, and *Forward* and the *Labour Leader* helped to take the NCF's message to a growing audience. The future of the ILP itself also continued to look somewhat brighter, as Willie Stewart noted in November 1917:

> The ILP has stood its ground through the war and the dark days of militarists' oppression. It has its sons in every prison and penal centres set apart for conscientious objectors to militarism. It has steadfastly and fearlessly fought for liberty and Socialism. Now it is reaping the rewards in increased membership and in the increased confidence of the industrial community.[92]

In March, 1918, Stewart was to report that the number of ILP branches had risen from 112 to 167, and the membership had swelled from just under 3,000 to 9,000, confirming his earlier predictions.[93]

During the last days of the war the mood in the ILP camp was buoyant and upbeat. Despite the threat of total collapse, the ILP's early unpopularity, its political isolation and its lone stand against the warmongers, the party had won through. It had taken on the 'Official' Labour Party when it 'defected to Militarism.' In the wake of the introduction of the Munitions Act, the Defence of the Realm Act, and finally the Conscription Acts, 'when the young men of the ILP, along with others ... had to face a new ordeal,' the party fought against the 'undermining of democracy'[94] Now the ILP was working to spread socialism throughout Scotland. Branches emerged in Inverurie, Buckie, Keith and Craigellachie: to cap it all, wrote Willie Stewart, 'the ILP is in Banffshire!' [95] The achievement was indeed remarkable, underlined by the fact that by 1918 the Scottish ILP was providing about a third of the party's total British membership.[96]

Conscientious objectors in peacetime

Despite the formal end of hostilities in 1918, the struggle for the ILP and *Forward* seemed far from over. In the first place, they were faced with the task of mobilising opinion to fight for the repeal of the Military Service Act. Also, along with the NCF, they were greatly concerned with the concessions to militarism contained in the Education Act, which allowed Local Authorities to introduce camps, drills, and special military lessons in schools. Meanwhile, a further concern was the continuing plight of the COs, whose continued imprisonment remained 'a challenge to whatever sense of justice still remains in this country.' [97]

In March 1919, the campaign to free the COs was stepped up, when *Forward* printed an article, 'The Quiet Safety of Prison', written by W. J. Chamberlain. The article was a response to 'the cruellest slander' ever uttered against the COs in prison, made by Sir George Cave, the late Home Secretary, who had argued that some preferred the 'quiet safety of prison to the more strenuous life of the soldier in the trenches.' For Chamberlain, this was a deliberate attempt to 'mislead the public' as to the true facts of the conscientious objector's case. Sir George Cave knew only too well, argued Chamberlain, that the only choice open to the COs was not between prison and the trenches, but between prison and the 'acceptance of work of national importance'.[98]

Chamberlain wrote of his own experiences of prison and noted how the COs and 'soldier prisoners' – those on active duty convicted of serious crimes – were mixed almost 'fifty-fifty'. For about a week or more, these soldiers thought they were better off than in the trenches. But as the weeks went by, the prison regime began to 'break their resolve', and they petitioned the War Office for 'remission of sentence', which was nearly always granted 'on condition that the prisoner went back to the front.' Chamberlain added: 'every man gladly accepted this condition in order to escape from the horror of the prison regime.'

In April it was reported that the government intended to release 'all COs who had served two years or more' – a move welcomed by the editors of *Forward*, who reminded readers of their duty to these men on their return. They would require 'careful attention, nourishing food, and a good holiday' in order to restore them to good health. To this end a committee was formed comprising the ILP, SLP and NCF and others, to raise £4,000 to help returning COs who would be back among them within the course of a fortnight. Ironically, in the following edition, a front page editorial spoke scathingly of Mr Lloyd George and his 'party' and their seeming opposition to Churchill's proposed Conscription Bill, which aimed to continue and extend the principle of military conscription in Britain. 'If we are not careful', they advised, 'the party that gave us conscription (saladed with trickeries about conscientious objection and attestation) will sweep back into power on a No-Conscription ticket!'[99]

At a meeting at St. Andrews Halls, Glasgow on 11 April 1919, a large crowd turned out to hear various speakers at a rally calling for 'the Abolition of Conscription and the release of all Conscientious Objectors'. One of the speakers was W. J. Chamberlain, himself only recently released, who recalled:

> They had been accused of being afraid of their skins, but it was a remarkable fact that since the fighting had stopped 240 men had been offered comparative freedom if they would just put on Khaki before demobilisation, and not a single man would accept the offer.[100]

Compulsory military conscription was finally abolished in December 1920, just under five years after it was introduced. For those who hoped it would 'flush out hordes of slackers', it had proved disappointing. In the first six months numbers enlisting fell to around 40,000 per month, less than half the rate of recruitment under the voluntary system.[101] In all, there had been around 16,500 conscientious objectors to conscription in Britain, but only around 1,500 of these were absolutists, and a full five months after the war had ended some 1,300 were still in prison.[102] As Martin Ceadel argues, although they only numbered 0.33% of the total of all other conscripts plus volunteers, 'they had a public impact out of proportion to their numbers.'[103]

For those war resisters still in prison, release eventually came, but many were to serve out their sentence in full. Despite the severity of the sentences and the conditions that many were to endure, they were still victimised in many other ways. 'Displaying a conspicuous pique', states DeGroot, 'Parliament disenfranchised all conscientious objectors for five years (beyond the enactment of the 1918 Representation of the People Act), unless they could prove that they had performed work of national importance.'[104]

Conclusion

In conclusion, the ILP as a political organisation maintained its anti-war stand throughout the Great War, and in the years after its end continued their fight against British militarism and campaigned to abolish conscription. Within Scotland, the ILP had first embarked upon their anti-war mission for political purposes. Where International Socialism failed at the outbreak of war, Scottish war resisters were to provide an alternative tradition for cultivation by later generations of socialists.[105] Moreover, there was 'much goodwill' reported between conscientious objectors and 'conscientious assentors' who had volunteered for armed service in Scotland. One such volunteer wrote from the trenches to a CO in Scotland, just days before he was killed: 'Your situation is worse because you are so misunderstood.' [106]

Finally, the ILP quest for international peace also had a near religious quality about it which may also have assisted its eventual recovery in Scotland. This was perhaps most eloquently put by one Glasgow minister, quoted in *Forward* in September 1919. He made reference to the ILP's ethical and international outlook during the war, and in particular its stand against conscription and militarism. He concluded: 'that they [the ILP] were the purest Christian institution in the city.' [107]

By the time the war was nearing its end, *Forward* reviewed the progress which the ILP had made over the previous four years. Because of a successful 'Home Front Offensive', it stated, the number of branches had now risen to 201 and the membership had increased to over 10,000.[108] In February 1915 there had been fears that the ILP's anti-war message would be 'misunderstood' and that this would adversely affect the party's fortunes. In the event, many thousands of ordinary Scots had listened to the ILP's anti-war message and by the end of the hostilities *Forward* could proudly proclaim: 'the ILP in Scotland lives, and in 201 towns and villages bears witness to the vitality of the Socialist Movement'.[109]

Notes

1. A. J. P. Taylor, *English History 1914 to 1945* (Oxford, 1981), pp. 1–2.
2. *Forward*, 22 Aug. 1914.
3. *Ibid.*, 14 Feb., 22, 29 Aug., 4 Sept., 17 Oct. 1914.
4. D. Hayes, *Conscription Conflict: The Conflict of Ideas in the Struggle for and against Military Conscription in Britain Between 1901 and 1939* (London, 1949), p. 248.
5. *Ibid.*, p. 257.
6. *Ibid.*, p. 266.
7. *Forward*, 1 Mar. 1919.

8. W. Marwick, 'Conscientious objection in Scotland in the First World War', *Scottish Journal of Science,* i (Jun. 1972), p. 157.

9. *Ibid.*

10. *Forward,*19 Mar. 1918.

11. C. Harvie, 'Before the breakthrough, 1888–1922', in I. Donnachie, C. Harvie and I. S. Wood (eds), *FORWARD!: Labour Politics in Scotland 1888–1988* (Edinburgh, 1989), p. 25.

12. *Ibid.,* p. 24.

13. *Daily Record,* 11 Aug. 1914.

14. C. Harvie, *No Gods and Precious Few Heroes: Scotland 1914 to 1980* (Edinburgh, 1981), pp. 10, 24; Harvie, 'Before the breakthrough', p. 21.

15. *Dundee Advertiser,* 8 Nov. 1914, quoted in R. Finlay, 'Imperial Scotland: Scottish National Identity and the British Empire, 1850–1914' (unpublished paper), p. 18.

16. Harvie, 'Before the breakthrough', p. 21.

17. *Ibid.*

18. *Glasgow Herald,* 31 Aug. 1914.

19. R. Harrison, 'The War Emergency Worker's National Committee 1914–1920', in A. Briggs and J. Saville (eds), *Essays in Labour History 1886–1923* (London, 1971), p. 219.

20. N. Milton, *John MacLean* (London, 1973), pp. 76–7.

21. *Ibid.,* p. 78.

22. *Glasgow Herald,* 10 Aug. 1914.

23. *Forward,* 15 Aug. 1914.

24. *Labour Leader,* 13 Aug. 1914.

25. *Forward,* 13 Aug. 1914.

26. Harvie, 'Before the breakthrough', p. 24.

27. *Forward,* 13 Feb. 1915.

28. *Ibid.,* 5 Sept. 1914.

29. *Ibid.,* 17 Sept. 1914.

30. *Ibid.,* 31 Oct. 1914.

31. Hayes, *Conscription Conflict,* p. 150.

32. *Glasgow Herald,* 8 Dec. 1914.

33. *Ibid.,* 18 Nov. 1914.

34. *Daily Record,* 1 Dec. 1914.

35. *Forward,* 21 Nov. 1914.

36. *Ibid.*

37. *Forward,* 28 Nov. 1914.

38. Hayes, *Conscription Conflict,* p. 249.

39. *Ibid.,* p. 251.

40. J. Rae, *Conscience and Politics: The British Government and the Consciencious Objectors to Military Service, 1916–1919* (Oxford, 1970), p. 12.

41. *Ibid.,* pp. 83–4.

42. Harvie, 'Before the breakthrough', p. 23; Marwick, 'Conscientious objection', p. 159.

43. *Forward,* 2 Jan. 1915.

44. *Ibid.*

45. *Ibid.*

46. Marwick, 'Conscientious Objection', p. 160; S. J. Brown, '"A solemn purification by fire": responses to the Great War in the Scottish presbyterian churches 1914–19', *Journal of Ecclesiastical History,* xlv (1994), pp. 82–104.

47. *Forward,* 21 Nov. 1914; Marwick, 'Conscientious objection', p. 160.

48. *Ibid.,* 21 Jan., 13 Feb. 1915.

49. *Ibid.,* 13 Feb. 1915.
50. *Ibid.*
51. *Forward,* 13, 27 Mar. 1915.
52. *Ibid.,* 17, 24 Apr. 1915.
53. *Aberdeen Evening Express,* 6 Apr. 1915.
54. *Forward,* 29 May 1915.
55. *Ibid.,* 21 May to 12 Jun. 1915.
56. Hayes, *Conscription Conflict,* p. 161.
57. *Ibid.,* pp. 218, 224–5.
58. *Forward,* 12 Jun. 1915.
59. Hayes, *Conscription Conflict,* p. 230.
60. *Glasgow Herald,* 5, 17 Jan. 1916; *The Scotsman,* 17 Jan. 1916.
61. Hayes, *Conscription Conflict,* p. 233.
62. *Labour Leader,* 25 Feb., 18 Mar. 1915; *Forward,* 13 Mar. 1915.
63. *Forward,* 20 Nov. 1915.
64. *Ibid.,* 28 Apr. 1917.
65. *Ibid.,* 27 Nov. 1915.
66. *Ibid.*
67. *Ibid.*
68. *Forward,* 18 Dec. 1915.
69. *Ibid.,* 19 Feb. 1916.
70. *Ibid.,* 26 Feb. 1916.
71. *Berwickshire News,* 29 Feb. 1916.
72. *Forward,* 4 Mar. 1916.
73. *Ibid.*
74. *Ibid.*
75. Harvie, 'Before the breakthrough', p. 23; Marwick, 'Conscientious objectors', p. 157.
76. *Forward,* 4 Mar. 1916.
77. *Ibid.,* 1 Apr. 1916.
78. *Ibid.,* 29 Apr. 1916.
79. *Ibid.,* 25 Mar. 1916.
80. Rae, *Conscience and Politics,* p. 98.
81. *Forward,* 1 Apr. 1916.
82. Rae, *Conscience and Politics,* p. 99; *Glasgow Herald,* 16 Mar. 1916.
83. *The Northern Scot and Moray and Nairn Express,* 8 Jul. 1916.
84. *Ibid.,* 2 Aug. 1916; Information from Leslie's daughter, Mrs Margaret Short, Dec. 1996.
85. Harvie, 'Before the breakthough', p. 23.
86. James Maxton, 'War resistance by working class struggle', in J. Bell (ed.), *We Did Not Fight* (London, 1935), pp. 213–22.
87. *Ibid.,* p. 220.
88. *Forward,* see weekly feature 'Round the Tribunals', Mar. 1916 to Apr. 1917.
89. *Ibid.,* 28 Sept. 1916.
90. A. Marwick, *The Deluge: British Society and the First World War* (London, 1965), p. 81.
91. Hayes, *Conscription Conflict,* p. 260.
92. *Forward,* 10 Nov. 1917.
93. *Ibid.,* 19 Mar. 1918.
94. *Ibid.,* 26 Oct. 1918.
95. *Forward,* 2 Nov. 1918.
96. Harvie, 'Before the breakthrough, p. 24.

97. *Forward,* 22 Mar. 1919.
98. *Ibid.,* 1 Mar. 1919.
99. *Ibid.,* 19 Apr. 1919.
100. *Ibid.,* 12 Apr. 1919.
101. J. Stevenson, *British Society 1914–45* (London, 1990), pp. 64–5; Taylor, *English History,* pp. 54–5.
102. *Forward,* 12 Apr. 1919.
103. M. Ceadel, 'Attitudes to war: pacifism and collective security', in Paul Johnson (ed.), *Twentieth Century Britain: Economic, Social and Cultural Change* (London, 1994), p. 223.
104. G. J. DeGroot, *Blighty: British Society in the Era of the Great War* (Harlow, 1996), pp. 312–13.
105. Hayes, *Conscription Conflict,* p. 226.
106. Marwick, 'Conscientious objection', p. 160.
107. *Forward,* 27 Sept. 1919.
108. *Ibid.,* 26 Oct. 1918.
109. *Ibid.*

CHAPTER FOUR

Fighting and Bleeding for the Land: the Scottish Highlands and the Great War

Ewen A. Cameron and Iain J. M. Robertson

THE MASSIVE EXPANSION of military recruiting by the British state in the second half of the eighteenth century was crucial in establishing the military identity of the Scottish Highlands. In this period landowners took advantage of government bounties to recruit men from their estates. This activity aided their rehabilitation in the eyes of the state and they exploited the process of recruiting to reorganise their estates. It has been demonstrated that the military industry was at least as important as kelping and fishing in the establishment of crofting communities. Further, it has been shown that Highland landowners in this period used the vestigial power of clanship to present themselves as potential recruiters.[1] For the purposes of this chapter, these points are important for two reasons. Firstly, the connection between recruiting and the land issue was long established: as will be discussed below, the idea of gaining land in return for military service became an important part of the rhetoric of crofters and cottars in the period of the Great War. Secondly, the legacy of recruiting was important for landowners as well as crofters and cottars: it allowed them to place their activities in recruiting in 1914 in an established historical context. Cameron of Lochiel, for instance, was instrumental in raising four new Service battalions of the Queen's Own Cameron Highlanders (QOCH) in 1914 and constantly referred to the history and traditions of the 79th regiment, the forerunner of the QOCH, raised by Allan Cameron of Erracht. Thus, in his view, the martial tradition of the Scottish Highlands was harnessed for the British state in the second half of the eighteenth century and only had to be rekindled in 1914 to be of service once more.

Developments in the nineteenth century, however, were problematic for those concerned to present an unbroken history of Highland military enthusiasm. Although the Highland regiments continued to perform effectively in theatres such as the Crimea, the Indian Mutiny and Egypt, Scottish recruiting was, in Hanham's words, 'simply not keeping up with population growth'.[2] In the Highlands there was a different relationship between recruiting and demography. Population growth had been checked by mid-century and there was a widespread perception that the Highlands were not living up to expectations in terms of recruiting. This became controversial during the Crimean War: recruiting came after forty years of peace, during which time Highland society had undergone a dramatic and traumatic transformation.[3] Nevertheless, the long tradition of viewing the Highlands as a distinctive recruitment area persisted. In the late Victorian period this often descended into sentimentality.[4] The Highland regiments, although they were decreasingly composed of Highlanders, were seen as something to be defended. This was abundantly clear during the controversy over army reform in he early 1880s when the Highland regiments and their tartan paraphernalia escaped lightly.[5]

Yet the myth of the Highland soldier could also be adapted to fit new economic and agrarian realities. The Lovat Scouts, for example, raised as a personal initiative of Lord Lovat during the South African War, demonstrated that the skills required to service the commercialised sporting economy of the Highlands could be utilised for military purposes. Lovat believed that Highland stalkers and ghillies, skilled in the use of telescopes, could be put to good use in South Africa. The unit was utilised once again in the Great War, with many members of the Scouts at the forefront of the new and grisly art of sniping.[6]

The chapter which follows will fall into three parts. The first part will consider the rhetoric of recruiting, the second the changing attitude to the war as losses began to mount, and the third examines popular protest over the land issue. The principal theme running through the discussion will be the link between promises held to have been made during recruiting campaigns and expectations of land settlement. In this regard, a distinction will be noted between the rhetoric of recruiting at a national and at a local level.

Recruiting

This section analyses a selection of the rhetoric used in the recruiting campaigns in the initial stages of the Great War in the Highlands. An attempt will be made to relate the experience in the Highlands to the wider context of recruiting in 1914. An important point to bear in mind here is that recruitment was located in the public domain and took place at a national level. The basic context for this discussion is the appeal made by Lord Kitchener in 1914 for an extra 100,000 recruits.

It has been argued that it was significant that the existing regimental structure was used for this expansion of the army rather than the creation of new regiments. This allowed old loyalties and emotions to be deployed and this was particularly important in the Scottish Highlands.[7] As emphasised below, quite different bargains were perceived to have been made at a local level. Notwithstanding the fact that the rather romantic notion of the 'rush to the colours' has been questioned by historians, it is beyond doubt that in a quantitative sense, the recruiting campaigns in 1914 were extraordinarily successful, especially in August and early September.[8] Of particular significance here, alongside motives more complex than that of simple patriotism, was the role played by local identities and loyalties.[9] This was especially relevant in the Highlands, where the vestiges of clan loyalty and a perceived martial tradition were added to the customary rhetorical devices of the recruiting campaign – namely, national loyalty and the need to demonstrate the vitality of voluntary recruiting in order to obviate conscription. Highland enthusiasm can be contrasted with other rural areas of Britain, most notably Welsh speaking parts of Wales. In Ireland, although it is important not to exaggerate from an uncritical acceptance of nationalist propaganda, recruiting was running behind Highland levels. Of course, the Highland experience was an element of the wider picture of buoyant Scottish recruiting in 1914.[10]

The leadership of the recruiting campaign in the Highlands was taken up by members of the traditional land-owning families. The tenurial role of landowners had been under threat in the Highlands since the 1870s, but in 1914 they still had latent powers of political and social leadership.[11] In late August, Cameron of Lochiel published a letter in the local press informing readers that he had been commissioned to raise a battalion. In this letter he emphasised his own personal role in the recruiting process, but he could not avoid the dilemma posed by the scattered nature of the Highland population:

> I want to raise a thousand Highlanders for my own battalion and I have no doubt I shall have little difficulty in doing so; but, having regard to the fact that Highlanders are now scattered all over the face of the earth, I must specially appeal to the officials and committees of the different Highland county and clan societies in Glasgow, Edinburgh and elsewhere to assist me in my endeavours by becoming my recruiting agents.

He went on to refer to the physique of the Highlanders and his determination to organise companies and platoons according to local districts, before concluding by referring to the 'untarnished standard of the Camerons'.[12]

After the initial recruiting boom had passed, renewed appeals for men were made. One such, by the Duke of Argyll in December 1914, is worthy of examination:

> Through causes purely economic, of which the growth of the Dominions is the chief, there are no longer such great surplus populations in the Highlands of Argyll and its Isles. By the lifting of his finger or his Cross of Fire, MacCailein cannot perhaps raise the men he once could have done, but he thinks the old spirit, hardly really dormant, is yet alive amongst his vassals, whose forbears so often rallied round the Kings of Old.[13]

Like Lochiel, the Duke was attempting to renew vestigial loyalties by glossing over the recent traumatic history of the Highlands. In his case, emigration was camouflaged by the phrase 'the growth of the Dominions' and depopulation was rationalised as the loss of 'surplus' population.

A more eccentric line was taken by Macdonald of Clanranald, whose forbears had been proprietors in the Uists and on the western seaboard but had lost their lands in the first half of the nineteenth century. The family had a Jacobite heritage and he made interesting use of the ethnic origins of the Hanoverians to argue:

> I will ask you to remember what happened to our ancestors after the '45 and how brutally they were treated by "Butcher" Cumberland, and his Germans, when the fortunes of war were against them. The Germans by their behaviour in Belgium and other places, which, owing to their immense forces, they have been able, at present, to overrun, are showing that they are quite as brutal now as Cumberland and his men were then.[14]

Of course, not all Highland regiments recruited exclusively from the Highlands. We have already noted how both Lochiel and Argyll referred to a perceived wider community of Highlanders in urban Scotland and beyond. Recruiting of Princess Louise's (Argyll and Sutherland Highlanders) took place in such Lowland towns as Dumbarton, Greenock and Port Glasgow. The QOCH made a considerable and successful effort to recruit in Glasgow. Lochiel spoke at meetings of Highland and Clan Societies in Glasgow in early September 1914. In November the regiment marched through Glasgow, was paraded at Ibrox at a Rangers versus Queen's Park match – football fans had been perceived as being reluctant to join the colours – and one hundred recruits were secured.[15] Further evidence of the wide appeal of the Highland regiments comes from the fact that a company of the 5th Battalion QOCH was formed from the employees of the Glasgow Stock Exchange, and a company of the 6th Battalion from the students of the University.[16]

As we have already noted, these early campaigns were highly successful in raising large numbers of men. To the existing regular and territorial battalions, the recruiting campaigns of 1914 added three new (or Service) battalions of the Seaforths, four new battalions of the QOCH and four new battalions of the Argylls.[17] These new battalions, regarded with some suspicion by professional soldiers, would not see active service until the summer of 1915. Their introduction to the front line and consequent losses completely altered the popular perception of the war in the Highlands.[18]

Changing attitudes to the war

Recruiting took place against a background of continuing activity in the industrial and agricultural economies and, indeed, competed for labour with these activities. In a rural area such as the Highlands, the main problem was to ensure that recruiting did not interfere with the gathering of the harvest. The efforts expended to minimise this conflict support the notion that the 'flight from the land' was not as serious as many considered it to be at the time.[19] The Harris Tweed and fishing industries were, however, adversely affected by the outbreak of war, but the kelp industry experienced a revival as supplies of potash from Germany were cut off.[20]

Socially, we have already noted the way in which the outbreak of war and the initial recruiting campaigns were overlaid with references to the martial tradition of the Highlands and to the histories of the various regiments involved. This was added to the national rhetoric of the war as a moral crusade. The *Inverness Courier* frequently repeated and augmented this statement by noting that this united response was evident 'even in Ireland'.[21] For one recent historian: 'This innocent, gullible generation still believed in heroes, duty and the glory of war. War was not a disaster but an opportunity, a chance to prove oneself and do one's bit.'[22]

Without necessarily endorsing the notion of a 'gullible' generation, it is possible to recognise that the rhetoric, if not the reality, of these notions was evident in a distinctly Highland context. Here, the heroism and glory that was appealed to was that of the Highland regiments in the past, and especially in the French Wars. The *Oban Times* reported in August 1914: 'Not since the Inveraray soldiery left for Belgium and fought at Quatre Bras and at Waterloo, nearly a hundred years ago, have the residents of the Royal Burgh exhibited such military enthusiasm.'[23] The paper was to return to the theme later in the year when it equated the death of Captain Allan Cameron, the younger brother of Cameron of Lochiel, to the 'glorious end of Colonel John Cameron of Fassifern at Quatre Bras'.[24]

In early 1915, in a renewed appeal for men, the *Inverness Courier* played on both the vestigial loyalty to clan and the exploits of Highlanders in the service of Britain:

> If an islesman enlists, depend upon it, he will follow Lord Lovat or Lochiel, for they are the militant representatives of two great Highland families to whom Highlanders and Islesmen ever looked to for leadership ... The country still appeals for men. The call has gone forth to these straths and glens from whence were drawn the warriors who fought under Wellington in the Peninsula, who stood by the grave of the gallant Moore on the ramparts of Corruna, and took a notable part in upholding their country's honour on a Belgian plain a few years later.[25]

Later in the year it was asserted of the men of the Hebrides that, 'the virtue of patriotism in them is not a growth of yesterday. It is a noble heritage from a race of ancestors whose deeds of valour on continental fields find a prominent place in the pages of history.'[26]

Lord Lovat, speaking at a recruiting meeting in Dingwall in September 1915, referred to the war as a 'glorious opportunity' for the young men of Ross-shire, and in the early months of the war, there was frequent reference to glory in the discussion of individual and collective losses.[27] For the landlord classes, loss was presented in the context of the heroic military tradition of their respective families.[28] In a more collective sense, the losses among the regulars of the Camerons with the British Expeditionary Force (BEF) at Mons and Aisne were presented in a similar manner: 'the courage and bravery of these Highland warriors has always been to some extent their undoing. They fall but they never yield.'[29] This attitude continued into 1915: the second battle of Ypres was ranked alongside Waterloo and Blenheim 'for glory and effect', and it was declared that 'it will long be remembered as one of the most glorious in the annals of the British army.'[30]

This was a period when the war was idealised and romanticised. Indeed, it was seen as a 'glorious opportunity' – a theatre of conflict for the demonstration of heroism. Typical of such attitudes was a letter from Sir Iain Colquhoun, published in the *Oban Times* in late 1914. In December 1914 the redoubtable Sir Iain, a 'prodigious walker', former boxing opponent of the Crown Prince of Germany and a 'lover of all things Highland', recovering from the removal of no less than 130 pieces of shrapnel from his side, wrote to friends in the following terms:

> Just to let you know that I am frightfully fit and enjoying the whole thing. The casualties all around are pretty heavy, I'm afraid, and our officers are a bit fewer. However, the battalion has fought simply splendidly, and that is all that matters.[31]

Such celebration and glorification was not to last, however. In late April 1915 a despatch from General French concerning the second battle of Ypres was published under the heading 'A Fateful Battle'. The *Inverness Courier* remarked that the despatch would help to 'awaken the nation to a full sense of realities and responsibilities of the situation' and further pointed out that:

> In drawing aside for once the veil and permitting the nation to see the nature of the terrible life and death struggle in which our men are at this very moment engaged in, the government has acted wisely ... the fate of nations is trembling in the balance.[32]

With the commitment of the Kitchener armies to Europe in the summer of 1915, and especially with their first major deployment in the front line at the Battle of Loos in late September, the perception changed irrevocably.[33] Highlanders were given a major role in the offensive in the late summer of 1915.[34] Two divisions, the 9th and the 15th, were to be involved in the battle and there were no less than five battalions of the QOCH involved, including three Service Battalions. The losses sustained by these battalions were immense.[35] There had been widespread suspicion among the officers of the regular army about the new troops, but in the aftermath of the Battle of Loos a concerted effort was made to present an impression of them as disciplined soldiers who had performed with the utmost bravery in the face of demoralising losses. The chapters on the battle in the official history of the QOCH are replete with testimonials to the new armies from serving officers. One officer was reported to have said of the 7th Battalion of the QOCH, that he 'could not have imagined that troops with a bare twelve months training behind them could have accomplished it.'[36]

The reaction to the battle at home was quite striking and most of it centred around the exploits of the 7th Battalion who had advanced far beyond their immediate objective, the capture of Hill 70, and had become cut off from their support and suffered terrible losses. The *Inverness Courier* initially gloried in the exploits of the Camerons but then began to rail against censorship when it became unclear as to whether the early gains made by the Camerons had been subsequently lost.[37] Such was the interest in the battle, that the *Inverness Courier* printed a penny pamphlet with its reports of the action. The introduction to this work hoped that:

> these tales of the deathless deeds of the Camerons may prove an incentive to such of the young and fit in the Highlands as have not yet joined the colours, and so help to fill up with Highlanders the depleted ranks of this most gallant regiment.[38]

Although, in the longer term, this battle would be used as the source for new myths about the invincibility of the Highland regiments, it did induce a more realistic attitude to the war at home.[39] This was so not only because of the scale of the losses, but also because it spread war losses all over the Highlands and the battle had involved soldiers of 'not more than seven months standing'.[40] The battle has also been presented as a peculiarly Scottish enterprise due to the large number of Scottish troops involved. The official history of the QOCH records that the battle of Loos was 'one of the greatest in the History of Scotland'.[41]

Thus far an attempt has been made to interrogate the rhetoric of the war. The following section will attempt to explore the reality of that rhetoric as it affected the ordinary Highlander. The quite different strategies used by recruiters at a more local and personal level will be emphasised. The medium used for this exploration is, perhaps, one of the best when concerned with 'history from below', that of acts of popular protest.

Protest and the land issue

If the concerns of military recruiters and the perception of the war changed over time, the domestic concerns of the Highlanders they recruited, remained remarkably consistent. Highlanders wanted enhanced access to land. For crofters this usually took the form of enlargements to their existing croft, while for cottars the demand was invariably for crofts. This section will attempt to demonstrate that a conjunction of the frustration engendered by the failure of government to meet crofters' and cottars' demands, the act of going to war, and, above all, the rhetoric of recruiting, brought about a revival in acts of protest and an expansion in the typology of protest, on a scale not seen in the Highlands since the 1880s.

Largely due to the inability of successive governments to legislate fully to meet the demands of crofters and cottars, the land issue in the Highlands continued to engender much political activity. Indeed, less than three years before the outbreak of war the Small Landholders (Scotland) Act came into operation. This act created very high expectations among crofters and cottars that large amounts of land were about to be redistributed in their favour. Unfortunately, these expectations could not be met. As a consequence of bad drafting and the lack of financial resources – weaknesses redolent of earlier equally flawed legislation – the land settlement operation was singularly ineffective in the period 1912 to 1914. With the onset of war, what land settlement there was, was wound down; nevertheless, criticism of the 1911 Act did not cease. Indeed, in 1916 the Scottish Land Court, the body created to oversee the implementation of the Act, condemned it in its Annual Report.[42]

This official criticism sanctioned renewed political activity on the land issue. At the 1916 AGM of the Inverness Liberal Association, for instance, J. G. Mackay, a veteran land campaigner, condemned the Act and concluded that:

> Highlanders at home and abroad had shown themselves to be loyal citizens of the Empire and had answered the call. The bitterest opponent of land reform could now see the injury done to the country by denuding it of its peasantry.[43]

This latter comment is an interesting echo of nineteenth century arguments that Highland depopulation was compromising national strength.

Political activity on this question continued to develop. In December 1916 a Highland Land Settlement Association was formed in Glasgow, for the particular purpose of 'settling soldiers and sailors upon the land'.[44] In October 1917, T. B. Morison, the Solicitor General, declared that Highlanders 'were entitled to expect that the land question in the Highlands would be settled once and for all'. Morison also used the argument that the Highlands were a vital reservoir of soldiery and that Highland land settlement was vital for 'national safety'.[45] These consensual points were augmented by the Secretary for Scotland, Robert Munro. Speaking in his native Easter Ross, Munro argued:

> Peer and peasant, castle and cottage were nearer one another and

understood one another better that they ever did in the history of
our land, because they were united in a common heroism and
suffered in a common grief.[46]

Moreover, this appeal to a wider constituency can be seen as part
of a deliberate attempt by politicians to use the war as a device to
take the bitterness and conflict out of the land issue. In his October
1917 speech, Morison argued that he 'was sure they would all be willing to forget past struggles and the bitterness of controversies', and
further:

> If ... the effect of the war would be to solve our Highland land prob-
> lem, let them make the most of the opportunity. Though they would
> do well to forget the bitterness of old controversies, let them not
> forget the lessons of past experiences and past mistakes, and let them
> aim at a land settlement on broad lines and on an extensive scale.[47]

War, however, did not solve the Highland land problem. In the short
term at least, it exacerbated it. We have already noted that the 1911
Act occasioned much political opposition at the national level. At the
regional and local level the characteristic response of the land-working
population to the frustrations engendered by a continuing lack of land
was, from the 1880s, the forced seizure of land. The institutions linking
the local and national, the social and political, were the Highland Land
League and the Highland Land Settlement Association.[48]

The generally accepted pattern of protest has suggested that it was
at its most intense during the period delineated by The Battle of the
Braes and the establishment of the Congested Districts Board (1881–
1897). More recently, however, attention has been drawn to
twentieth-century protest. The period between 1897 and 1914 is now
recognised as a significant link between earlier events and the intense
period of disturbance in the years immediately following the Great War.
Indeed, the full extent of protest after 1918 has only recently been
documented.[49]

As demonstrated by Table 1 and Appendices 1 and 2, there was a
significant expansion of events of protest in the post-1914 Highlands.
For the period 1897–1914, forty-two instances of protest are recorded,
confined principally to the Western Isles. However, after 1914, and after
1918 especially, it is possible to document over 500 separate events and
recognise that protest had spread to areas previously quiescent, such as
Caithness, Perthshire, Mull and Tiree. This represents a return to levels
of protest commensurate with that of the early stages of the Land Wars

Table 1: *Comparative Rate of Occurrence of Incidents of Protest* *

	1897–1914		post-1914	
	Raid	*Threat*	*Raid*	*Threat*
Barra and Vatersay	8	4	8	26
South Uist	7	2	11	21
North Uist	2	0	22	53
Harris	2	0	15	43
Lewis	4	1	18	75
Skye	1	7	14	89
Sutherland	1	2	3	22
Elsewhere	0	1	3	81
TOTALS	25	17	94	410

* The choice of categories is intended to reflect the uneven distribution of occurrence of protest across space, and recognise the concentration of protest in the islands of the Outer Hebrides, particularly pre-1914. It is important to recognise also, that for the period after 1914 the typology of protest was not confined to threats to seize and incidents of land seizure, but should include other, previously unrecognised, types.[51]

and, as such, must challenge the notion, advanced by Withers, of a continuing contraction of protest into '*Pura Scotia*'.[50]

While it is now no longer possible to assert that acts of protest ceased with the onset of war, it is equally important to accept that the act of going to war acted as a catalyst for disturbance. At first sight, the act of going to war would appear to be significant on a number of levels.[52] Attention has already been drawn to the geographical expansion of protest after the cessation of war. In addition, it is apparent that war removed much of the fear of imprisonment consequent upon land seizure and altered the sympathies of some local and national authorities towards the landless. Finally, the provisions and use of the Defence of the Realm Act (DORA) created a new form of protest.

One aspect of DORA was the recognition that maximisation of food production involved an element of central control and compulsion. The intention was to encourage an increase in productivity, in terms of areas under cultivation and in stocks held.[53] In the Highlands the drive to maximise production was often interpreted by the local Agricultural Executive Committees, charged with implementing DORA under direction from the Board of Agriculture, as an opportunity to return areas within deer forests to agriculture. Furthermore, when attempting to do this, they argued that because it would be inappropriate for the landlord

or the sporting tenant to be compelled to turn to agriculture, and unsat-
isfactory to bring in an agricultural tenant from outwith the region, then
the only people suitable to undertake this expansion were the local crofting
tenantry. Consequently, when attempting to return deer forests to agriculture, local Agricultural Executive Committees predominantly turned to
local crofters. Access was given via voluntary or compulsory agreements
between crofters and landlords over grazing or cultivation rights.[54]

The principal motive behind this decision to turn to the crofting
tenantry, however, was not a search to find the most efficient and
appropriate means of maximising food production. Rather, it was an
attempt to pacify a local population during a national emergency – an
attempt to give the crofting tenantry temporary access to land which
they had been agitating for and threatening to seize, and which existing
legislation did not encompass. The 1911 Small Landholders Act had
covered deer forests, but at the same time, allowed high compensation
awards to landlords. A decision was made during the war years that
schemes in deer forests could not proceed under this Act. This motive
was never overtly stated by Board of Agriculture officials, but is implicit
in the way in which, in many instances, officials would turn to DORA
in response to threats to seize land, once peace time legislation had
proved inadequate.[55]

Tenancy arrangements were for three years. There was, therefore,
only one period of tenancy, and the provisions of the Act ceased with
the end of the war. After the war, while some tenants agreed to relinquish
the land and some proprietors continued with voluntary agreements, at
other forests the tenants refused to return the land. It is this action, an
expression of the desire to regain and retain land, which can be considered
as protest.[56] The Wester Bunloit (Drumnadrochit) crofters refused to
give up their occupation and, according to a report obtained by the
Board of Agriculture, approximately 300 sheep were illegally grazed in
the forest in 1921 and 1922. The report concluded that the 'crofters
are very determined … the estate are quite alive to this fact and … it
will prove impracticable if not impossible to get them removed'. Illegal
utilisation of the forest continued until at least 1924 when, during the
course of negotiations with the Board over possible purchase, the Estate's
agents alleged that extensive and deliberate damage had been done to
the forest.[57]

The crofters based their refusal to quit upon a tradition of past
occupation and customary inheritance.

From time immemorial until the Deer Forest era of about 60 years ago, our ancestors held a grazing ... a portion of the Deer Forest ... Since we were ruthlessly deprived of our grazing, we have presented many applications ... for restoration of our former grazing rights ... but our applications have been consistently refused. As far as the estate is concerned we have now exhausted all peaceable means of obtaining restitution.

This attitude firmly identifies the act of refusal as an act of protest and is identical to the principal motivating beliefs underlying many of the land seizures of this period, and, indeed, earlier events.[58]

This echo of the past notwithstanding, the bulk of the evidence thus far supports the view, suggested by Hunter, that in 1918 a new and distinct phase of protest began.[59] When investigated at a more local level, however, it would seem that a number of continuities with pre-war protest do exist. Nevertheless, we need to recognise also, that Highland disturbance was rooted in a complexity of causes. In virtually every instance of protest after 1914, where sufficient evidence is available, the group decision to act was made from a combination of motives, with individual participants entering into protest for different reasons. Finally, while not always sharing motives, individuals entered into protest for reasons that would have been recognisable to their counterparts from earlier generations: the same motives, the same pressures and the same causes underlay and generated events before, during and after the Great War.[60]

The one exception to this, however, may well have been responsible for the significant expansion of protest evident immediately after the war. This was the belief that, as part of the recruitment drive, the promise had been given that land would be made available for the landless. In this context, and in terms of the effect on acts of popular protest, it is important to note that the significance of the promise lies not in whether it was actually made, but in the fact that crofter and cottars *believed* that it had been made; *believed* that they had been promised land in return for military service. With the end of the war and demo-bilisation, the demand for land, given the economic conditions of the time, far exceeded the capabilities of agencies of government – specifically the Board of Agriculture for Scotland – to meet it. This caused much frustration. The perceived failure to fulfil the expectations of those who went to war and, indeed, the relations of those who went to war, generated many acts of protest across both time and space. In July 1919, for instance, applicants for land from Gribus, Mull, wrote:

We should like to point out to the Board of Agriculture that the Government during hostilities made definite promises towards settling ex-members of H.M. Forces on the land ... if the Board do not see their way clear to constitute small holdings we propose seizing the land.[61]

Having said that it is the belief in the promise that is significant, it is equally important to recognise that the promise does appear to have been made. As Leneman notes, 'the pledge of land for men who served in the war was an intrinsic part of government policy.'[62] Moreover, and perhaps more importantly, there is direct evidence to show that such pledges were being made by local authorities and recruiting agents within the Highlands. In December 1920 the Board of Agriculture's local officer for North Uist reported his conversation with those who had seized land at Lochmaddy. They had 'joined up ... on account of the direct promise made ... by Captain Beaton, of land.' This promise had not been fulfilled. The direct consequence of this was the decision to seize land. Similarly, in South Uist, the Drimore raiders claimed that their raid was prompted by the lack of action on a 'definite and precise promise of land made to them ... when they joined up for service.' They believed that 'if they were in default of law and order' then 'so were others in not fulfilling the promise of land made.'[63] They believed that local recruiting agents had a moral obligation to meet their promises.

This sense of a moral obligation is apparent not just among the land-working population. It was expressed also by some local authorities and appears to have altered their own attitude to the crofting tenantry and to the justice of claims to land. In July 1920, the Rev. Roderick MacGowan wrote from the Free Church manse, Kiltarlity, that the local ex-servicemen 'have a claim on me, because as Chairman of a Tribunal I sent a good many of them away to War, and following the government I promised them land on their return.' He was later to write supporting the threat to raid made by the ex-servicemen.[64]

In 1917, a similarly sympathetic view came from a local Justice of the Peace in Mull. He wrote complaining of the failure of government agencies to support the parents of servicemen and believed that

you may depend on having trouble in the critical months of May and June when potatoes cannot be got. As one who had a great deal to do with recruiting and persuading parents to let their sons join the colours, I feel bound to call attention to this dilettantism by which these noble and self sacrificing parents may suffer hunger and deprivation.[65]

There can be little doubt, then, that in direct local recruiting the promise of land was made and believed. Furthermore, there is also little doubt that the failure to carry out these promises generated acts of protest. When we explore this in greater detail it becomes clear that the relationship between protest and the expectation of land in return for war service functioned on a number of different levels.

As has already been noted, at a local level the belief in the promise contributed directly and unequivocally to the decision to undertake protest. Thus, in December 1921, cottars from Torrin, Skye, wrote that 'we have been promised the land, we fought for it, so we think we are now entitled to get it.' They subsequently raided it, were imprisoned, but were eventually given holdings on the land they believed they had been promised.[66]

Alongside the purely local, it is important to recognise that, contained within the relationship between the promise of land and acts of popular protest, there existed a local/national dialectic. Crofters and cottars took what they believed to be the promise of land made by individuals, agencies and institutions of national government, and transferred it to the specifically local, applying it to land to which they believed they had a legitimate claim, via past inheritance and customary occupation. In May 1920 for instance, crofters from Knockintorran, North Uist, wrote to the Scottish Secretary that:

All the crofters in the said township have decided ... to take possession of the part of Paiblesgarry ... which was taken from them by James MacDonald, tenant of Paiblesgarry ... why did we send our sons to fight for this country if it wants to deprive us of our existence ... they look on the land that was treacherously taken from them as their own to the present day.[67]

The belief that the government had promised them the land was one of the ways crofters and cottars sought – consciously or unconsciously – to legitimate their agitation for land. It was also a 'modern' adaptation and a means of maintaining the belief in the promise of continued occupation over time and space. Moreover, this legitimisation was not confined to direct promises of land but encompassed a wider and more generalised political rhetoric. This is apparent in the agitation for land at Lairg, where correspondents wrote to the Scottish Secretary:

some of them have fought for their country, and they are prepared now to fight for their rights at home, a course which they never expected when the promise was made that this country would be made a place fit for heroes to live in.

This is evident also on Tiree, where applicants for land wrote that 'if the Board will grant us two acres and the grazing of one cow we will be satisfied but otherwise we will take possession ourselves.'[68] Here again, it is important to appreciate that the significance of the promise lies not with whether it was actually made but with the fact that crofters and cottars believed that it had been made.

Finally, and perhaps most interestingly, it is apparent from a number of instances that crofter and cottars felt that the act of going to war brought an entitlement to land. This is an idea with deep roots in the Highlands. Indeed, it has recently been argued that, as early as 1760, 'the concept of land for military service was well understood'.[69] As viewed through acts of protest after 1918, this took a number of forms. Often those attempting to gain land would base their actions upon the belief that 'every man who has served his country ... is entitled to get a comfortable home in his native country ... for which he has fought and suffered.' The sentiment is present also in the belief that fighting for your country justified fighting for a home in that country. Finally, there is evidence to show, as at Drimsdale, South Uist, that raiders believed, quite boldly and directly, that 'as we fought pretty hard for it, it's our land now.'[70] Views such as these draw upon the ancient belief that land was gained for chief and clan by the power of the sword. With the increasing integration of the Highlands into the British space economy this notion was transmuted into fighting for 'your country'. And yet, residues of the older belief persisted, specifically in the form of land being 'fought for' and to which individual members of the land working population were entitled. Once land was unforthcoming, these twin beliefs formed a principal motive for acts of protest.

The principal function of the promise of land in return for military service in the Great War was as a recruiting device, both locally and nationally. Crofters and cottars believed it, and with the war's end, expected to gain land. The end of the war saw the passage of the Land Settlement (Scotland) Act, a much more efficient piece of legislation than the 1911 Act, but one which was still unable to redistribute land according to the precise nature of the demand put by crofters and cottars.[71] When agencies of government were unable to meet demand for land, expectation turned to frustration and the frustration generated land raiding on a scale not seen in the Highlands for forty years.

Conclusion

We were promised these farms when we fought and bled for it. [72]

This chapter has sought to explore the relationship between military recruitment and acts of popular protest immediately after the Great War. At first glance, any connection between the two would appear to be slight. Recruitment focused upon the martial tradition of the Scottish Highlands and the heroism and glory associated with earlier military activities. Popular protest was based upon a desire to reclaim land – land to which crofters and cottars believed they were entitled through past inheritance and customary occupation.

At second glance, however, important links emerge. The key to recognition lies in the rhetoric of recruiting, which drew heavily upon notions of 'tradition'. This is apparent both in terms of those who were doing the recruiting – members of the traditional land owning families – and in the language utilised. The call to arms was based upon an appeal to locality and past loyalties, and on a vestigial clan tradition. In drawing upon these and continuing them into the twentieth century, recruiters also maintained the well-established link between military service and land. This was, in part at least, responsible for maintaining the crofting tenantry's 'traditional' belief in an entitlement to land. Indeed, it has previously been demonstrated how residues of these beliefs became entwined with the supposed martial inheritance of ordinary Highlanders. For the crofters and cottars, land was equated with freedom, both individual and collective. Land represented home, and was something to which all were entitled by past occupation, present right and as a right gained by war service. Once land was not forthcoming, protest followed.

There remains the question as to whether the promise of land was actually made. In recruitment speeches made at regional level and reported in the press, the promise does not appear. Nevertheless, evidence has been presented here in which local officials admit to making such a promise. Resolution of this contradiction lies with the fact that officials often said they followed the national government's lead. What this appears to indicate, is the increasing integration of the Highlands into the British space economy and the recognition that, increasingly, conflict in the Highlands was tri-partite: between crofting tenantry, landowners and agencies of national government.

The relationship between the promise of land in return for war service and acts of land seizure functioned at a number of different levels and on a number of different scales. The promise was made overtly at a local level. As such it was directly and unequivocally responsible for generating acts of protest. But at the same time, the promise was also expressed in more general terms at a national, political level. Crofters and cottars took this political rhetoric and applied it to the specifically local as one means of legitimising their actions. Finally, in the same way that the military industry was as important as kelping and fishing in the establishment and maintenance of crofting communities, the rhetoric of military recruiting was, in part at least, responsible for the maintenance of the belief within those communities of a right and entitlement to land, ultimately generating acts of land seizure.

Notes

The authors are grateful to Prof. Hew Strachan for a number of constructive suggestions.

1. A. Mackillop, 'Military Recruiting in the Scottish Highlands, 1739–1815: the political, social and economic context' (University of Glasgow, Ph.D. thesis, 1995).
2. H. J. Hanham, 'Religion and Nationality in the Mid-Victorian Army', in M. R. D. Foot (ed.), *War and Society: Historical Essays in Honour of J. R. Western, 1928–71* (London, 1973), p. 163.
3. *The Times*, 21 Sept. 1855; *The Scotsman*, 24 Sept. 1855; 'Nonsense about the Highlands', *The Spectator*, 29 Sept. 1855, pp. 1004–5.
4. Lt. Col. J. Macinnes, *The Brave Sons of Skye* (Edinburgh, 1899).
5. H. Strachan, *The Politics of the British Army* (London, 1997), pp. 204–6.
6. *Inverness Courier*, 5, 9, 16 Jan. 1900; F. Lindley, *Lord Lovat: A Biography* (London, 1935), pp. 75–81, 171–96; M. L. Melville, *The Story of the Lovat Scouts, 1900–1980* (Edinburgh, 1981), pp. 4–8, 28–33; H. Hesketh-Prichard, *Sniping in France* (London, 1994), pp. 103, 107.
7. Strachan, *Politics of the British Army*, p. 208.
8. V. W. Germains, *The Kitchener Armies* (London, 1930), is the traditional account. Complexities have been added by P. Simkins, *Kitchener's Army: the Raising of the New Armies, 1914–16* (Manchester, 1988); I. F. W. Beckett, 'The Nation in Arms, 1914–18' and C. Hughes, 'The New Armies', both in I. F. W. Beckett and K. Simpson (eds), *A Nation in Arms: a Social Study of the British Army in the First World War* (Manchester, 1985), pp. 1–35, 100–25.
9. J. M. Winter, *The Great War and the British People* (London, 1986), p. 30; G. J. De-Groot, *Blighty: British Society in the Era of the Great War* (London, 1996), pp. 42–53; K. Grieves, '"Lowther's Lambs": rural paternalism and voluntary recruitment in the First World War', *Rural History*, iv (1993), pp. 55–76.
10. C. Parry, 'Gwynedd and the Great War, 1914–18', *Welsh History Review*, xiv (1988–89), pp. 78–117; T. Denman, '"The red livery of shame": the campaign against army recruiting in Ireland, 1899–1914', *Irish Historical Studies*, xxix (1994–95), pp. 208–33; E. Spiers, 'The Scottish soldier at war', in H. Cecil and P. H. Liddle (eds), *Facing Armageddon: The First World War Experienced* (London, 1996), pp. 314–15.
11. E. A. Cameron, 'The Political Influence of Highland Landowners: a reassessment', *Northern Scotland*, xiv (1994), pp. 27–45.

12. *Inverness Courier*, 28 Aug. 1914.
13. *Oban Times*, 5 Dec. 1914.
14. *Ibid.*, 12 Sept. 1914.
15. *Inverness Courier*, 8 Sept., 10 Nov. 1914; C. Veitch, '"Play Up! Play Up! and Win the War!"', football, the nation and the First World War, 1914–1915', *Journal of Contemporary History*, xx (1985), pp. 370–6.
16. *Souvenir Booklet of the Sixth Cameron Highlanders* (London, 1916), p. 11; Simkins, *Kitchener's Army*, p. 71.
17. E. A. James, *British Regiments, 1914–18* (London, 1978), pp. 103–8.
18. *Inverness Courier*, 1 Dec. 1914.
19. DeGroot, *Blighty*, p. 86; P. E. Dewey, 'Agricultural labour supply in England and Wales during the First World War', *Economic History Review*, xviii (1975), pp. 100–12; see also P. E. Dewey, 'Food production and policy in the United Kingdom, 1914–18', *Transactions of the Royal Historical Society*, 5th Ser., xxx (1980), pp. 71–89; *Ross-shire Journal*, 14 Aug. 1914; *Inverness Courier*, 21 Aug., 4 Sept. 1914; 5 Jan. 1915.
20. N. A. Johnson, 'How the War Affects the Hebrides', *Inverness Courier*, 20 Oct. 1914; 'The Present Winter in the Hebrides', *Inverness Courier*, 5 Jan. 1915; 'The Highland Season – How the War Affects it- A Dull Town', *Inverness Courier*, 18 Sept. 1914; for the revival of the kelp industry see *Inverness Courier*, 23 Apr. 1915; 14 Mar., 30 May 1916; *Oban Times*, 29 Aug., 10 Oct. 1914; 10 Apr. 1915; 17, 24 Feb. 1917.
21. *Inverness Courier*, 4 Aug. 1914; see also 7, 21 Aug. 1914.
22. DeGroot, *Blighty*, p. 53.
23. *Oban Times*, 15 Aug. 1914.
24. *Ibid.*, 3, 10 Oct. 1914.
25. 'The Appeal for Recruits – What the Hebrides have done', *Inverness Courier*, 12 Mar. 1915.
26. Johnson, 'Hebrides', *Inverness Courier*, 12 Mar. 1915.
27. *Inverness Courier*, 4 Sept. 1914.
28. *Ibid.*, 3 Nov. 1914; 5 Mar. 1915; *Oban Times*, 13 Mar. 1915.
29. *Ibid.*, 2 Oct. 1914.
30. *Ibid.*, 5 Mar. 1915.
31. *Oban Times*, 26 Dec. 1914.
32. *Inverness Courier*, 27 Apr. 1915.
33. *Ibid.*, 27 Apr. 1915.
34. Hughes, 'New Armies', p. 113.
35. *The 79th News*, No. 133, Jan. 1916, p. 87; J. W. Sandilands, 'A Year's Command', *The 79th News*, No. 134, Apr. 1916, pp. 157–9; *Historical Records of the QOCH* (7 vols, Edinburgh and London, 1909–62), iv, p. 84.
36. *Historical Records*, iv, pp. 285–6; R. B. Talbot Kelly, *A Subaltern's Odyssey: Memoirs of the Great War, 1915–17* (London, 1980), pp. 50, 58–61. We are grateful to Dr James L. Macleod for this reference.
37. *Inverness Courier*, 1, 5, 12, 15, Oct. 1915; *Oban Times*, 16, 23 Oct. 1915.
38. *The Cameron Highlanders at the Battles of Loos, Hill 70, Fosse 8 and the Quarries* (Inverness, 1915).
39. J. Buchan, *A History of the Great War* (4 vols, London, 1921), ii, pp. 313–24; P. Warner, *The Battle of Loos* (London, 1976), pp. 53–4; L. Macdonald, *1915: The Death of Innocence* (London, 1993), pp. 538–44; M. Gilbert, *First World War* (London, 1994), pp. 196–201; J. E. Edmonds, *History of the Great War based on Official Documents, Military Operations, France and Belgium, 1915, Battles of Aubers Ridge, Festubert and Loos* (London, 1928), pp. 196, 199, 399.
40. *Inverness Courier*, 8 Oct. 1915.

41. *Historical Records*, iv, 281; J. Ewing, M.C., *The History of the 9ᵗʰ (Scottish) Division, 1914–19* (London, 1921), pp. 40–1.
42. E. A. Cameron, *Land for the People? The British Government and the Scottish Highlands, c.1880–1925* (East Linton, 1996), pp. 163–4; *Oban Times*, 22 Jul. 1917.
43. *Inverness Courier*, 11 Feb. 1916.
44. *Ibid.*, 1 Dec. 1916.
45. *Ibid.*, 5 Oct. 1917.
46. *Ibid.*, 9 Oct. 1917.
47. *Ibid.*, 5 Oct. 1917.
48. *Ibid.*, 1 Dec. 1916.
49. J. Hunter, *The Making of the Crofting Community* (Edinburgh, 1976), pp. 131–83; C. W. J. Withers, *Gaelic Scotland* (London, 1986), pp. 351–89; E. A. Cameron, '"They will listen to no remonstrance": land raids and land raiders in the Scottish Highlands, 1886 to 1914', *Scottish Economic and Social History*, xvii (1997), pp. 43–64; I. J. M. Robertson, 'The Historical Geography of Social Protest in Highland Scotland, 1914–c.1939' (University of Bristol, Ph.D. thesis, 1995), pp. 125–71.
50. Withers, *Gaelic Scotland*, p, 17.
51. Robertson, 'The Historical Geography', pp. 101–24.
52. This is a question examined in depth elsewhere. See, I. J. M. Robertson, 'The effect of the First World War upon events of popular protest in the Scottish Highlands' (forthcoming).
53. A. Marwick, *The Deluge* (London, 1991 edn), p. 287.
54. Robertson, 'Historical Geography', pp. 117–21; L. Leneman, *Fit for Heroes? Land Settlement in Scotland after World War One* (Aberdeen, 1989), pp. 5–19.
55. Department of Agriculture and Fisheries for Scotland [DAFS], 35809/1, 35809/3, Glenmore. Please note that on the request of DAFS, and because these remain active files, all names have been withheld from DAFS material.
56. I. J. M. Robertson, 'Governing the Highlands: the place of popular protest in the Highlands of Scotland after 1918', *Rural History*, viii (1997), pp. 112–14; DAFS, 74141, Land Settlement Procedure, 27 Jan. 1926.
57. DAFS, 40928, Balmacaan, letter from estate solicitors, 9 Jan. 1924.
58. Robertson, 'Historical Geography', pp. 92–7; DAFS, 40928, Balmacaan, copy letter sent by solicitor, 13 Jan. 1922; Report from Sub-commissioner to Board of Agriculture, 24 Mar. 1922; Report from Sub-commissioner, 12 Sept. 1922.
59. Hunter, *Making of the Crofting Community*, p. 195.
60. Robertson, 'Historical Geography', p. 88.
61. DAFS 3682/1, Balmeanach, letter to Board of Agriculture, 31 Jul. 1919.
62. Leneman, *Fit for Heroes?*, p. 205.
63. Scottish Record Office [SRO], AF67/65, N. Maclean to Board of Agriculture, 14 Dec. 1920; AF83/207, same to same, 11 Dec. 1920.
64. SRO, AF67/150, Rev. R. MacGowan to Scottish Office, 3 Jul. 1920.
65. SRO, AF83/287, Estate Management Files.
66. SRO, AF67/157, Torrin Cottars to Scottish Office, 16 Dec. 1921.
67. SRO, AF67/152, Malcolm and 16 others to Board of Agriculture, 17 May 1920.
68. SRO, AF67/65, Donald Mackay and others to the Scottish Office, 2 Mar. 1920; AF83/358, John Macaulay and others to Board of Agriculture, 16 Apr. 1920.
69. Mackillop, 'Military Recruiting', p. 166.
70. SRO, AF83/634, W. J. Macleod to Board of Agriculture, 7 May 1918; AF67/65, Donald Fraser to Scottish Office, 7 Nov. 1918; AF67/152, Drimsdale raiders to Board of Agriculture, 11 Nov. 1919.
71. Cameron, *Land for the People?*, pp. 166–90.
72. SRO, AF67/65, Malcolm MacDonald and others to Scottish Office, 24 Jan. 1921.

Appendix 1

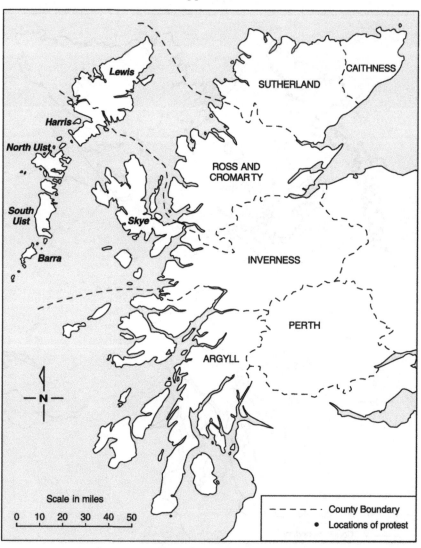

Appendix 2

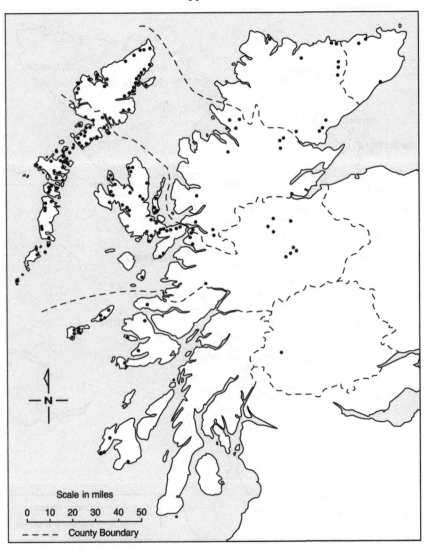

Sources: S.R.O. AF67, S.R.O. AF83, D.A.F.S. files, Oral interviews

'Be Strong and of a Good Courage': the Royal Scots' Territorial Battalions from 1908 to Gallipoli

Ian S. Wood

NOT FOR THE first time since August 1914, Princes Street in Edinburgh echoed to the pipes and drums and the tread of marching feet as yet another locally raised infantry battalion took its leave of the city. It was 16 June 1915 and the 16th Battalion of the Royal Scots were marching to the Waverley Station on the first stage of their journey to the killing fields of the Western Front. At the station, a local newspaper noted, 'There was a great deal of bustle and save for a few weeping women folks, everybody was in high spirits, the men singing and cheering and the crowd giving them an enthusiastic send off.' [1]

Marching at the head of the column were Heart of Midlothian footballers, whose recruitment to the 16th had been a great coup for the battalion's 'raiser' and commanding officer, Sir George McCrae. Indeed, the 16th were always known simply as 'McCrae's Battalion', one of the many contributed by the army's oldest line regiment to Lord Kitchener's New Army. McCrae had been well-known before 1914 for his tireless work on behalf of the Territorial Army, raised by act of parliament in 1908. Owner of a highly successful drapery and outfitting business and an advanced Liberal in his politics, McCrae had made the easy transition to the new territorial force from long years of service with the volunteer rifle regiments originally raised in 1859.

The Volunteers had been hugely popular in Victorian Scotland because they seemed to embody a civic and liberal militarism, uncontaminated by the brutality of a regular barracks army and the influence of aristocratic officers. McCrae was very typical of local entrepreneurs of reforming instinct who rose through the Volunteer movement, and Edinburgh's close-knit commercial and professional world was strongly represented in its officer corps. The men they led were from the commercial and manufacturing labour force. 'All over the country', the volunteer movement's historian has written, 'working men were entering the force in financial and organisational dependence on their employers.'[2]

Along with the militia and the mounted yeomanry, both raised in the late eighteenth century, the volunteer regiments constituted the bulk of Britain's home based defence troops at the end of Queen Victoria's reign. The army's manpower crisis during the Boer War posed hard questions for the War Office, and a Royal Commission on the Militia and Volunteers set up in 1903 surveyed the whole issue of reserve forces. Its criticisms of existing provision prepared the way for that improbable Liberal Secretary of State for War, Robert Haldane, to present his Territorial and Reserve Forces Bill to Parliament in 1907.

Haldane did this at a time when the case for some form of conscription was being strongly made in Britain by bodies like the National Service League, founded in 1902. He was alert to the strength of their case, as he was later to recall:

> Of course I knew, and I told the House of Commons so, that if a great war came we should probably have to resort to compulsory service in order to increase and keep up the Army. But in peace time all that could wisely be done was to perfect the organisation so that it could be used, if the necessity came, for expansion.[3]

Haldane never, in fact, thought of the Territorial Army as a force raised solely for home defence. He saw them as the second line behind the regular army, but pressure from the Liberal backbenches and from spokesmen for the Volunteers and Yeomanry forced him to retreat from his initial preference for the territorials to be liable for overseas service. This belief has been described as something, 'fundamental to his concept of their proper role', but under the legislation which received the royal assent, imperial or overseas service was an option, not an obligation, for those who enlisted in the new Territorial Army.[4] By 1913, just over 20,000 officers and men – under 10% of total territorial strength – had registered for overseas service in time of war, though many more of course would do so once war came.

Territorial service consisted of an initial four year engagement, statutory drills and a fifteen-day summer camp, attendance at which was paid at regular army rates. Recruitment started off well, peaking at a figure of over 270,000 officers and men in 1909, but then declining to just under 246,000 by September 1913.[5] Once the city Territorial Forces Association was set up under Haldane's act to administer his scheme locally, events in Edinburgh reflected this overall pattern. The Association represented the council, Edinburgh University, the Merchant

Company which funded and ran four of the city's fee-paying day schools, the regular army and local employers, as well as the Trades Council.[6] The Labour movement in many places was hostile to the new Territorial Army, but not in Edinburgh, though the Trades Council representative successfully pressed the case for a fair wage clause to be applied to all contracts entered into by the association with local employers.[7]

Four years later, however, the manager of the local St Cuthbert's Co-operative Society – a very large wholesale and retail employer in the city – informed its workers that they must either resign from their territorial units or forfeit their jobs. This had to be taken up at a meeting of the Association, partly because it came at a time when enlistment had passed the high point of 1909 and problems were starting to be acknowledged.[8] Figures were still good, but fell short of establishment levels set by the War Office, so that securing maximum summer camp attendance remained a problem. As early as 1906, the Territorial Association's recruiting committee had written to local employers urging them to grant all reasonable facilities to employees for camp duty. Seven major banks, eleven insurance companies and twenty manufacturing firms all replied positively, but a fundamental manpower problem remained.[9]

The Territorial Army's inability in Edinburgh and elsewhere to meet the full enlistment quotas demanded of it may have owed something to the National Service League's increasingly vocal campaign for conscription. Leading figures in the League, like Field Marshal Lord Roberts, became increasingly critical of the Territorials. 'Discipline alone can confront discipline on the field of battle', he declared in a letter to *The Times* early in 1912.[10] This was an implied criticism of the territorial force. Roberts had intially supported the Territorials' formation, but went on to claim that many in the Territorial Army, in fact, accepted the League's case and that nearly a quarter of all members of the County Associations belonged to it.[11] By 1913 a growing number of these bodies were indeed identifying themselves with the League and voicing their growing alarm at the young age of many territorial recruits and the low levels of re-engagement among those who had completed their first four-year term of service.[12]

Another problem in the minds of some active figures in the Territorial Army was the extent to which its recruitment had quickly become working-class. Perhaps in Scotland this should not have been a surprise, given the Volunteer movement's history. Sir George McCrae in Edinburgh offered his explanation of this to the Liberal Secretary of State for War, Sir John Seely, in November 1913:

We are having a very stiff time as regards recruiting in Edinburgh ... I feel that the middle class man is shirking the duty and that we are becoming more and more dependant on the artisan to keep the numbers up. The middle class fellow gets his fortnight's holiday – at least his pay is not stopped. He therefore sacrifices only his leisure or convenience (i.e. by camp attendance). The artisan is in a much worse position. He gets only a week's holiday during which his pay stops.[13]

This was a situation, McCrae argued, that made it very hard for a working-class recruit to take the full two weeks for camp training, since his pay for doing it would be well short of the wages he would forfeit over and above his holiday week. McCrae called for a doubling of the rate of pay for the second week, in effect a bounty to maximise attendance and thus the unit cohesion and efficiency which a full-length camp could promote. These results would of themselves, he argued, contribute to higher enlistment levels.[14] One of Edinburgh's local newspapers supported his views, while arguing more still would have to be done to reach all social classes. It also registered support for some form of compulsory part-time service:

If young men can stand idly by or spend their Saturday afternoons shouting at football matches and their evenings sitting in picture houses while their brother citizens attend their drills and firing practice and devote their leisure to making themselves useful in the defence of the Empire, they would have no reason for surprise or complaint if they were made to meet their liabilities in some other way.[15]

McCrae continued to press his recommendations, but the War Office needed more convincing and some civil servants there had their doubts. One of them, Edward Bethune, a Private Secretary, wrote to Seely, arguing that while there was merit in the McCrae plan,

the more money we pay directly in doles to the territorial the more we get away from the voluntary system and the more we begin to tap the class of man who really cannot afford voluntary soldiering. That class of man would be far better in the Regulars if he has a taste for soldiering.[16]

Thus, in his view, such success as territorial recruiting had achieved might even be keeping suitable men out of the regular army. The target group for territorial enlistment in Bethune's view were 'a better class of citizen, men who can afford to sacrifice a little time and money to voluntary service and the more we recruit from the artisan class the more difficult it becomes to get the other.'[17]

A town clerk's army?

Bethune was perhaps less than just to the range of recruiting achieved by the Royal Scots territorial battalions in a city where class distinctions were as sharply defined as in Scotland's capital before 1914. James Connolly, who had done regular service with the regiment, famously described the city of his youth as

> largely composed of snobs, flunkies, mashers, lawyers, students, middle-class pensioners and dividend-hunters. Even the working-class portion of the population seemed to have imbibed the snobbish would-be respectable spirit of their betters.[18]

Yet Edinburgh had a working class, much of it appallingly housed and employed in relatively large scale industries like rubber manufacture, brewing, printing and engineering. However, in stark contrast to Glasgow, there was a far higher proportion of the population employed in professional, financial and legal services.[19] For this reason among others, no 'Red Forth' would emerge in Edinburgh, though in fact a strong Labour movement already had.

Territorial recruitment was, in a real sense, an extension of this social structure. When mobilisation began after war was declared in 1914 one Royal Scots Battalion, the 4th, was labelled straight away in a written account of its service: 'Professional and city men, clerks, mechanics, shop assistants, teachers, students and gentlemen of leisure filled the ranks.'[20] It was grouped into companies to reflect broadly these categories, though it also had a Post Office and civil service company.[21] Another battalion, the 7th, which was to join the 4th at the Dardanelles after dreadful loss of life in the Gretna railway disaster, recruited heavily from dock workers in the Port of Leith, as well as miners from the East Lothian coalfield.

Some battalions were thought of in terms of their connection to Edinburgh's fee-paying schools. The 5th Battalion recruited heavily amongst George Heriot's former pupils, while the kilted 9th Battalion did so among boys who had been Heriot's fiercest rival on the rugby field, George Watson's.[22] Many of these young enthusiasts were lawyers, accountants or employed in banks and insurance companies and eligible for commissions through their education and often service in their school cadet forces. However, there was a limit to the number of officers needed, thus many of them served happily in the ranks or as NCOs.

Such figures held little interest for Kitchener once he became Secretary of State for War in August 1914. His dislike of the Territorial Army was instinctive and inveterate, one of his biographers has written, and this certainly influenced his initial view of the role it could play in the war.[23] Kitchener had been abroad during the debate over its creation in 1907 and 1908, but on his return to Britain was quickly influenced by the view that an annual camp and one drill a week was an inadequate way of giving military training to civilians. Too many territorial soldiers, in his view, looked upon their military duties as a mere diversion from the social life of their unit, and he also distrusted the civilian element in the administration of what he referred to as a 'town clerk's army.'[24]

Territorial recruitment was never a foolproof system in terms of Haldane's objectives in his 1908 legislation. In Edinburgh, as elsewhere, the shortfall between actual enlisted manpower and required establishment figures laid down by the War Office had, in the final weeks of peace, not been closed. On 30 June 1914, the General Purposes Committee of Edinburgh's Territorial Force Association reported overall numbers in the city's battalions of the Royal Scots as being 81.6% of the War Office target figure, but 82 men in that month alone had failed to re-enlist after completion of their four-year term.[25] In the city and adjacent areas, 6,104 men were registered as enlisted either in Royal Scots Battalions or artillery and other units.

These numbers grew rapidly after August 1914, as more men joined territorial units with which they could identify, either through their workplace or where they lived. But Kitchener's hostility caused problems. Local unit orders for kit and equipment were often overruled by the War Office, regular army instructors were transferred away from territorial battalions to units of the New Army which Kitchener wanted both to create and dominate. By mid-December 1914 territorial battalions had only 240,000 rifles of the 400,000 they needed.[26] Soon, however, Kitchener had to revise his views, as units whose members had taken the Imperial Service Obligation to serve overseas went into action in France and fought bravely there, while recruitment at home to territorial battalions increased at a rate parallel to that for the New Army.

Gallipoli

As casualty lists lengthened on the Western Front, the call for volunteers became ever more insistent. Early in January 1915, a meeting in Edinburgh's North British Hotel, organised by the Royal Scots Recruiting Committee, was told that a total of 104,000 'enlistable' men existed in Edinburgh and Leith.[27] Thirty thousand of these had been recruited, one speaker declared, but the audience of 'one hundred and sixty gentlemen representative of all classes and parties' were assured that this was far from sufficient.[28] The recruiting committee, whose patron was the former Liberal Prime Minister, Lord Rosebery, declared its intention to co-operate fully with the local Territorial Forces Association and announced an intensive programme of meetings. The historian, Professor Richard Lodge of Edinburgh University, an executive committee member of the Territorial Forces Association, was the main speaker, warning the city's young men against complacency as the tide of German conquest spread across France, Belgium, Poland and Russia.[29]

One essential requirement was to persuade serving territorial soldiers to sign up to the Imperial and Overseas Service obligation. This now met with marked success. However, men who did this could not be posted away without the consent from their parent battalion – a valuable factor in maintaining the very local cohesion of territorial units. Some of Edinburgh's Royal Scots Battalions took longer than others to reach a full war footing in manpower terms, but the regiment's 4th Battalion led the way, reaching a figure of forty-two men over its required strength by January 1915.[30]

Councillors, politicians of all parties, lawyers and employers vied with each other to be seen on recruiting platforms, with men of the cloth also to the fore. Exhortations to enlist reverberated from the city's many pulpits, especially at territorial battalion church parades. In February 1915 the United Free Church made its assembly hall on the Mound available for a service and reception in honour of the Royal Scots 9th Battalion. The preacher of the day, Dr Kelman, told the soldiers and many of their parents, that the conflict in France

> was not merely a fight of Britain against Germany but of love against hate, or Christ against anti-Christ, and the true meaning of the war came to this, that certain ancient paganisms had asserted themselves against all that Christian Europe loved and honoured.[31]

Some of those active in the Edinburgh recruiting campaign showed an almost addictive enthusiasm for it. Sir George McCrae was a prime example of this. While he remained active in the Territorial Forces Association, his raising of the Royal Scots 16th Battalion was an important contribution to Kitchener's New Army. The unit was constantly on show at recruiting rallies and church parades in the city and it was rumoured that his success was tempting McCrae to consider raising another battalion. There were those who felt this would be premature and could cause recruitment to be spread too thinly over too many units: by May 1915 McCrae's zeal was even being criticised in the local press.[32]

Some commentators on the recruitment situation drew a distinction which they claimed existed between Edinburgh and the Port of Leith. Leith men were described in the local press as more willing to enlist than employers were to let them go. In February 1915 one third of the port's 3,000 dockers were reported as having joined up, with the locally based 7th Royal Scots Territorial Battalion being the first choice of many of them. Moreover, the 7th also successfully recruited from many other trades, as well as shipping offices and waterfront warehouses.[33] There was, of course, competition from the New Army Battalions, but the 7th Battalion's very popularity dealt a dreadful blow to the port when it was involved in the Gretna railway disaster of 22 May 1915.

In this worst of all accidents in British railway history, over two hundred officers and men of the battalion were either killed or burned to death when their troop train, headed for Liverpool – where the battalion was to embark for the Dardanelles – was destroyed in a high-speed collision.[34] The bodies of many of the victims were carried back to the battalion's Dalmeny Street drill hall and later buried with full military honours in a cemetery a mile or so away. In local newspapers the port's awful loss at Gretna was presented as a penalty to be paid for successful recruitment and as a challenge for its unenlisted men to keep faith with the victims of the disaster. The economy of Leith dictated a high level of reserved occupations in docks, shipyards and railways and this, it was argued, simply put the onus on more men to join up, preferably with the 7th Battalion. Alternatively, serving territorials who had not already done so were encouraged to take the Imperial Service Obligation.[35]

The carnage of Gretna merely delayed the 7th Battalion on its way to a destination that would cost it even more lives. Reinforced from other units, it arrived at the Dardanelles close behind the 4th Battalion in mid-June 1915. Their landfall was on Cape Helles where British and ANZAC troops had clawed their way ashore on 25 April. Helles was a coastline beautiful to view at a distance against the clear waters of the

Aegean and was famed for its variety of spring flowers which vanished quickly in the arid heat of summer. It was formed largely by precipitous cliffs, flanked at their base by narrow beaches and intersected by rocky 'nullahs' or gullies leading up to higher ground made up of scrub-covered ridges which gave a perfect field of fire to Turkish snipers and artillery.

Since April, this unyielding terrain had become the cockpit of one of the First World War's boldest ventures. It was a gamble conceived of by Winston Churchill, among others as a way to prise the war open from the bloody stalemate of the Western Front, by knocking out the Kaiser's Turkish ally and securing a Black Sea supply route to Russia. Reality on the peninsula soon mocked such hopes. Battalion after battalion was fed into attritional attacks on well-prepared Turkish positions which had survived naval shelling before the landings. These proved lethal obstacles for youthful Edinburgh Territorials whose very basic fieldcraft had been learned in the lea of Salisbury Crags and Arthur's Seat and at a few summer camps.

One Royal Scots Battalion, the 5th, had been in action since just after the original landings as part of the 29th Division. Their losses were already serious when the 4th and 7th Battalions, brigaded with the wholly Territorial Scottish 52nd Lowland Division, first went into action. This was their initiation into a netherworld. Here the stench of the unburied dead drifted down the gullies to the water's edge and the heat was more suffocating than they would have been prepared for, even given the time they had served in Egypt or on the island of Mudros *en route* to the peninsula. Disease was already taking its toll among troops whose best, though often basic, efforts at sanitation were constantly disrupted by enemy fire. Apart from typhoid and cholera, the worst affliction was a form of enteric dysentery, quickly designated 'the Gallipoli gallop' because it kept its victims running to the latrine trenches until they ended up crawling there or simply fouling themselves where they lay until stretcher parties could reach them.

William Murray, an Edinburgh accountant and a survivor of the 4th Battalion, recalled how his company resorted simply to propping the worst cases on planks laid across the latrines until medical help was to hand.[36] Conditions like these, of course, worsened the plague of flies which tormented all who served on this ill-fated front. Dr William Ewing, Minister of Grange United Free Church in Edinburgh, a chaplain with the 52nd Division, wrote later of the constant companionship of these flies. In his dug-out, he recalled:

the table was black with them. They came down upon our food

like a hive of bees. When you ventured to take a helping they rose with an angry buzz and violently contested the passage of each bite to your mouth. Their activity was prodigious. They explored your eyes, nose, mouth and ears. If you tried to write they crawled over the paper and over your fingers till you could hardly hold the pen.[37]

The Royal Scots had to learn to live with all of this as well as the ceaseless attention of Turkish gunners and marksmen before they were committed to a major offensive with a companion unit of their brigade, the 7th Scottish Rifles or Cameronians. This was yet another attempt to strengthen and widen the allies' foothold on Helles, in which infantry of the 29th Division would also take part. Scheduled for the morning of 28 June, the attack's purpose was to force the Turks back up Gulley Ravine, as it was known on British maps, in order to threaten their hold on the critical hilltop position of Achi Baba from which constant artillery fire could be directed at the allies.

Turkish troops were securely dug into the ravine and everything depended on effective artillery fire preceding the infantry assault. However, as a Royal Scots regimental history published ten years later made very clear, this was not on offer: 'Our cannonade commenced punctually at 9am but no shells fell on the trenches to be attacked by the 4th and the 7th Royal Scots.'[38] The only covering fire was from the attacking battalion's own machine guns. This account went on to confirm:

the men of the 156th Brigade probably did not realise that their task was in the nature of a forlorn hope, in that they were asked to attack trenches garrisoned by men over whom superiority of fire had not been obtained.[39]

In France or Flanders it would have been suicidal even for experienced infantry and so it was for the Royal Scots and Scottish Rifles. Cheering as they went up and over their parapets and relying on rifle, bayonet and grenade, they ran forward into a storm of Turkish fire backed up by artillery from further up the ravine. The initial momentum of their attack carried them further than the Turks had thought possible. Some survivors of the charge recalled, with something close to horror, the ferocity which seized them as they reached the outer line of enemy trenches. One Lieutenant in the 4th Royal Scots wrote later of how, 'all that is savage in one seemed to be on top', and of how he had even hurled himself against Turkish corpses in a section of captured trench, 'hacking their faces with my feet or crashing my rifle into them.'[40]

Made in Scotland: land, sea and air. Scottish industry was in the forefront of producing the instruments of modern warfare.

Mark IV tank with 105hp Daimler engine. Beardmore collection. *Reproduced with permission from Glasgow University Archives and Business Records Centre.*

Parkhead Gun Factory. Beardmore collection. *Reproduced with permission from Glasgow University Archives and Business Records Centre.*

HMS *Agamemnon* prepared for launch, 1906. Scottish steel manufacturers William Beardmore and Co. had been closely linked with the pre-war armaments industry and were to remain solvent through government orders. The battleship illustrated fired the opening salvoes in the bombardment of the Dardanelles in February 1915. Beardmore collection. *Reproduced with permission from Glasgow University Archives and Business Records Centre.*

Beardmores also became one of the most important constructors of rigid airships by the end of the war. The R34 airship, laid down at Inchinnan on 9 December 1917, was best known for her double crossing of the Atlantic in 1919. Beardmore collection. *Reproduced with permission from Glasgow University Archives and Business Records Centre.*

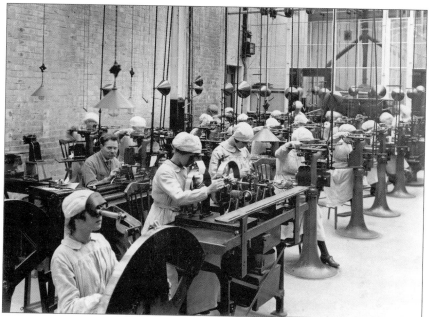

Women at work: the Engraving Department at Barr and Stroud. The women in the foreground are dividing rangefinder scales. Scottish women helped meet the demand for labour which arose from the mobilisation of substantial sections of the male workforce. *Reproduced with permission from Glasgow University Archives and Business Records Centre.*

Women at war: women were also in uniform. Miss J. G. Cadell, 4th Edinburgh Voluntary Aid Detachment (VAD), 814 MT Company (*c.* 1916). *Reproduced with permission from United Services Museum, National Museums of Scotland.*

THE LAST GOOD-BYE. 1916.

Women at home: A more traditional view of women's wartime role offered by Joseph Gray, war artist of *The Graphic. Reproduced with permission from the United Services Museum, National Museums of Scotland.*

Two faces of the recruiting drive.

1st Battalion Black Watch in pre-war finery march up Edinburgh High Street (*c.* 1914). *Reproduced with permission from the United Services Museum, National Museums of Scotland.*

One year on. Soldiers returned from the trenches, clad in animal-skin jerkins, greet prospective recruits during the winter of 1915. *Reproduced with permission from the United Services Museum, National Museums of Scotland.*

Men of the Royal Scots join in worship at a Sunday morning parade (*c.* 1914). *Reproduced with permission from the United Services Museum, National Museums of Scotland.*

Saturday afternoon soldiers: Glasgow's prestigious territorial battalion, the 5th Scottish Rifles (Cameronians), listen attentively at a pre-war training camp. The inspecting officer, Major Macalister, was killed by machine-gun fire while trying to regroup his men at High Wood on 20 July 1916. The battalion's casualties on this day were 407 officers and men. Bowman collection. *Reproduced with permission from Glasgow University Archives and Business Records Centre.*

Captain Alan G. Cameron, 1st Battalion, 79th Queen's Own Cameron Highlanders. Killed in action at the Battle of the Aisne, 25 September 1914. The Highland press compared his death to the 'glorious end of Colonel John Cameron of Fassifern at Quatre Bras'. *Reproduced with permission from the United Services Museum, National Museums of Scotland.*

John Ross of the Lovat Scouts, 1914. Not only was he a soldier in the Great War, but he had also been involved in a land raid at Scuddaburgh in the north of Skye in 1911. *Reproduced with permission from Dr Ewen A. Cameron (his grandson).*

Frontispiece from *The First Hundred Thousand*, 1916 edition. *Reproduced with permission from the United Services Museum, National Museums of Scotland.*

More popular images of the Scottish soldier:

"I jined the army for tae fight they Germans, and no for tae be learned to scrub floors."
'Jock', 1915–17, by Charles Johnson Payne (Snaffles). *Reproduced with permission from the United Services Museum, National Museums of Scotland.*

'. . . a very gallant officer and Scotsman'. 'A Heilan' Lad', 1915–17. *Reproduced with permission from the United Services Museum, National Museums of Scotland.*

'Accept my greetings aye sincere,
To wish you joy and all good cheer.
I would that I were with you,
But ... as yet that cannot be.
I send my hearty greetings,
  To you across the sea.'

Christmas and New Year card, 1918–19, 3rd Battalion, Queen's Own Cameron Highlanders. *Reproduced with permission from the United Services Museum, National Museums of Scotland.*

Concentrated firing and explosions ignited dry scrub and bushes and many wounded men burned to death where they lay before stretcher bearers could help them or drag them clear. As the casualties mounted, 29th Division units were hurled in to press the attack forward. The 4th and 7th Battalions of the Royal Scots were joined by their own 5th Battalion, as well as the Dublin Fusiliers. They too sustained terrible loss of life as the Turks, though forced to abandon some of their trenches, fought back with all the tenacity they had shown since the start of the campaign. Night came mercifully to cloak a scene of horror, 'a bloody sunset closing a day of bloodiness', one survivor wrote afterwards. Lieutenant O'Hara of the Dublin Fusiliers, who had fought alongside the 4th Royal Scots, later confided in writing to his fiancé that, 'we were in a condition bordering on lunacy when it was over.'[41]

The 4th and 7th Battalions of the Royal Scots paid an appalling price for their part in the 28 June attack. Only three of the 4th Battalion's officers came out of it alive and unwounded and its Commanding Officer, Lieutenant Colonel Dunn was among the first to be killed, dying of his wounds where he fell. Together with the 7th, losses in killed and missing were put at 337 men with almost 300 more wounded. The 5th Battalion, as well as the Cameronians, also suffered heavily from an operation which, though it took more ground than might have seemed credible given the circumstances, achieved little in strategic terms and should never have been ordered without adequate artillery support.

Official communiqués eventually claimed 28 June as a victory for the allies' cause, but divisional and surviving battalion commanders began to question the worth of further frontal attacks by daylight until drastic improvements in the artillery and ammunition situation could be guaranteed. Their doubts however, had little impact on the 8th Corps commander who had overall responsibility for operations on the 28th. This was the Ayrshire General Sir Aylmer Hunter-Weston who was later to represent his county in Parliament for almost twenty years in the Unionist interest. Officers of the 4th and 7th Battalions and their Brigade staff were particularly incensed by a remark he made to the effect that he had welcomed the use of the territorials on the 28 June as a good way of 'blooding the pups'. Major General Egerton, the 52nd Division commander, was so angered by this breezy metaphor from the hunt that he made his feelings known to Sir Ian Hamilton who had overall command of ground forces.[42]

Hamilton privately sympathised with Egerton, but nonetheless filed a report on him to Kitchener at the War Office in London, describing him as 'highly strung and apt to be excitable under stress'.[43] Subsequent to this, Egerton was invalided off the Peninsula as an exhaustion case, a victim of his inability to think of the former schoolboys, insurance and shipping clerks, bank tellers and postal workers of battalions like the 4th Royal Scots as merely disposable cannon fodder. Hunter-Weston, it seems, remained undaunted by fresh attempts to take Turkish positions like Achi Baba, but heat-stroke and exhaustion overtook him and he was granted sick leave in July. A year later he was to command another infantry corps with catastrophic results during Haig's offensive on the Somme.

Edinburgh's territorials remained so wasted by their losses that, for part of the time left to them on Cape Helles, the 4th Battalion amalgamated with what remained of the 7th until new drafts arrived from home. They saw it through, holding off repeated Turkish counter attacks on what little ground had been taken since the first landings, and retrieving and burying their dead when and where they could. In late July Dr Ewing conducted a memorial service for all from the 52nd Division who had fallen on and since the 28 June. He later described it:

> The stars were very bright, but the night was dark, and we could see each other only as shadows. The enemy seemed to enter into the spirit of the thing, and left us absolutely in peace. So there, in the trenched valley, alive with armed men we held our service. We sang familiar words, a few of the lads with good voices standing by and acting as a choir. *All people that on Earth do Dwell, The Lord's my Shepherd* and *O God of Bethel* were sung with deep feeling. As the music floated away on the night breeze it seemed to rouse the interest of others and attracted by the strains many dim figures moved silently towards us from the surrounding battalions, considerably swelling our congregation. How our hearts were stirred as we thought of the brave men gone, who had so often worshipped with us in the Grange and the old Cathedral. One felt in a peculiar way a sense of their presence, so we prayed that we might be worthy to cherish the memory of these heroic friends and comrades.[44]

Casualties

As the casualty lists from 28 June, as well as subsequent and prior actions, began to reach Edinburgh and to appear in the local press, the grim reality of the city's sacrifice was brought home to families and streets, schools and offices, workshops and warehouses from which the Royal Scots had raised their territorial battalions. Newspapers vied with each other in the solemnity of their tributes to the fallen. The *Scotsman* declared:

> Our ancient capital has never been deaf to the call to arms in our country's hour of need. Toll for the opening of the Dardanelles has been freely drawn from our poorest streets and classes and from the households of the foremost and most active citizens.[45]

The *Evening Dispatch* on the same day reacted very similarly, singling out the 4th Royal Scots because of the swathe which its death roll had cut through the city's legal and commercial community:

> In its ranks are many former pupils of such schools as George Watson's College, not a few of whom joined after the outbreak of the war. There is something at once inspiring and pathetic in the fate of these young fellows. They had grown up together almost from infancy, sitting on the same bench at school, romping in the playground together, running shoulder to shoulder on the football field, and then after the parting that comes at the end of school life, finding themselves side by side once more on the field of battle, playing the biggest game that men have ever played.[46]

A slightly different emphasis was given by the *Evening News* when its leader writer invoked an aspect of Edinburgh history no longer celebrated as part of the city's douce and respectable self-image:

> The Royal Scots is a glorious regiment but the citizen battalions have added to its laurels. The ancient fighting spirit of Edinburgh, which gave the city the questionable advantage of having the fiercest mobs in Europe, had been renewed for the benefit of the barbarous Huns and their savage allies the Turks and nobly have the sons of Edinburgh fought for a clean and just cause.[47]

Casualty lists lengthened relentlessly as more bodies were found and identified and as hospitals reported the names of those dying of their wounds. Day after day the photographs of the fallen were carried in the *Dispatch* and *News* – the faces forever young, smiling out under their glengarries. Brief details were usually printed along with the photographs and they mirror for us the social structure of a city where class categories were sharply defined in terms of neighbourhood and occupation, yet blurred too by the nature of territorial recruitment. In a battalion like the 4th Royal Scots, insurance managers, lawyers, and teachers enlisted and served very often with identical rank to postmen, delivery boys, or warehousemen. This, of course, was simply because there were initially not enough officers' commissions to go round. This was a situation that altered rapidly on 28 June.

The localism of Edinburgh's economy and its labour market shows vividly through these baleful statistics from a distant peninsula of which most of the city's people would never have heard before 1915. Boys who left their board schools before 1914 would tend to find work often within walking distance of where they lived with their parents. If this was in Fountainbridge or Gorgie it would be with the North British Rubber Company; if in the Old Town or Holyrood Road then it would be with Younger's Brewery or perhaps one of the big printing works further south on the edge of Arthur's Seat, like Thomas Nelson. One of their employees, a storeman, James Jackson, was killed with the Royal Scots 5th Battalion at Gallipoli on 28 June. He lived five minutes away from the Parkside works in an East Crosscauseway tenement with his wife and six children. In the *Evening Dispatch* he appeared not in uniform, but as a rather formal figure in a suit and stiff collar.[48]

The daily listings of officers killed reads like a roll-call of the city's fee-paying schools, as well as its legal and business families. Sir George McCrae's son, who worked in his father's business, was one of the Royal Scots 4th Battalion officers killed in Gallipoli. Another was a city lawyer, Major J. N. Henderson, who bled to death from terrible wounds sustained in the initial phase of the 28 June attack. 'A splendid soldier and a proper toff', was the verdict on him from a private soldier who was able to tend him briefly before he died.[49] Badly wounded close by him, was Lieutenant P. F. Considine, third son of the owner of a noted New Town law firm. Aged twenty-two when he died in a hospital in Malta, he had been a rugby player and athlete at Merchiston Castle, a boys' boarding school in the city.[50]

Another old established firm whose owner lost a son was the auctioneers, Lyon and Turnbull. He made available to the local newspapers the letter he received from a battalion chaplain after the body of his son, a Lieutenant in the 5th Royal Scots, was located and identified some time after his death in action. The letter describes his burial and a wooden cross being left to mark his grave and went on: 'It must be some consolation for you in the midst of your sorrow to know that your son died bravely leading his men in as gallant a charge as has ever been known in British history.'[51]

Along with the daily listings of dead and wounded came personal accounts of the Gallipoli fighting, sent in some cases directly to the local press or passed on to it by the families of those serving on the peninsula. The Chaplain, Dr Ewing, sent a sombre letter to be read out to his congregation which was made available to *The Scotsman* for publication. He wrote:

> The sights I have seen will never be erased from memory. To realise what war is you need to see the procession of fine, high-spirited young fellows, maimed, bleeding and dying, and spend hours with them in the improvised hospital tents. Then you get some conception of what this strife costs.[52]

A Portobello man wounded in action wrote home of his rescue by battalion stretcher bearers: 'It is wonderful what the human body can endure on active service, where life is stripped of all its sacredness and where blood is spent as freely as water.'[53] He also recalled some of what he had seen in the dressing station where his wounds were treated:

> They brought in a poor fellow next morning who had been shot in the head. He was alive and no more and I thought how merciful it was that folks at home were spared the full reality of what it means to be "killed in action" or to have died of wounds.[54]

Recollections like these cut raggedly across the constant editorials in the local press acclaiming the regiment's exploits and supporting appeals for yet more recruits.

As realisation deepened of what the fighting at Gallipoli had cost Edinburgh, churches began to hold special services of intercession for those of their congregation already enlisted and on active service. One of these in mid-July 1915 was at St Cuthbert's at the West End of Princes Street. This thriving church served the Fountainbridge and Haymarket areas as well as Lothian Road and the fashionable West End of the New Town. It had an active Boys Brigade company through which, before the war, many boys had transferred to the Royal Scots Territorials when they were of age. A total of over 360 members of the parish were listed in a special publication to mark the service along with the units they had joined.

The order of service invoked an ancient God of battles to give all of them courage and resolution, 'not for the increase of our glory but for the preservation of freedom and for the glory of Thy holy name.'[55] Special prayers followed for the fallen and those still to fall, 'that they might look death in the face with level eyes and die as good soldiers of Jesus Christ.'[56] The Rev. Norman Maclean, the minister responsible for the order of service, left nobody in doubt about his personal support for the war. He was not unusual in that respect among the city's clergy, but some were already becoming more directly threatening to those not yet enlisted. At a Royal Scots recruiting meeting at the end of July, the Rev. L. Maclean Watt told his audience that, 'he could not get ten men in his church of serviceable age and if he found them to be there he would make it impossible for them to stay there.'[57]

Serving territorial soldiers who had yet to accept the overseas service obligation began to be sharply reminded of the need to re-examine their position, especially if they were unmarried or simply married without children.[58] As the Gallipoli casualty lists grew, the language of recruitment propaganda became more strident and accusing. The *Evening News* declared, 'Many districts from apathy and it may as well be said from stupidity, have not done their duty. Scotland is not free from these black spots. They must be shamed into yielding up their shirkers if necessary.'[59]

Young enough to go

In this changed atmosphere, conscription was already being discussed, and indeed Edinburgh Trades Council voted in favour of it in late May 1915 on the grounds that Kitchener's latest call for another 300,000 men was unlikely to be met and that sacrifices under a voluntary system were unfairly shared.[60]

Moral blackmail had always had a place in recruiting propaganda, but it now became more frequent as the urgency both of keeping faith with those sacrificed at Gallipoli, and in France too, was driven home in renewed appeals for more men. In poster form these were displayed everywhere and faithfully carried in the local newspapers, especially the *News* and *Dispatch* with their much larger sales than *The Scotsman*. 'Have you a weak heart or just a faint heart?,' one appeal on behalf of the 6th Royal Scots asked its target audience: 'Better men than you have given up better jobs than yours and 'listed in the Royal Scots. Wake up man! Wake up and buck up and roll up today to the Recruiting Station.'[61]

Fear of not having employment to return to is thought to have influenced the degree to which enlistment levels varied from area to area over the 1914 and 1915 period, but recruiting appeals in Edinburgh were briskly dismissive of such anxieties.[62] 'Never mind your present job, laddie. There will be lots of jobs after the war', a 5th Battalion appeal declared: 'Hun-hunting with the Royal Scots is a man's job and you are jolly lucky to get the chance of it.'[63]

Young men not wanting to be separated from girl friends and sweethearts were treated with particular scorn, and one of their favoured summer courting places in the city's south side, the Blackford Hills, was ridiculed in another appeal:

Are you still suffering from Apronstringitis, laddie? Some young men are. You see them on the Blackfords every night! But Apronstringitis is easily cured. Oh yes! It means parting with the lady for a while, but she will gladly agree to your going if you tell her it is your duty to go. Your duty to her and your sisters too.[64]

At other times fear and hatred of a supposedly sub-human foe was used to lurid effect, as on another 5th Battalion poster:

What if a big drunk German stalked into your house looking for loot – looking for loot, laddie, and ready for rape – what would you do then? The poker, eh? No! No! Your own Lee-Enfield rifle with a shining bayonet would be the only cure for him. Of course you would be able to use it too, quick and clever. The Royal Scots would teach you that. They are waiting to teach you now, and wondering why you haven't 'listed long ere this.[65]

In a city with so many families now in mourning, the language used in their constant calls for more men could be unfeeling, especially when parents and wives were told to play their part. One choleric Royal Scots major was reported as telling a recruiting meeting:

It was a scandal that it should be necessary to appeal to young men to come forward as a favour to fight for their country. He appealed to fathers and mothers to bring pressure upon their sons every day. Let them cut down their rations or make their beds harder and thus force them to join their comrades. He also called upon young married women to urge their husbands to join the colours.[66]

'Squire nagged and bullied, till I went to fight under Lord Derby's scheme', Siegfried Sassoon wrote of those in 1915 who 'attested' their readiness to be called up when required under an initiative launched by one of the great aristocratic 'raisers' of the New Army. In Edinburgh, however, there were still young men averse to being bullied in the summer of a year in which voluntary enlistment was well past its peak. This emerges from some particularly cutting exchanges in the letter pages of the local press.

A patriotic correspondent signing himself as A. M. wrote with indignation of what he called the Saturday night 'Princes Street parade' of non-uniformed men of military age whom he saw strolling with friends and going into picture houses. In the space of an hour or so, A. M. claimed to have counted 500 men eligible for service and this too when a major recruiting meeting was being held in Holyrood Park. The least that picture houses could do, he concluded, was to raise admission prices for such obvious 'slackers'.[67]

A. M. got a prompt answer in the paper's next issue from a writer who signed his letter simply as 'a slacker' and declared himself to have been one of a group of five young men in civilian clothes who had entered a Princes Street picture house during the period of A. M.'s Saturday night surveillance. Of the five, he wrote, that one was a soldier on leave, while two others had in fact volunteered but been turned down on medical grounds. A fourth was the British-born son of a German interned in 1914 under the Defence of the Realm Act, whose brother had been discharged from the army after service on the Western Front for asking for the full separation allowance for his mother. 'My friend cannot be expected to gush over our military authorities', this correspondent declared, adding that he too had failed the army's medical requirements.[68]

As for himself, this letter writer went on to say, 'I am a slacker and am entitled to be one'. Rather than going to the pictures, he and his friends

> might have spent the evening in Princes Street collecting statistics about the number of men (Can A. M. be one?) who "only wish they were young enough to go" but secretly thank God they are just over the age limit.[69]

Another contributor to this correspondence stressed the dilemma of the younger brothers of already enlisted men who were often under severe pressure to stay and help parents who might be invalids or in real need of their wage. Others pointed out that the non-uniformed 'shirkers' in Princes Street and elsewhere could well be men in essential occupations and forbidden to enlist, as well as those with medical rejections from the army.[70]

For those with really difficult home circumstances who deferred the decision to volunteer, as well as the simply unmilitary who stayed put until conscription in 1916 removed any choice from them, the social pressures from ceaseless and increasingly hectoring recruiting propaganda must have been hard to bear. The cynicism created by it was not confined to those who avoided volunteering, something made clear in verses written by a Scot, Ewart Alan Mackintosh from Easter Ross who was killed on the Western Front in 1917:

> Lads, you're wanted, go and help;
> On the railway carriage wall

Stuck the poster, and I thought
Of the hands that penned the call.

Fat civilians wishing they
'Could go out and fight the Hun'
Can't you see them thanking God
That they're over forty-one? ...

Better twenty honest years
Than their dull three score and ten.
Lads, you're wanted, Come and learn
To live and die with honest men ...

Take your risk of life and death
Underneath the open sky.
Live clean or go out quick –
Lads, you're wanted. Come and die.[71]

A survivor

Even though its days were numbered, the voluntary system could still raise new drafts who went out from the depots to reinforce the Royal Scots at Gallipoli. Fighting dragged on bloodily until the year's end, as did arguments in London over whether or not to abandon the whole enterprise. Churchill, though he had been the principal political casualty of the campaign, continued to put the strategic case for it after his enforced resignation from the Admiralty in May 1915. Recriminations went on as new scapegoats were sought and in November, Kitchener himself went out to report on the case for an evacuation. By then a severe winter had set in on Cape Helles and at Suvla Bay where further landings had been made in August.

The flies and fever abated only to be replaced by bitter cold and blizzards which inflicted new privations on all units before the final withdrawal took place in January 1916. In perhaps the one really well planned operation in a disastrous venture, the Royal Scots Territorials were shipped off Cape Helles with the rest of the British, ANZAC and French forces. Huge quantities of supplies were set alight as the last troops left, and as their ships slipped anchor off the peninsula great fires could be seen burning on an abandoned battlefield where so many had fallen to gain so little.

Symptomatic of this cost was the shrunken spectre of the Royal Scots 4th Battalion. In May 1915, 30 officers and 941 other ranks had embarked at Liverpool, the battalion's full strength apart from just one doubter who deserted on the quayside.[72] Eight months later one captain, a medical officer and just one hundred and forty-eight men of other ranks were evacuated.[73]

One private of the 4th who got away with the rest of its survivors was James Edgar Wood, this contributor's father. Born and raised in Rosebank Cottages, between Morrison Street and Fountainbridge, he had volunteered at once for overseas service. On 28 June, he went into action at Gulley Ravine with many of his friends from school, St Cuthbert's Church, the Boys Brigade and the Post Office where he had worked before the war. Before embarkation, all of them were issued with pocket size New Testaments bearing the regimental crest and the injunction to 'be strong and of a good courage for the Lord thy God is with thee whithersoever thou goest'. Nearly all the members of his platoon signed the fly-leaf of his copy though it remains badly stained with blood from a wound which was to trouble him for the rest of his life.

Notes

The author would like to thank the staff of the National Library of Scotland, Edinburgh Central Library, the Scottish United Services Library at Edinburgh Castle, the Scottish Record Office, the Public Record Office at Kew, and all at the Royal Scots Club in Edinburgh for their invaluable help in the preparation of this chapter.

1. *Edinburgh Evening News*, 17 Jun. 1915.
2. H. Cunningham, *The Volunteer Force* (London, 1975), p. 21.
3. R. B. Haldane, *An Autobiography* (London, 1929), p. 195.
4. P. Dennis, *The Territorial Army 1906–1940* (Woodbridge, Suffolk, 1987), p. 19.
5. I. Beckett, 'The Territorial Force', in I. W. Beckett and K. Simpson (eds), *A Nation in Arms: A Social Study of the British Army in the First World War* (Manchester, 1985), p. 129.
6. Scottish Record Office [SRO], MD/11/1, Minutes of City of Edinburgh County Territorial Force Association, 13 Jan. 1908.
7. SRO, MD/11/1, Minutes of Edinburgh County Territorial Force Association, 29 Apr. 1908.
8. SRO, MD/11/2, Minutes of Edinburgh County Territorial Force Association, 29 Oct. 1912.
9. Lieut-Col Etheridge, *The Territorial Army: What it is and why you should join it* (Edinburgh, 1909), pp. 45–6.
10. *The Times*, 8 Jan. 1912.
11. *Ibid.*
12. Dennis, *Territorial Army*, pp. 23–4.
13. Public Record Office [PRO], WO 32/11242, McCrae to Seely, 16 Nov. 1913.
14. *Ibid.*
15. *Edinburgh Evening News*, 22 Nov. 1913.

16. PRO, WO 32/11242, Bethune to Seely 3 Dec. 1913.
17. *Ibid.*
18. R. Dudley Edwards, *James Connolly* (Dublin, 1981), p. 7.
19. J. Holford, *Reshaping Labour: Organisation, Work and Politics – Edinburgh in the Great War and After* (London, 1988), pp. 16–17.
20. Lieut-Col R. R. Thomson MC, *The Fifty-Second Lowland Division 1914–1918* (Glasgow, 1923), p. 10.
21. See also, Etheridge, *Territorial Army* p. 28.
22. J. Ewing, *The Royal Scots 1914–1919* (Edinburgh, 1925), vol. 1, pp. 3–11.
23. P. Magnus, *Kitchener: Portrait of an Imperialist* (London 1958), p. 290.
24. T. Royle, *The Kitchener Enigma* (London 1985), pp. 262–3.
25. SRO, MD 11/5, General Purposes Committee City of Edinburgh's Territorial Forces Association, 30 Jun. 1914.
26. Dennis, *Territorial Army*, pp. 32–3.
27. *The Scotsman*, 6 Jan. 1915.
28. *Ibid.*
29. *Ibid.*
30. *Ibid.*, 14 Jan. 1915.
31. *Ibid.*, 16 Feb. 1915.
32. *Edinburgh Evening News*, 22, 24 May 1915.
33. *Ibid.*, 20 Feb. 1915.
34. J.M. Cameron, 'The Quintinshill (or Gretna) Rail Disaster', *The Gallipolian: Journal of the Gallipoli Association*, lxxix (1995), pp. 11–19.
35. *Edinburgh Evening News*, 26 May 1915.
36. William Murray, interviewed by author, 20 May 1987.
37. Ewing, *Royal Scots*, vol. 1, p. 152.
38. *Ibid.*
39. *Ibid.*, p154.
40. N. Steel and P. Hart, *Defeat at Gallipoli* (London, 1994), p. 206.
41. R. Rhodes James, *Gallipoli* (London, 1965), p. 230.
42. *Ibid.*, p. 231.
43. *Ibid.*
44. Thomson, *Fifty-Second Lowland Division*, p. 75.
45. *The Scotsman*, 8 Jul. 1915.
46. *Edinburgh Evening Dispatch*, 8 Jul. 1915.
47. *Edinburgh Evening News*, 9 Jul. 1915.
48. *Edinburgh Evening Dispatch*, 23 Jul. 1915.
49. L. Weaver, *The Royal Scots* (London, 1915), p. 242.
50. *Edinburgh Evening Dispatch*, 21 Jul. 1915.
51. *Ibid.*, 17 Jul. 1915.
52. *The Scotsman*, 5 Jul. 1915.
53. *Edinburgh Evening News*, 3 Sept. 1915. Also available in, *Royal Scots Casualty List 1914–1918*, Vol. 7, Royal Scots Club, Edinburgh.
54. *Edinburgh Evening News*, 3 Sept. 1915.
55. *Parish Church of St Cuthbert's, Edinburgh Roll of Honour, July 1915* (Edinburgh, 1915), p. 12.
56. *Ibid.*, p. 13.
57. *Edinburgh Evening News*, 31 Jul. 1915.
58. *Ibid.*, 19 May 1915.
59. *Ibid.*
60. *Ibid.*, 26 May 1915.

61. *Ibid.*, 24 Jul. 1915.
62. Beckett, 'Territorial Force', pp. 9–10.
63. *Edinburgh Evening Dispatch*, 13 Jul. 1915.
64. *Ibid.*, 22 Jul. 1915.
65. *Ibid.*, 15 Jul. 1915.
66. *Ibid.*, 26 Jul. 1915.
67. *Ibid.*, 12 Jul. 1915.
68. *Ibid.*, 13 Jul. 1915.
69. *Ibid.*
70. *Ibid.*, 14 Jul. 1915.
71. T. Royle (ed.), *In Flanders Fields: Scottish Poetry and Prose of the First World War* (Edinburgh, 1990), pp. 81–2.
72. R. Westlake, *British Regiments at Gallipoli* (London, 1996), p. 1.
73. *Ibid.*, p. 4.

CHAPTER SIX

Confrontation and Withdrawal: Loos, Readership and 'The First Hundred Thousand'

Gordon Urquhart

"It's a tremendous opportunity for our section of 'K(1),'"
continued Wagstaffe. "We shall have a chance of making
history over this, old man."
... Then suddenly his reserved, undemonstrative
Scottish tongue found utterance.
"Scotland for Ever!" he cried softly.[1]

THE GREAT WAR has been cited as the catalyst for the birth of
modernism and the revival of Scottish literature which centred on
MacDiarmid, Gunn and others. This Scottish Literary Renaissance was,
however, one of 'high art' and dealt with the war in retrospect. The
present chapter concerns itself with literature reflecting contemporary
popular sensibilities, which offered the reading public current representations of the Scot at war. J. J. Bell, already established as a story
teller of some renown, added to his 'Wee MacGreegor' sequence with,
Wee MacGreegor Enlists, recently republished.[2] Although less remembered, the work of Captain R. W. Campbell was well-received at the
time: his Glaswegian character 'Spud Tamson' became, according to
Moira Burgess, 'a national figure for a time.'[3]

This chapter focuses on another writer with Edinburgh – rather than
Glasgow – connections, albeit with an international reputation. John
Hay Beith had been a schoolmaster at Fettes Academy and was an
occasional contributor, as 'Ian Hay', to *Blackwood's Magazine*. After
giving up teaching to concentrate on writing, he proceeded to add to
his reputation as a light novelist. Already a territorial army officer since
1908, he enlisted in the 10th Argyll and Sutherland Highlanders on the
outbreak of war. This unit, pseudonymously 'The Bruce and Wallace
Highlanders', was to provide the backdrop for his most famous novel,

The First Hundred Thousand, published first in serial form in *Blackwood's*. Written by 'The Junior Sub', it started in November 1914, following immediately after Ian Hay's *Happy-go-lucky*, another school story from his accomplished pen. Though not initially 'propaganda' in an official context, its potential for being part of the government's Waterloo House operation was spotted. *Blackwood's* was offered assistance in publication and soon had a best seller on their books. Within a year of publication, it went on to sell 115,000 copies in Britain and the colonies, and 350,000 in the United States.[4]

A comedy of military manners

The First Hundred Thousand is considered in this paper in three ways. Firstly, Hay's use of metaphor and humour is examined in order to define his readership. Secondly, *The First Hundred Thousand* is analysed as a 'letter home' from the front to the first group of intended readers, the families of the New Army soldiers, bringing into play issues of morale, information, nationality, class, ideology, and finally, salvation and sacrifice. Thirdly, Hay's representation of the battle of Loos as a site where fact and fiction interplay is dicussed.

Metaphor is, in literary terms, a device which describes the new in terms of the old by comparison. Metaphor, therefore, serves to facilitate a transition from the known to the unknown. For Kitchener's army, which suddenly thrust a tenth of a million men into a new way of life, a whole new culture waited to be understood. For those at home, explanations were necessary. In answer, Hay offered the public school as the metaphoric vehicle with which to comprehend the army life.

Buitenhuis is succinct:

> The tone ... is farcical. Practical jokes are always in order; emotion must never be expressed; high sentiments are out. The more senior officers are the equivalent of housemasters and usually nicknamed (Waggers for Wagstaffe is typical); the junior officers are the prefects, and the men are partly grown-up versions of the younger boys – down to the unwashed knees beneath the kilts.[5]

Yet 'farcical' obscures a great deal of pathos, sentiment and erudite wordplay – comedy of manners might be a better allusion. But Buitenhuis' understanding of Hay's expression of the social strata is impressive. Such a trope would be comprehensible to the predominantly middle-class readership of *Blackwood's*, though it was also, by necessity, a reflection of a literal truth. Lieut. Col. Croft, a friend of Hay's, would take over command of the 9th Scottish Division, in which Hay had served. Writing in 1919, he recalled that, by 1917

> we had pretty well reached bed-rock for officers in the British Army. And here I want to put it on record that that I did not hold that deprecatory view of our officers, who were, I considered, just as good as ever, for the following reason. Most of them had received a public school education. It matters not even if it was a day school; the fact remains that that all those boys had the public school spirit. Now that public school spirit is a priceless asset in war, for as everyone knows, the boy learns to play for his side, to forget his own little self. And when later he comes to us knowing that, he has learnt half the duties of an officer, and furthermore he has imbibed that spirit of leadership with his mother's milk. We must encourage that public-school spirit in England.[6]

Although this umbrella metaphor would seem, for the officer class at least, to be tending towards the literal, lesser descriptive metaphors can prove enlightening with regard to class. *Blackwood's* readership was predominantly white collar: 'The firing trench is our place of business – our office in the city, so to speak. The supporting trench is our suburban residence', wrote Hay in the *First Hundred Thousand*.[7] He continues in a parody of what we would now call 'estate agency speak', as the humour ameliorates the harshness of trench life. Similarly, when the character Mucklewame meets a French sentry for the first time, they 'regard one another with shy smiles, after the fashion of two children who have been introduced by their nurses at a party.'[8] The 'nurses' is a sure class signifier, as is the description of waiting to go up the line. Here, the soldiers '(snap) our fingers with impatience, like theatre-goers in a Piccadilly block, whose taxis have been held up by the traffic debouching from Berkeley Street.'[9]

Locales, as well as class, are deterministic factors in the choice of metaphoric vehicle. The bursting of start shells overhead is described as being, 'Just like the Crystal Palace on benefit night!'[10] However, 'dug-outs compare unfavourably with a flat in Knightsbridge', serving to remind the reader that irrespective of his Scottish affiliations and subject matter, Hay's readership was predominantly metropolitan.[11]

The main focaliser, who provides the vision through which the story unfolds, is Bobby Little, a young officer. As a kind of 'everyson', he becomes the channel for identification and *The First Hundred Thousand* is his *bildungsroman*, an extension of his university career. Through his eyes, we are shown the regiment in training, as Hay demonstrates a clinical understanding of the mechanisms of morale.

John Baynes, in his *Morale – a Study of Men and Courage* lays the ground rules for morale, with special reference to the Second Scottish Rifles at the Battle of Neuve Chappelle. The first condition of morale is cheerfulness, which is transmitted in almost every section of Hay's novel, and especially in the ironic humour of the officers.[12] Irony is seen as being an essentially British quality. The introduction to the French edition of *The First Hundred Thousand*, stresses this point and urges its readership to try to make an effort, 'in order to understand the thoughts of a friend'.[13] Irony is, it continues, 'by no means a sign of levity or poverty of heart. When an Englishman speaks of "Our Brother Boche" or of "The kind Hun" there is much indignation beneath such sweetly ironic epithets.'[14] It should, therefore, be borne in mind that irony is a euphemistic device.

Baynes goes on to discuss individually the signs, or absences of signs, of morale. Firstly:

> In peacetime, or out of the line, one of the best guides is saluting. To walk into a barrack or camp where morale is high is obvious to any experienced officer in the first two minutes. About three smart, cheerful salutes give the clue. Where soldiers have good officers, whom they trust, they are happy. Having good officers, they salute them well and their salutes are properly returned. It is as simple as that.[15]

It is not far into *The First Hundred Thousand* that the rules of military etiquette come under discussion by a group of novice junior officers. They painstakingly debate the rules of saluting, determined to extract the underpinning methodology in what is, for them, a mystifying ritual. Their examples become absurd:

> "What does a Tommy do," he inquired, "if he meets an officer wheeling a wheelbarrow?"
> "Who is wheeling the barrow," enquired the meticulous Struthers – "the officer or the Tommy?"[16]

They consult the aptly named Captain Wagstaffe to provide a solution. He replies in a written bill, which is posted in the ante room:

> *Correct procedure.* – The soldier will immediately cant the swill tub to an angle of forty-five degrees, at a distance of one and a half inches above his right eyebrow. (In the case of the Rifle Regiments the soldier will balance the swill-tub on his nose.) He will then

invite the officer, by a smart movement of the left ear, to seat himself in the wheelbarrow.[17]

Ultimately, for all the ribbing, the saluting ritual is reinforced. All Baynes' conditions are met in considered sequence in Hay's narrative: turn-out, treatment of visitors, hygiene and sick-parade attendance. Cheerfulness pervades all the examples.

Yet behaviour is another barometer:

> it has to be seen in perspective. Certainly no unit with good morale has continual cases of bad discipline. On the other hand, some of the soldiers in a first class battalion may from time to time cause annoyance by becoming troublesome in their local town. The experienced officer knows almost by instinct whether the trouble is due to poor morale or high spirits. Good soldiers have a bit of devilment in them, and it is no good becoming alarmed at occasional outbursts of misbehaviour.[18]

In the austerely, yet ironically, titled chapter 'Crime', the unsophisticated Bobby Little, learns from the monosyllabic Captain Blaikie as he presides over the reviewing of the conduct sheets. The reader is implicitly invited to offer judgement, while becoming familiarised with both the individual characters and the stereotypes. Crime in the army, we are told, means a great many things. Private Dunshie refuses to wash a floor:

> "I jined the army for tae fight they Germans, and no for tae be learned to scrub floors -"
> "Sirr!" suggests the Sergeant Major in his ear.
> "Sir!" amends Private Dunshie reluctantly, "I was no' in the habit of scrubbin' the floor mysel' where I stayed in Glesca'; and my wife would be affronted." [19]

Private McNulty is charged with destroying Government property:

> "I was sittin' on my bed, with the knife in my hand, cutting a piece bacca and interfering with naebody, when they all commenced to fling biscuits at me. I was keeping them off as weel as I could; but havin' a knife in my hand, I'll no deny but I gave twa or three of them a bit cut." [20]

Humorously delaying closure, 'biscuits', we and Bobby Little eventually find out, are small square mattresses. McNulty is reported to the Commanding Officer, but – we are relieved to hear – will probably just be fined.

Private Robb, drunk and singing, was lifted by the Military Police:

"... Want to go to the front, don't you?"
"Yes, sirr." Private Robb's dismal features flush.
"Well mind this. We all want to go, but we can't go till every man in the battalion is efficient. You want to be the man who kept the rest from the front – eh?" ...
" Good boy, that," remarks the Captain to Bobby Little, as the contrite Robb is removed. "Keen as mustard. But his high water mark is somewhere in his boots. All right, now I've scared him."[21]

This heart-warming wisdom is juxtaposed with the subsequent ingress of Private McQueen, 'an unpleasant- looking creature with a drooping red moustache and a cheese-coloured complexion'.[22] He has been:

"Drunk – beastly drunk – four times in three weeks. Always dirty and insubordinate. Always trying to stir up trouble among the young soldiers. Been in the army before haven't you?"
"No."
"That's not true. Can always tell an old soldier on parade. Fact is you have either deserted or been discharged as incorrigible. Going to be discharged as incorrigible again. Keeping the regiment back, that's a real crime."[23]

Not only is the reader given insight into the sagacity of the officers as decision makers, but the conditions under which morale can thrive in this imaginary body are also revealed. The reader becomes concerned for the soldiers' welfare, for they know that with good morale nothing bad can happen to them. The real morale question was on the home front, but this was one way in which the 'gang-show' exhibited its 'more than ordinary practical value', as Hay's obituary in *The Times* expressed it.[24]

However, as Finkelstein attests, *Blackwood's* also had an extensive readership amongst the military while on active service, and a 'spirit of emulation' is inculcated through *The First Hundred Thousand*. Bobby Little is proffered as being the medium for the process. As a Brigadier General wrote, 'it puts matters in a way that would appeal to young officers infinitely more than any of the recognised books.' It seems also to have played a direct part in the official modernisation of the Army. The artist responsible for the book's frontispiece mentioned that, 'A few weeks ago in a lecture on Military matters we were recommended to read *The First Hundred Thousand* as being the book – so it has become a Corps handbook – and the ordinary textbooks on "Field Service", "King's Regulations", etc. are out of date.'[25]

Thus, the other purpose was as an explicative text on both fronts. Hay, in pedagogic mode, offers insights into the realities of army life, thereby satisfying curiosity on the home front. However, by extending them to the point of absurdity, he makes them humorous. In the chapter, 'Olympus', Hay satirises the army's supply logistics with a sideswipe at what Fussell calls, 'Forms rhetoric'.[26]

For instance, in the case of machine gun washers – by the way, in applying for them, you must call them *Gun, Machine, Light Vickers, Washers for lock of, two.* That is the way we always talk at the Ordnance Office. An Ordnance officer refers to his wife's mother as *Law, Mother-in-, one* – you should state when the old washers were lost and by whom; also why they were lost, and where they are now. Then write a short history of the machine gun from which they were lost, giving date and place of birth, together with an exact statement of the exact number of lines fired ... adding the name and military record of the pack animal which usually carries it ...[27]

The discussion of 'Olympus', is reminiscent of the logistical excesses in Joseph Heller's *Catch 22*. The tangled web of bureaucratic administration, would have struck a muted, but recognisable, chord with a middle-class white-collar readership. Similarly, Hay in his desire to clarify, variously lists and describes men and officers' field kit,[28] bomb-types,[29] an average day in the trenches,[30] leisure activities[31] and types of letters home. The latter include the field service postcard which has, Fussell says, 'the honour of being the first spread exemplar of that kind of document which uniquely characterises the modern world: the "Form."'[32] Lampooned by Owen, Waugh, Heller and others for their reductionist, dehumanising effect, Hay – through the censoring pen of Bobby Little – is minimal in his critique:

He [the card writer] is not allowed to add any comments of his own. On this occasion, however, one indignant gentleman has pencilled the ironical phrase, "I don't think!", opposite the line which acknowledges the receipt of a parcel. Bobby lays this aside, to be returned to the sender.[33]

Again, the order is validated, teased, but strengthened in response. By extrapolation, a great deal of the humour in the text comes from the interplay between these two registers: the informality of the soldiers and the narrator's summative closure in ameliorative terms, and in frequent militaristic rhetoric. For example, while out on exercises,

Dunshie, tired of the game and needing a cigarette, offers himself up
as hostage to Mucklewame on sentry duty.

> The hospitable Mucklewame agreed, and Scout Dunshie, overjoyed
> at the prospect of human companionship, promptly climbed over
> the low wall and attached himself, in the *rôle* of languishing captive,
> to Number Two Sentry-Group of Number Three Piquet.[34]

Taken in its original format of the magazine episode, this closure serves
to seal the humanity of the soldiers within the shell of the martial
envelope. The last word is always given to the Army.

In the ranks

Born in Manchester of Scottish parents, Hay was a 'Scottophile' from
an early age. According to *The Times*, this he demonstrated in his writing:
in a style of humour that is 'pawky', and 'a strain of lively and ceremo-
nious sentiment which trembled on the verge of sentimentality.'[35]
Though these can be considered typical of the literature of the age,
particularly commensurate with the 'kailyard school', he himself has a
vital notion of national characteristic. ('Finally we are Scotsmen, with
all the Scotsman's curious reserve and contempt for social airs and
graces.'[36]) However, these characteristics, as we have seen, were not
necessarily in accord with army life. 'Scotland' was an exclusive club,
admission only to the most select. When Captain Blaikie is killed, he is
described as 'a very gallant officer and Scotsman', which, however it is
read, ameliorates the second category. He describes his unit out on
exercises, on a route march in England:

> Suddenly far in the rear, a voice of singular sweetness strikes up
> *The Banks of Loch Lomond*. Man after man joins in, until the swelling
> chorus runs from end to end of the long column. Half the battalion
> hail from the Loch Lomond District, and of the rest there is hardly
> a man who has not indulged, during some Trades Holiday or other,
> in "a pleesure trup" upon its historic, but inexpensive waters ... On
> we swing full throated. An English battalion, halted at a cross-roads
> to let us go by, gazes curiously upon us. *Tipperary* they know, Harry
> Lauder they have heard of; but this song of ours has no meaning
> for them. It is ours, ours, ours.[37]

We are thus linked to Neil Munro's reported sighting of Hay on Loch
Lomondside, 'trudging in front of his platoon, his shoulder covered by
an old waterproof sheet, which spouted rain down his kilt and legs. He

was carrying the rifle of a dejected Tommy who limped behind him in the first section of fours.'[38] The vision is mocking, but compassionate. Yet Hay is desperate to transform reality into something as lustily inclusive as myth.

As Bobby Little is for the officer group, Mucklewame, though to a lesser extent, is point of entry for the 'other rank' identification. He is described, as 'an esteemed citizen of Wishaw ... a rank and file man by instinct and training, but he forms a rare backbone for K(1)', thus cast as a particularly regional 'everyman' of Kitchener's army. He is not bright: Army scouts, he attests, "gang oot in a procession on Setterday efternoons, sirr, in short breeks"'. He is clumsy: he perforates Aldershot's water main while practising entrenching. However, unlike Campbell's Glaswegian, as we shall see later, Hay's Scottish working man – for that is who his soldiers are – is a glorious creation: 'off-handedly brave' as Buitenhuis puts it, loyal and hardworking. He is variously described as respectable, conscientious, punctilious.[39] To denigrate him would be to give the game away, for, like Shakespeare's mechanicals, he has his dramatic purposes – much of the broad humour is at his expense. He has, like some of Scott's creations, a name with illustrative qualities: the recruit with the flat feet is called McSplae; Private Mearns is from Aberdeen; the divisional scout is McSnape. The diligent miners Ogg and Hogg, who call Fosse Eight at Loos, a 'bing', are always portrayed in industrious duofold.[40] However, unlike the officers, whose eloquence offers insight, the soldier is sketchily drawn, and inspires little curiosity, with one exception.

McOstrich, the Ulsterman, is a figure writ large, like the drunkard discussed earlier, but not yet excluded; the 'outsider' within:

a dour, silent, earnest, specimen ... [who] keeps himself to himself. He never smiles. He is not an old soldier, yet he performed like a veteran the very first day he appeared on parade. He carries out all orders with solemn thoroughness. He does not drink; he does not swear ... As a matter of fact he is not a Scotsman at all, though five out of six of us would put him down as such. Altogether he is a man of mystery; but the regiment could do with many more such.[41]

As an illustrative anecdote, we are shown him felling Private Burke, who made a 'contemptuous and ribald reference to the Ulster Volunteers and their leader.' Hay continues enigmatically: 'Plainly, if [he] comes safe through the war, he is prepared for another and grimmer campaign.' But the character's most brutally unlikely of pseudonyms – which Hay mischievously introduces with, 'as unlikely as it seems' – alludes to a technique for avoidance.

His reappearance is deferred until the final chapter at the Battle of Loos.

> McOstrich, the Ulster visionary, was there, six paces ahead of any other man, crooning some Ironside canticle to himself ... The men pressed on, at a steady double now. McOstrich was the first to go down. Game to the last, he waved encouragement to his mates with a flailing arm as they passed over his body.[42]

The paradox resolves itself in death, at the hands of a common enemy, yet the paragraph is designed to provoke ridicule: 'crooning' seems fey and incongruous in the warlike context. The use of 'game' offers itself up as a play on words, and 'flailing' seems to corroborate the birdlike allusion. In a battle where nearly all the other named characters escape alive, all tropes seem to contrive to devalue this sacrifice. The conclusion that McOstrich is a cipher for a particular ideological position on a current discourse – that of Irish Republicanism – cannot be avoided.

Similarly, early in the book, the conversion of the 'reformed revolutionary', McSlattery, sets the collusional tone and exhibits the Scottish egalitarianism discussed earlier:

> "If I had kent all aboot this 'attention' and 'stan'-at-ease', and needin' to luft your hand tae your bunnet whenever you saw yin o' they gentry-pups of officers goin' by – dagont if I'd hae done it, Germans or no! (But I had a dram in me at the time). I'm weel kent in Clydebank, and they'll tell you there that I'm no the man to be wastin' my time presenting airms tae kings or any other bodies."[43]

So much for McSlattery's rant, but Hay cannot resist a more eloquent delineation of the 'Before' position. Using the narrator's privileged omniscience, however, he possibly blunders into misplaced irony.

> In the lower walks of the industrial world Royalty is too often a mere name. Personal enthusiasm for a sovereign whom they have never seen, and who often in their minds is inextricably mixed up with the House of Lords, and capitalism, and the police, is impossible to individuals of the stamp of Private McSlattery. To such, Royalty is simply the head and corner-stone of a legal system which officially prevents a man from being drunk and disorderly, and the British

Empire an expensive luxury for which the working man pays while the idle rich draw the profits.[44]

Such is the fortitude of the dramatic build-up, that the denouement is telegraphed. During a Royal review, McSlattery has an epiphany:

> For a moment - yea, more than a moment – keen Royal eyes rested upon Private McSlattery, standing like a graven image, with his great chest straining at the buttons of his tunic.
> Then a voice said, apparently in McSlattery's ear -
> "A magnificent body of men, Colonel, I congratulate you."
> A minute later McSlattery was aroused from his trance by the sound of the Colonel's ringing voice -
> "Highlanders, three cheers for his majesty the King!"
> McSlattery led the whole Battalion, his glengarry high in the air …
> "Yin mair, chaps," he shouted" – for the young leddy!"[45]

Hay again provides the punchline to frame the incident: 'And yet there are people who tell us that the formula, O.H.M.S., is a mere relic of antiquity.'[46]

A cognate sentiment appears in R. W. Campbell's melodramatic poem, *The Making of Mickey McGhee* (1916), where the eponymous hero is of similar stock to McSlattery:

> Life had made him a rebel. He was a nomad from the slums,
> Who'd only come for the drink and the bread, and not for the
> soul of the drums.[47]

But, the narrator tells us, he begins to learn that the army offers an egalitarianism of effort, and thus a chance of betterment-by-association:

> And how the sons of Princes and Peers are pals of men like he,
> Sharing with manly pleasure the skirmish, the march and the
> spree.[48]

Nevertheless, unable to cope with discipline, he strikes an officer, and while in gaol is given a chance to contemplate his debauched life:

> Would he go back to Sarah, the "Model" and things of sin?
> These were the thoughts that sent his head into a swirling din.
> Then the good that's in the vilest whispered, "No lad, stick it out;
> The Army is kind to the sinner, and the men that the merchants
> clout."[49]

On his release, he goes on a binge and is called up for 'criming'. But Mickey is given another chance.

"Come! On your word of honour – you're going to play the game!"
"Yes, Sir" said Mickey, the sinner, his heart in a righteous flame.
But the battle was stiff and uppish; he was fighting the sins of
sires,
And the craving for drink was hellish – like raging passions' fires.[50]

However, fate provides a turning point and 'Providence' comes to Mickey's aid.

Then came the Ultimatum – War and freedom from lures,
An outlet for hidden glories; the chance that murders or cures.[51]

Mickey's division is active in the retreat from Mons, where he is heroic in hand-to-hand combat.

Their rounds were fired and vanished; all that was left was the
steel,
As they rose with a cheer and plunged it home into the swine
who squeal.
Gad! what a noble ending – plunging then warding the blows,
Smashing the heads with the butt-ends, ripping the hearts of their
foes.[52]

Hidden within the carnage, is the prolepsis which carries the denouement of the tale. In the attempt to save a wounded officer, Mickey is bayoneted by an enemy soldier. Mickey and his Captain die side-by-side. The scene switches to Sarah, weeping in the 'Model':

And her pride is a silver medal, a letter and statement of pay,
From the man who cherished her dearly, and saved on a "bob" a
day.
Ten pounds to this woman called Sarah – crude, yet kind as a
dove,
Whose charity in the mean streets gained her a soldier's love.[53]

In both stories it is the Army, and indeed war, that provides salvation; in McSlattery's case from socialism; in McGhee's from loose-living. For McGhee, however, it seems the only way out of the poverty trap was through death. The theme of redemption from poverty is recurrent in Campbell's work, through *Private Spud Tamson* (1915) to *Jimmy McCallum* (1921). Recognising the war as a watershed, his search for a solution to Glasgow's social problems shows a constantly evolving perspective, examined through the genre of popular fiction. Strangely, there exists very little examination of Campbell's *oeuvre*.

Loos: the unwanted battle

The climactic event for Hay's troops in *The First Hundred Thousand* is the Battle of Loos. Hay's representation would have been a point of access for all New Army readers, for it was here that they – including Hay's unit in the Scottish 9th Division – got 'blooded'. In his book, *The 10th Battalion Argyll and Sutherland Highlanders, 1914–1919*, Sotheby defers to Hay, 'An early history of the 10th Battalion Argyll and Sutherland Highlanders has already been presented to the world, by the inimitable writings of "Ian Hay" in his *First Hundred Thousand.*' [54] He then uses that as justification to abridge the early days of the unit's action, despite Hay's own preclusion that, 'The reader is hereby cautioned against regarding this narrative as an official history of the Great War ... the characters are fictitious but the incidents described all actually occurred.' [55]

This polarisation gives clear illustration of Hayden White's dictum. 'Literature', he says, 'is ... viewed as being more or less realistic, depending on the ratio of empirical to conceptual elements contained within it.' [56] We are, therefore, given the sense that Hay's 'truth' of the battle is somewhere between a dryly factual military history and an adventurous backdrop in which the established characters can act.

There are, of course, many 'truths', particularly about the Battle of Loos. This battle has generated an abundance of discourses and subsequent conclusions. For Hay it was 'The Battle of the Slag-Heaps'; for Liddell Hart it was 'The unwanted battle'. Kitchener saw the joint Anglo-French manoeuvre, under his direction, as a strategic sop to the French in order to secure for himself the post of Commander-in-Chief of the Allied Forces.

Although it was keenly anticipated as being the breakthrough on the Western Front, Sir Henry Rawlinson noted: 'It will cost us dearly and we will not get very far.' [57] It was, he said, 'ill-fated' through a lack of shells, cover and even an adequate amount of support troops. The rationed bombardment used insufficient ammunition to break the German defences. Haig's anticipated use of gas was initially barred by the wind direction. Later, when the gas was released, it drifted over the German trenches on the right, but not to the left where, in some places, it even blew back. Many British soldiers were poisoned by their own gas. For Hay's ingenue warriors 'in close up', understatement seems to be the order of the day: Wagstaffe was affected by the somewhat romantic sounding 'lachrymous shell', but 'nothing to signify.' [58]

It was, however, the machine guns that proved costly for the Scottish Divisions at Loos. The German regimental diary describes 10,000 men walking in ranks across open territory, 'offering such a target as had never been seen before, or thought possible. Never had the machine gunners had such straightforward work to do, nor done it so effectively. They traversed to and fro across the enemy's ranks unceasingly.' [59]

Having been pinned down under machine gun fire, Hay's combatants are blasé:

> "What were your sensations, *exactly*?" asked Kemp.
> "I felt just as if an invisible person were tickling me," replied Ayling, with feeling.
> "So did I," said Kemp. "Go on." [60]

The transformation is of lethal hot metal changed to the frolics of a mischievous imp. This serves to remove the dread of the German guns to fairyland, via nursery floor. The conversation – enquiry, offer and confirmation – conducted, of course, mid-battle, would serve to counteract any re-communicated terror from returnees. [61]

In such times of despair, rumours are rife: 'there was a report that the German General in charge had said that his machine gunners had refused to fire another shot. They were so filled with bitter remorse and guilt at the corpses at Loos.' [62] This may even have been corroborated in a German regimental diary which notes how, when the fifth British attempt at a push had failed, they were allowed to retreat in peace: 'No shot was fired at them ... for the rest of the day, so great was the feeling of compassion and mercy.' [63] Hay's assailants, left to hold the most forward position, doubly outflanked and last to fall back, are given no such humanitarian consideration when surrendering the ground so expensively won, but are loquacious in retreat:

> "We shall have a cheery walk back, I *don't* think!" murmured Wagstaffe.
> He was right. Presently the withering fire was opened from the summit of the Fosse, which soon began to take effect in the ill-protected trench ...
> "... This enfilade fire from the Fosse is most unpleasant. (I fancy that one went right through my kilt.) Steady there on the left: don't bunch whatever you do. Thank heaven there's the next line of

trenches, fully manned. And thank God, there's that boy Bobby tumbling in unhurt!"[64]

Captain Johnstone of the field ambulance observed a resurgence after Loos in, 'definite hysterical manifestations (mutism and tremors) ... particularly in many of the younger members of Kitchener's New Armies, the volunteers of eighteen and nineteen.'[65] While unhurt in body, Bobby, 'who had neither eaten nor slept since the previous dawn, was nibbling chocolate, and shaking as if with ague.'[66] He is suffering nascent shell shock.

In a brief moment of repose, the officers debated the course of the battle:

"I wonder what they will do with us next," remarked Mr. Waddell ...

"If they had any sense of decency," said Major Kemp, "they will send us back to rest a bit, and put another Division in. We have opened the ball and done a lot of dirty work for them, and have lost a lot of men and officers ..."

"I should be more inclined to agree with you, Major," said Wagstaffe, "if only we had a bit more to show for our losses."[67]

Major Kemp guesses that the plan was to occupy the German resources, while 'our French pals on the right are pushing him off the map. At least that's my theory: I don't pretend to be in touch with the official mind. This battle will go on for a week or more, over practically the same ground.' For a while, this is what happened, with the German Guard Corps coming to reinforce Vimy Ridge, to the south. However, the French also sustained heavy losses, which allowed the German Army time to strengthen resources to the rear. The ten days of Kemp's best guess became a total of twenty-one days – The British Army sustained losses of 60,392 to the German army's 20,000. Liddell Hart summarises:

Never were novice divisions thrown into a vital stroke in a more difficult or absurd manner, and in a greater misconception of the situation in all quarters ... This amply explains their subsequent failure ... That in courage they were not lacking that much is clear, and equally that its fruits were reduced by their rawness, by that of their staff still more.[68]

Confusion, deceit and covert ambition made pawns of the British soldiers. As the official history has it, The Battle of Loos, 'had not improved the general situation in any way and had brought nothing but useless slaughter of infantry.'[69]

Slaughter, however, was outwith Hay's lexis. Morale was dented, but still reformed. With the main focaliser safe and continuity assured, the narrative goes into summary: the cycle of attack and counter attack and the contingency measures inherent in war. Many of the soldiers are 'Over the Hill', but the book ends with most of our heroes still intact.[70]

Market forces demanded a sequel. The Somme was to provide the climax for *Carrying on – After the First Hundred Thousand*, published as a book in 1917, by which time Hay had long since left 'for home and later went to the United States on a lecturing tour.'[71]

Loos, according to MacIntyre, with some understatement, was a 'disappointing' battle: 'If 1 July 1916 and the Somme are forever engraved on the nation's consciousness ... 25 September 1915 and Loos are remembered particularly in Scotland ... There was hardly a home, and certainly not a village, that did not know somebody at Loos.'[72] This is corroborated by Hay himself, describing an 'imagined community':

> Englishmen are fond of saying, with the satisfied air of men letting off a really excellent joke, that everyone in Scotland knows every one else. As we study the morning's role of honour, we realise that never was a more truthful jest uttered. There is not a name on the list of those who have died for Scotland which is not familiar to us. If we did not know the man – too often the boy – himself, we know his people, or at least where his home was ... Scotland is small enough to know all her sons by heart ... Big England's sorrow is national; little Scotland's is personal.[73]

In a country so staunchly founded on myth, the mythic significance of Loos, far outstripping Culloden in terms of Scottish carnage, is an absence in the Scottish core. It has a silent continuity, evoked only tangentially and caught out of the corner of the eye, but offering a resolution to the schism in Scottish identity.

In his 1995 short story, 'Beady Eyes', John Cunningham explores a relationship breakdown in modern Scotland. The final page describes the bus journey from Edinburgh to Glasgow, and the return to the old lover:

> By the time we get to the M8, I'm seeing the poppies on the roadside in a haze of sleep and the droning cosy vibration of the bus. Before it makes its halfway stop at Harthill, we pass a place where they're landscaping mounds of earth into pyramids. They'll

be covered with grass and bushes probably. The bare earth's almost completely shaped now and a digger is perched on the slope doing the final smoothing with its delicate arm.

It changes about here, at Harthill, a slight difference but no special place, like a border crossing, it changes here in the frontierland, the no man's land of undulating central plateau. We cross an invisible ridge about Harthill, other than the crest of the road. Everyone in the bus must feel it, more or less; they slump back in their seats for the second half – we've crossed over. I can't help thinking somehow of the trouble they're having in Shotts prison must be connected with the situation, the poor guys being affected perhaps dragging over the nerve each time they cross their cell, doing time in this twitchy no-man's-land. We go up the hill to Kirk o' Shotts. Over to the right black mounds and nothing much, to the left graveyard, fields and wood but – the bus angles down and there are the towerblocks and spread of Glasgow.[74]

The symbols are consistent: poppies, the drowsiness, the repetition of 'no man's land', the waiting men and the notional 'going over the top'. Even the martial connotations of 'Shotts' corroborate the allusion. The first part of the last sentence reads like a scout's report from Loos – a view from a distance, as if through field glasses.

'More than mere momentos'

In conclusion, it is worth considering the thesis postulated by Cairns Craig in his essay, 'The Body in the Kit Bag'. He suggests that it was with the First World War that Scottish literature regained its sense of history, lost since the excesses of Culloden. All writing between those dates is 'ahistorical' lacking any sense of its own national identity; forsaking historical narrative by subsuming it within the Anglo-British Empire. However destructive the experience of the Great War, it represented the possibility of a new beginning, a new engagement with the forces of history, a reconnection of Scotland with the real dynamics of the external world.[75]

The true value of *The First Hundred Thousand* is, then, as the story of that agency at the historical moment of its rebirth. The repetition of the word 'history' in the book, as evidenced in the quote at the head of this chapter, is indicative of the enthusiasm for that reclamation, which Hay – in his role as proxy – attempts to convey. In his role as 'war correspondent', Hay realises the uncertainty, but relishes the importance of his mission. The closing paragraph of the first part promises that, 'Whether Part Two will be forthcoming, and how much of it there will be, depends on two things – the course of history, and the present historian's eye for cover.'[76]

In addition to the magazine serial reader, another kind of reader, perhaps less intended, suggests itself. Any second-hand book shop in Scotland will probably have at least one copy of *The First Hundred Thousand* and possibly some of Hay's other books. My own copy has Hay's obituary from *The Times* and accompanying photograph pasted inside with other related ephemera: information on Kitchener, the famous pointing poster and so on. My copy of *Carrying On*, once owned by one John McLeod, is covered with a protection of thick brown paper, with the title typed on the outer cover and handblocked on the spine. Evidently both books were much valued by their original owners and provide, in one instance, context, and in the other, the craving for permanence. Dressed up like testaments, perhaps even venerated as being an artery of 'truth', they are more than mere mementoes. Although the fluctuations in historiography may have changed the interpretation of the texts, for the original owners, 'facts' were secondary. This, the books seem to offer, is what it was like and how it felt to be there.

The survivors once again duck down below the historical parapet and return to the anonymity of the static community, having 'done their bit'. In the absence of any conflicting representations – or maybe even despite them – Hay's books were cherished and offer a patina of blandishments to sweeten the fading memory.

Notes

1. I. Hay, *The First Hundred Thousand* (Edinburgh, 1927), p. 282.
2. J. J. Bell, *Courtin Christina – Wee MacGreegor Enlists* (Edinburgh, 1993).
3. M. Burgess, *The Glasgow Novel: A Survey and Bibliography* (Motherwell, 1986), p. 23. See R. W. Campbell, *Private Spud Tamson* (Edinburgh, 1915).
4. D. Finkelstein, 'Blackwood's Magazine in World War One', in J. Treglown and B. Bennet (eds), *Grub Street and the Ivory Tower: Essays on the Relations between Literary Journalism and Literary Scholarship* (London, forthcoming 1998). All references to Finkelstein's work are taken from the pre-publication draft and are hence unpaginated.
5. P. Buitenhuis, *The Great War of Words – Literature as Propaganda 1914–18 and After* (London, 1989), p. 113.
6. Lieut. Col. W. D. Croft, *Three Years with the 9th (Scottish) Division* (London, 1919), p. 95. The reader is best referred to P. Fussell, *The Great War and Modern Memory* (London, 1977), for an extended discussion of this motif and several others in *First Hundred Thousand*. See particularly pp. 24–9.
7. Hay, *First Hundred Thousand*, p. 90.

8. *Ibid.*, p. 176.
9. *Ibid.*, p. 287.
10. *Ibid.*, p. 203.
11. *Ibid.*, p. 209.
12. The exception is the chapter '... and some fell by the wayside'. This chapter details the death of 'Wee Pe'er' through – as Finkelstein observes – 'officer neglect'.
13. I. Hay (trans. Georges Richet and Emile Herzog), *Les Premirs Cent Mille (K.1.)* (Paris, 1916), p. 8. The translation is my own.
14. *Ibid.*, p. 8.
15. J. Baynes, *Morale – a Study of Men and Courage* (London, 1967), p. 94.
16. Hay, *First Hundred Thousand*, p. 40.
17. *Ibid.*, p. 42.
18. Baynes, *Morale*, p. 95.
19. Hay, *First Hundred Thousand*, p. 31.
20. *Ibid.*, p. 30.
21. *Ibid.*, pp. 33–4.
22. *Ibid.*, p. 34.
23. *Ibid.*, p. 35.
24. *The Times*, 23 Sept. 1952.
25. Finkelstein, 'Blackwoods'.
26. Fussell, *Great War*, p. 179.
27. Hay, *First Hundred Thousand*, pp. 122–3. Croft, *Three Years*, p. 3, notes that Hay was a machine-gun officer. Hence the example is given added vitality through personal experience.
28. Hay, *First Hundred Thousand*, pp. 194–9.
29. *Ibid.*, p. 212.
30. *Ibid.*, pp. 216–42.
31. *Ibid.*, pp. 256–62.
32. Fussell, *Great War*, p. 179.
33. Hay, *First Hundred Thousand*, p. 264.
34. *Ibid.*, p. 107.
35. *The Times*, 23 Sept. 1952.
36. Hay, *First Hundred Thousand*, p. 15.
37. *Ibid.*, p. 12.
38. T. Royle (ed.), *In Flanders Fields: Scottish Poetry and Prose of the First World War* (Edinburgh, 1990), p. 175.
39. Buitenhuis, *Great War*, p. 113.
40. Hay, *First Hundred Thousand*, p. 285. Other characters in the text are Cox and Box, the engineers, and Cosh and Tosh, the rifle-range scorers. These characters, all defined by the physicality of their roles, are linked in function, like Carrol's 'Push-me-pull-you'.
41. Hay, *First Hundred Thousand*, p. 158.
42. *Ibid.*, p. 296.
43. *Ibid.*, pp. 21–2.
44. *Ibid.*, p. 19.
45. *Ibid.*, pp. 23–4.
46. *Ibid.*, p. 24.
47. R. W. Campbell, *The Making of Mickey McGhee* (London, 1916), p. 12.
48. *Ibid.*
49. *Ibid.*, p. 14. 'The model' is thoughtfully glossed as 'a common lodging house'.
50. *Ibid.*, p. 16.

51. *Ibid.*

52. *Ibid.*, p. 18.

53. *Ibid.*, p. 21.

54. H. G. Sotheby, *The 10th Battalion Argyll and Sutherland Highlanders 1914–1919* (London, 1931), p. xv.

55. Hay, *First Hundred Thousand*, p. i.

56. H. White, 'Fictions of factual representation', in *Tropics of Discourse* (Baltimore, 1978), p. 122.

57. Quoted in B. H. Liddell Hart, *History of the First World War* (London, 1970), p. 195.

58. Hay, *First Hundred Thousand*, p. 295.

59. Quoted in M. Gilbert, *The First World War* (London, 1994), p. 199.

60. Hay, *First Hundred Thousand*, p. 293.

61. As Haig noted, 'Some of the wounded had gone home and said that they had been given impossible tasks to accomplish and that they had not been fed'. Quoted in Gilbert, *First World War*, p. 201.

62. L. MacDonald, *1914–1918 – Voices and Images of the Great War* (London, 1988), p. 106.

63. Gilbert, *First World War*, p. 199.

64. Hay, *First Hundred Thousand*, p. 309.

65. Gilbert, *First World War*, p. 201.

66. Hay, *First Hundred Thousand*, p. 291.

67. *Ibid.*, pp. 297–8.

68. Liddell Hart, *History*, p. 201.

69. *Ibid.*, p. 203.

70. Carson Stewart of the Cameron Highlanders remembered: 'When they took the roll-call after Loos for those not answering, their chums would answer, "Over the Hill!"'. Quoted in MacDonald, *1914–1918*, p. 106.

71. Sotheby, *10th Battalion*, p. 15. Prior to 26 March 1916, Hay had been seconded from the army and was involved in government-sponsored propaganda work to precipitate America's entry to the war. He was later awarded the C.B.E. for this service. See Finkelstein, 'Blackwoods'.

72. C. MacIntyre, *How to Read a War Memorial* (London, 1990), p. 100.

73. Hay, *First Hundred Thousand*, p. 47.

74. J. Cunningham, 'Beady Eyes' in *Flamingo Scottish Short Stories* (London, 1995), p. 148.

75. C. Craig, 'The Body in the Kit Bag', in *Out of History* (Edinburgh. 1996), p. 35.

76. Hay, *First Hundred Thousand*, p. 166.

CHAPTER SEVEN

May 1915: Race, Riot and Representations of War

Catriona M. M. Macdonald

THEIR NAMES DO not appear on official casualty lists, but during May 1915 the following, and their families, became 'victims of war': Conrad Ahrweiler, hairdresser, English Street, Dumfries; H. C. A. Ramsdorf, jeweller, High Street, Dumfries; Charles Cleeberg and Charles Cleeberg jun., gut manufacturers, Lockerbie Road, Dumfries; Christian Feyerabend, pork butcher, High Street, Annan; William Ohlms, hairdresser, West Blackhall Street, Greenock; William Gaze, provisions merchant, Lynedoch Street, Greenock; Mrs E. Sieger, publican, West Blackhall Street, Greenock; William Eilert, hairdresser, Kilmacolm; Albert Becher, pork butcher, High Street, Alloa; John Frenz, pork butcher, South Street, Perth; Charles Kumerer, pork butcher, High Street, Perth; Mrs H. Liebow, hairdresser, South Street, Perth; Charles Gruber, pork butcher, Lothian Road, Edinburgh and H. Egner, pork butcher, Great Junction Street, Leith.[1]

Panikos Panayi, the foremost historian of the anti-German riots which took place across Britain in May 1915, has suggested that 'the incidents of this month resemble a Russian pogrom with the native population attempting to clear out aliens.'[2] In Liverpool, damage caused by the rioting was estimated at £40,000 and 200 'establishments' were gutted.[3] In Manchester, crowds numbered in their thousands smashed windows and looted shops, and in Salford thirty properties came under attack.[4] In London, 'out of the twenty-one Metropolitan Police Districts, only two remained free from disorder'.[5] In the capital 1,100 cases of 'damage and theft' were recorded, 250 people suffered injuries, and by October 1915 claims for damages amounted to £195,000.[6] Rioting also spread to Sheffield, Rotherham, Newcastle and various other provincial English towns. Yet, while the English riots have, admittedly, received little more than 'passing attention' from most historians, far less is known of the nature and the motive forces of the Scottish riots which took place in Greenock, Annan, Dumfries, Perth, Alloa and Leith.[7]

Panayi admits that 'each disturbance arose out of an individual set of circumstances and each took a unique course', yet there is an implicit suggestion in his work that the rioting of May 1915 should, nevertheless, be considered in its totality.[8] In his identification of a set of common causes, the search for 'patterns' in the riots and his appreciation of the events of this month as 'racial' disturbances, Panayi posits inclusive explanations.[9] Consideration of the Scottish riots, however, casts doubt on the unity or 'national' character of these disturbances and suggests that a new paradigm must be sought to explain the events of May 1915. In what follows, evidence of commonality will be challenged by attacking the 'universals' which Panayi employs to contextualise and explain the riots: namely, the influence of the press and the prioritisation of common causes, premised on the chronological coincidence of the riots.

The press, the provinces and the public

Two basic dilemmas must be addressed when attempting to explain the Scottish riots: namely, why there were relatively few and why they took place in the towns mentioned above. Alternatively, why were there not more, and why did they not take place in the major centres of population?

By failing to address unique aspects of Scotland's war experience, the common causes suggested by Panayi fail to address such critical questions. Fundamentally, the sections of the press which Panayi considers instrumental in fuelling the riots, stand in need of re-examination when one turns to the Scottish experience.[10] The focus of Panayi's analysis of press attitudes to Germans and enemy aliens in Britain falls largely on the Unionist press of Fleet Street, the controversial right-wing weekly, *John Bull* and the nationalist journals *Passing Show/Vigilante*, the *British Citizen and Empire Worker* and the *British Empire Union Monthly Record*.[11] Panayi admits that

we cannot necessarily prove that public opinion became hostile towards Germans, whether on the field of battle or on the Home Front, simply by repeating the point that the press constantly preached hatred of Germany and of its residents within Britain.[12]

However, much of his subsequent explanation of the influence of the press in the anti-German riots rests on connections and inferences drawn between the motives of the rioters and the perspectives of these newspapers and journals.[13] But, it remains unclear how many rioters read or had knowledge of these titles or, indeed, the extent to which the local presses in towns affected by the disturbances mirrored their anti-German rhetoric. At root, questions regarding the circulation, influence and political persuasion of the popular Scottish press – and the right-wing press which Panayi analyses – must be addressed.

In 1914 the Glasgow *Daily Record* advertised in Mitchell's *Newspaper Press Directory:*

> The 'Glasgow Daily Record; is NOT a 'provincial' newspaper. The 'GLASGOW DAILY RECORD' is a NATIONAL PAPER with a NATIONAL CIRCULATION. It is Scotland's 'Daily Mail'. It has a circulation larger than any other newspaper north of the Border.[14]

For the twelve months ending December 1912, the *Daily Record* boasted average certified daily sales of 154,053 at a time when the *The Times* was selling around 150,000.[15]

Over 300 separate titles were produced and printed in Scotland on the eve of war, ranging from well-known names like *The Scotsman* and the *Glasgow Herald*, to lesser-known local organs such as the *Crieff Advertiser* and the popular *Football Times*, published weekly by the Highlands News Company and established as recently as 1907.[16] However, as much of the research published to date has focused on the journals of Fleet Street, even mundane issues regarding the circulation and ownership structures of the Scottish press at the turn of the century remain something of a mystery. Circulation is a problem for most British press histories of these years. For statistics before the inter-war period, we must rely on erratic sources and a corpus of secondary literature which has subsumed the experience of the Scottish press with that of the English 'provincials'. Even the most reliable of the primary sources, the *Monthly Circular of the Advertiser's Protection Society* (from 1908), is notoriously inaccurate on the presses outwith Fleet Street.[17] Instead, in terms of published sources, we are forced to rely on occasional advertisements in journals such as *Advertising World* and the *Newspaper Press Directory;* the shady remembrances of retired editors, journalists and proprietors, and informed guesses from English academics, who mention Scotland's 'Fourth Estate' largely by way of courtesy. Newspapers were under no obligation to publish their average daily, weekly or annual circulations, and between the removal of the stamp duty in 1855 and the arrival of the Audit Bureau of Circulations in the 1930s, all but a small number 'jealously guarded the volume of their sales'.[18]

Yet a number of conclusions can be made. Generally, during the war years the geographical limits of the combined circulations of the Scottish presses coincided with Scotland's national boundaries and Scotland's most popular papers were contained within its borders. English and metropolitan titles had relatively limited circulations north of the border, casting doubt on the appropriateness of the epithet, 'national press', used by many historians to describe them. In addition to problems of distribution, it was also acknowledged by many that the circulation of English titles in Scotland suffered due to the long-standing popularity and distinctiveness of the 'native' Scottish titles.[19]

The popularity of local, evening and weekly Scottish titles was marked. In 1914 the *Dumfries and Galloway Standard* claimed an average weekly circulation in excess of 23,000, and by 1921, it claimed to sell over 27,000 copies, at a time when the population of the burgh of Dumfries stood at 15,728.[20] Glasgow's *Evening Times* boasted an average daily circulation of over 154,053 on the eve of the Great War, and in 1916 recorded fluctuating daily sales of between 135,000 and 369,000 copies.[21] Similarly, sales of Thomson's *Weekly News* reflected the popularity of the Scottish 'weekly', with sales rising from over 437,000 in 1910 to 644,525 by 1923.[22] For many rural communities, it was often such weekly titles, rather than the more famous dailies, which informed public opinion in these years.

The Scottish press, therefore, was a decentralised and fragmented entity during the war years. While some closures and amalgamations had already occurred, such trends were not as fully developed as they would become in the inter-war years, when the encroachment of London financiers posed cause for concern. Generalisations rooted in the metropolitan experience regarding the influence of the press – in a generic sense – are therefore highly questionable. This point is further enhanced when one looks to the political persuasion of the Scottish press.

From a survey of over two hundred Scottish newspapers in 1914, the vast majority – over 70% – were either Liberal or Independent. Even without pointing to their circulations, the influence they exerted over the framing and interpretation of war news in the subsequent four years was to be phenomenal. This 'liberal' bias accords well with the provincial English experience where, in 1910 over 61% of all provincial 1d. and ½d. dailies were either Liberal or Independent.[23] Yet such political bias is in stark contrast to the papers of Fleet Street. On the eve of war, only two morning dailies (*Daily Chronicle, Daily News*) were Liberal and controlled around 20% of the total circulation of the London dailies.[24] In the evening market the Liberals faired better, with around 40% of the total circulation of these titles. In the Sunday press, however, three of the five largest in this category had Liberal owners and took over 70% of the circulation.[25] In contrast to Scotland and the provinces, however, the ownership of the Fleet Street titles was in the advanced stages of concentration. In 1914, for example, Lord Northcliffe controlled 28.9% of the circulation of the London dailies.[26] Thus, while the political influence of the Fleet Street 'Press Barons' on the policy networks of Westminster was undeniably profound, questions remain about the extent to which their 'influence' touched the popular imagination of the nation in its widest sense.[27] As Alan J. Lee has made clear,

> The total circulation of the morning and evening provincial press, even though it cannot be precisely measured, was certainly far in excess of that of the metropolitan press, and where they were direct competitors it was the local paper which usually did best. It had the advantage of containing local news, and had often built up a hard core of readership over many years. Larger circulations, which the London dailies were after, depended to some extent on recruiting working-class readers, who were apt to stick to their weeklies, or the cheaper local evening paper.[28]

Despite the paucity of evidence, it seems reasonable to conclude that in any attempt to gauge the influence of the press on popular attitudes in Scotland at this time, a focus on the Fleet Street titles would – to say the least – be unhelpful, due to their geographically limited circulation, their concentrated ownership and their political bias, which directly conflicted with that of the majority of the press north of the border. Rather, it is suggested that it is in the manner in which the Scottish press mediated the national experience of 'total war' and, subsequently, how the local press mediated the Scottish perspective that the complex influence of the printed word north of the border is to be found.

Fighting in the 'fog of falsehood'

In 1919, George Outram & Co., the owners of the *Glasgow Herald*, published John Buchan's *The Battle Honours of Scotland, 1914–18*. Here Buchan wrote:

> When in earlier days war was proclaimed at the Cross of Edinburgh and all enemies were ordered furth of the kingdom, the decent citizen listened to the fan faronade and went about his business. War was no concern of his since our ancient foes of England had ceased from troubling. To find a parallel to the summons of August 1914, we must go back to the time when old and young were called to man the walls after Flodden; and that was but a local affray after all, for the news scarcely penetrated beyond the Highland

Line. But in that sunny and confused month of destiny there was a stirring to the uttermost islands. The answer came quick, and after four bitter years we can judge the greatness of it.[29]

As the Director of the Department of Information from 1917, Buchan's words are poignant. They reflect the manner in which the Great War blurred the distinctions between the home and fighting fronts and did as much to encourage a commitment to Scottish distinctiveness as re-affirm the unity of Empire.[30]

By focusing on the experiences of the localities where the Scottish anti-German riots took place, the inter-relationship between the local and the national, as evidenced in the pages of the local press, throws into sharp relief the way in which the war destroyed the boundary between the domestic sphere and the battle-field; collapsed geographical distinctions through the nature of personal experiences, and highlighted the ambiguities inherent in neat distinctions between truth, propaganda and falsehood.

As Miriam Cooke and Angela Woollacott have made clear, war in the twentieth century has begun to 'undo the binary structures that it originally put in place: home (female space) and front (male space); combatant and civilian.'[31] Such tensions acquired linguistic expression in the local press during the Great War: in the muddying of subtle editorial distinctions between 'leader' and 'report'; 'Letters Columns' and 'News from the Front'; 'Foreign News' and 'Local Gossip'.

Yet, while several variants were allowed to co-exist, one distinction could not be compromised: the distinction between 'them' and 'us', between enemy and friend. Several commentators have highlighted the importance of the demonisation of the German enemy in the British war effort, yet few have provided a sufficiently nuanced reading of the discourses evidenced in the press – taking account of the geographical and cultural specificity of the readerships involved – to account for the conflicting responses to war which are evident when we look below the level of the national.[32] During and before the riots of 1915, the local press in the areas affected by the disturbances negotiated the boundary between the near fictive entity of 'the German' in the popular conscious-ness and the lived experiences of the Germans who were part of the communities which they served. How the enemy was to be understood relied on the ways in which news from the battle-field was mediated by local circumstances: the state of the local economy, the political persuasion of the readership, the levels of recruitment in the area, and so on. Explanations for the riots of May 1915, at root, lie within this relationship and highlight the manner in which 'total war' is best understood as the sum of local experiences, rather than a structure imposed upon them.

A reversion to ancestral type?

All British newspapers were constrained during war-time by the Defence of the Realm Act, the operation of the Press Bureau after 6 August 1914, and later by the Department of Information (the Ministry of Information from February 1918).[33] No Scottish proprietor or editor – except for the shadowy figure of Sir Henry Dalziel (Reynold's News) – succeeded in achieving the level of influence of the Fleet Street 'Press Barons' and as a result, their story remains largely untold. For the small local newspaper, the public's absorption with the European theatre of war led to a reliance on official press releases, syndicated news and letters home from local soldiers at the front. For the larger interests, however, there were ways round such restrictions. In the early days of the war, for example, the *Glasgow Herald* reinstalled its twenty-four hour wire, secured its reporters a desk in the Press Bureau and, when correspondents were allowed to the Front after May 1915, shared expenses with the English *Daily Chronicle* by using joint correspondents.

Yet the pressures of war were as much psychological as material. Repeated complaints in the early days of war that the press was being starved of news led to a greater reliance on home news and a heavier dependence on myth to frame the war narrative which was emerging in the columns. With little of substance to go on, newspapers resorted to dramatising the events they were permitted to reveal by framing them in the traditions of epic and the heroic. Censorship and control, therefore, not only created capital in sensation, but in familiar and recognisable 'sign systems' through which readerships could make sense of war.

The Scottish press presented the war as discourse in a very real sense. With little alternative sources or readings of the war available, the media consensus which framed the news it presented, manufactured subject positions which relied on a series of opposites to acquire meaning: soldier/'conshie', striker/war-worker. What distinguished the Scottish press from the English perspective, however, was its creation of another 'us' against which 'them' could be explained and an understanding of 'them' which best fitted the interests of the common war effort and Scottish political sensitivities.

Due to the fact that the readership of the Scottish press largely coincided with Scottish national boundaries, and the dominance of the 'home-grown' periodicals was relatively unchallenged within its bounds,

1. Clincher Tyres advertisement. Source: *Glasgow Herald*, 23 January 1915.

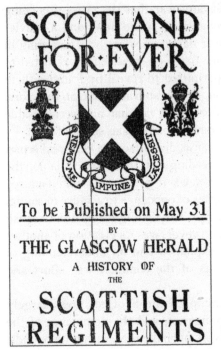

2. 'Scotland for Ever' advertisement. Source: *Glasgow Herald*, 25 May 1915.

A Scotsman's Catechism

WHO made this little Island the greatest and most powerful Empire the world has ever seen ?

Our Forefathers.

WHO ruled this Empire with such wisdom and sympathy that every part of it—of whatever race or origin — has rallied to it in its hour of need ?

Our Fathers.

WHO will stand up to preserve this great and glorious heritage ?

We will

WHO will remember us with pride and exultation and thankfulness if we do our duty to-day ?

Our Children.

Justify the faith of your fathers, and earn the gratitude of your children.

ENLIST TO-DAY!

God Save the King.

3. 'A Scotsman's Catechism'. Source: *Glasgow Herald,* 3 February 1915.

Wee Macgreegor.

WHAT HE THINKS OF IT

Paw (startled from reading the war news)—That's Wee Macgreegor's chap at the door !

Maw (turning very pale)—Naw; it's no' possible. Wee Macgreegor's in the trenches in France. His last letter said—

Paw (rising to open the door)—It'll be as weel to see what it is, ony wey.

Wee Macgreegor (six feet high, dressed in kilts, and wearing a corporal's stripe and an inscrutable Kitchener smile)—This is me, maw ! Nae greetin', noo ! I'm no' wounded. I've been promoted, and I'm gettin' a holiday hame.

Maw—Are ye sure ye're no' wounded? I've dreamed a hunner times ye were blawn awa'. Whit wey did they manage to send ye hame? I thocht they couldna ha'e dune wantin' ye. Have ye no' got pneumonia, or rheumatism, or frost bite?

Wee Macgreegor—No; jist promotion.

Paw—Hoots, wumman ! It wid tak' something stronger than frost to bite Wee Macgreegor.

Maw—Weel, come awa' and get some tea. Whit kind o' meat do ye get in the trenches? Gey puir stuff, I've nae doot; made by men buddies !

Wee Macgreegor—As much as ye can eat; and ye're aye stervin' wi' hunger at meal times.

Paw (admiringly)—Weel, you're a grand advertisement for them, ony wey. You sodger folk, ye ken, are in everybody's mind. Ye get socks, and chocolates, and mufflers, and National Funds, and—

Maw (vigorously)—And whit for no?" Wha could do enough for them? They do a thoosan' times mair for us than we could do for them.

Wee Macgreegor (with a far-away look in his eyes, and his smile tinged with melancholy)—Aye, that's true. Nae money peys for yon wark ! Nor rubies, nor pearls !

Wee Macgreegor's mother strikes the right note when she declares that our soldiers and sailors do a thousand times more for us than we can do for them. Let us help their wives and families to the utmost limit of our resources. Yesterday we received contributions amounting to £214 9s 9d. With the amount already acknowledged " The Glasgow Herald " branch of the National Relief Fund now stands at £48,851 9s 6d.

All subscriptions should be addressed to THE GLASGOW HERALD (National Relief Fund), Buchanan Street, Glasgow

Should an acknowledgment not appear within two days, it is requested that intimation be made of the amount sent and the date and place of posting.

Cheques and Postal Orders should be crossed, and made payable to George Outram and Co., Ltd. (National Relief Fund).

Subscription sheets can be had on application.

SUBSCRIPTION LIST.

Shillings.
Amount previously acknowledged ...... 972,739½.
Employees William Boardman and Co. &c./, Parkhead Works (19th and 20th week)
contributions........................ 2,4911½

4. Wee Macgreegor. Source: *Glasgow Herald,* 9 February 1915

the focus of the Scottish press on the generation of a Scottish perspective on the war was, perhaps, predictable. Indeed, there is a substantial corpus of evidence to prove that this was the case.

Even in the mundane case of advertising, the Scottish press used Scottish iconography to tempt its readers in identifying with a 'Scottish' war effort – either through a defensive patrotism or guilt – and parting with their pounds to prove it (Fig.1). In recruitment materials, again, the press appealed to Scottish sensitivities – here (Fig. 3) the religious sensibility – to encourage a peculiar vision of the Empire's struggle as a Scottish campaign.

Dialect also had its uses in shaping a Scottish vision of war (Fig. 4). A conventional tool of the press to intensify its empathy with its reading public, dialect – especially in the form of local poetry – presented a couthy, home-spun image of war in which the allies, in a very real sense, 'spoke the same language'.

Finally, in appeals to the past, the press legitimated the war through a reliance on precedent and tradition. Sidney Wood's appreciation of the Scottish military tradition is seminal in this regard. Yet, how it was transmitted and appreciated outwith the armed forces requires further attention.

Figure 2 is an advertisment for a three-shilling history of the Scottish regiments produced by the *Glasgow Herald* in 1915 – with a foreword by the Earl of Rosebery. From 1742 to the present (skilfully side-stepping 1745), it traces the Scottish military tradition in an attempt to frame the present – to place the contemporary Scottish experience at the end of a continuum stretching back centuries. Returning to Buchan, he considered the Scots to have been 'very conscious of our past',

> It dwells with us like a living memory. Bannockburn, and Flodden and Prestonpans are far closer to a Scots boy than Agincourt and Crecy to his English co-eval. Stories like that of Wallace or the heart of Bruce or the death of Montrose are almost a personal tradition.[34]

In attempting to explain how and why a separate Scottish press has persisted into the late twentieth century, its persistent fashioning of Scottish identity has come in for scrutiny and has been explained by an 'entrenched position', 'ow(ing) much to the local loyalties and national consciousness of (its) readers'.[35] War did much to legitimise the sense of nationhood reflected in the Scottish press by contextualising it as part of something bigger – by providing the context within which that sense of nationhood could be lived as well as read.

Yet war relies as much on perceptions of the enemy as of the national 'self' for meaning.

A significant minority

Comparing the numbers of Germans in Scotland and England at the turn of the century highlights important differences in Scotland's experience of this immigrant group.[36] While 50,599 Germans were recorded in England and Wales in the Census of 1901, in Scotland, only 3,232 were recorded, comprising 1.1% of all immigrant groups. Thus, whereas in England, the press in war-time could readily point to a significant enemy alien minority within the nation's bounds, in Scotland the supposed 'danger' seemed a lot less 'real'.

Moreover, when we turn to other migrant groups in Scotland, the volume of German immigrants in comparison to other groups is revealing. Even leaving the Irish to one side, German immigrants in Scotland in 1911 accounted for less than 5% of the country's immigrant European community. In some respects it could be suggested that such disparity between the English and Scottish alien populations is sufficient in itself to explain the relatively limited occurrences of anti-alien hostility north of the border. However, further insight is afforded when we look at the treatment of Germans in Scotland by the authorities during the war years.

In Britain, 'the size of the German community during the First World War declined from 57,500 in 1914 to just 22,254 in 1919.'[37] Under the terms of the Aliens Restriction Act of 1914 and the numerous Standing Orders which, over the course of the war years, increasingly restricted the freedoms of enemy aliens and naturalised British citizens, aliens throughout Britain found their lives dramatically changed. From August 1914 enemy aliens who were not interned could not travel more than five miles from their place of residence without a permit, and in 1916 this restriction came to be applied to all aliens. Prohibited areas were established within which enemy aliens could not reside without permission from the local chief constable, alien clubs and newspapers were shut down, enemy aliens were prohibited from owning firearms, wireless equipment and homing pigeons, and British-born wives of enemy aliens were re-patriated to their husband's country of origin.

By 1918 the repeated extensions which had been made to the prohibited areas in Scotland during the course of the war meant that a sizeable proportion of the Scottish land-mass – including the whole east coast – was covered by the strictest controls on alien residence and mobility. It could be suggested that the Scottish authorities' efficiency in implementing the government's directives on internment and re-location further reduced the fears generated by alien citizens 'at liberty' in Scotland and so reduced the risk and incidence of anti-German disturbances. As Appendix 3 makes clear, the Scottish Office, in co-operation with local chief constables, acted promptly in controlling the alien population of prohibited areas in the early days of the war. The Redford Barracks in Edinburgh and Stobs Camp near Hawick were both promptly utilised as internment centres, complimenting the English camps on the Isle of Man. By November 1914 there were only 35 male and 309 female enemy aliens in the prohibited coastal areas from Aberdeen to Berwick, compared with 736 male and 1,419 female enemy aliens in the areas from Berwick to Devonport.[38] Two months later, by January 1915, enemy aliens in Scotland – other than prisoners of war and those interned in concentration camps – numbered only 1,380 of whom 459 were men and 921 were women.[39]

Yet numbers alone do not reveal the true complexity of the Scottish experience. If they did, why was it that while Glasgow boasted 617 enemy aliens in November 1914 and experienced little in the way of serious disturbance; Greenock, with only 16 enemy aliens; Alloa, with only four enemy aliens and Perth with only 14, were the centres of hostility? Indeed, why was it that no riots were recorded in Hawick and in south Edinburgh, near the two major internment centres?

At least part of an explanation may be found in the political complexion of the Scottish press and the nature of the Scottish mission which the Scottish press preached in these years – in the imagined Scotland which fought the war at home. No publication in Scotland served the same jingoistic function north of the border as Horatio Bottomley's *John Bull* did in the south. While there is little evidence to indicate its circulation in the north, the lack of such a powerful media mouth-piece for the radical right in Scotland and the overwhelming Liberal sympathies of the Scottish press and the Scottish nation did much to restrain anti-alien outrages in the first two years of war, before Asquith's fall from grace. The support of the Scottish Liberal press for the government was, obviously, not guaranteed, but in this period of crisis most were reluctant to break the entente between the parties and desert Asquith's government. Very few directly challenged Haldane's role as Lord Chancellor, as many Unionist papers in the south did with such telling results, and only slowly – from around June 1916 – did the Unionist press become overtly critical of McKinnon Wood in the Scottish Office.[40] Direct attacks on the government's internment policy were, therefore, few in number and generally guarded.

The implication of this state of affairs was a distinctive Scottish Liberal Imperialism which was consolidated in the first two years of the war and used to frame the war experience in the columns of the press. Having learnt the hard way to play the patriotic card after the Boer War, the Scottish Liberal press presented a vision of the Great War which stressed its goals in terms of liberty and the rights of small nations. The smaller swing against the Liberals in the north after 1918 may partly be explained by the success of the Scottish press in the war years in delivering this message and resisting the more irrational jingoism of its English Unionist colleagues.

Its reaction to the German population in its midst was also telling. The Scottish Liberal press, in general, took longer in moving from condemnation of the German state to explicit attacks on the German people themselves and did so only during periods of heightened crisis. Its reporting of the riots of May 1915 is revealing. Following the Kentish Town riots in London, the Liberal *Daily Record*, carried the following editorial:

> it is not an uplifting spectacle to see this country descending to trivial and hysterical methods of vengeance and to retaliation in useless riot, for the foul crime of the *Lusitania*. Anti-German shop-looting, flagellation of Teuton fleshers and barbers may have righteous rage behind them, but they are no less futile than demeaning ... Unscrupulousness will not be killed by unscrupulousness ... Our virtue lies in keeping our heads, not in rivalling torture by torture; crime by crime.[41]

It concluded on what would prove to be an ill-founded optimistic note:

> We are glad to see that in Scotland, whose recruiting record is second to none – and therein lies the grand reprisal – a more dignified and judicial spirit is at work. Anger under restraint hits the directed blow, the telling blow ... The Government must be left to voice the feeling of the country.[42]

The level of consensus is telling when we turn to the *Glasgow Herald* which, a few days later, referred to the Scottish riots as 'a lamentable and discreditable phase of the war' and regretted that the 'epidemic of riot and destruction' had attacked some parts of Scotland.[43]

By contrast, it is revealing that in Perth, the scene of serious rioting in May, the overtly Conservative *Perthshire Constitutional and Journal* – a bi-weekly which had carried an editorial three days before the riot entitled 'A Race of Degenerates' – easily made the transition from attacking the German state to attacking Germans as a race apart. It noted:

Germans are the worst race of savages the world has ever known. All the vices to which mankind is prone seem to have been concentrated in the German people, mixed with the cunning and venom of a poisonous snake. With them crime has come to be regarded as a virtue ... The only way to get at Germany is for the Government to confiscate all German property in this country ...[44]

Yet, significantly, such sentiment in the local media is not replicated when we look at the press of Dumfries, Annan, Alloa, Greenock and Leith – the sites of the other Scottish riots.

Avenging the Lusitania?

During August 1914, a public notice printed in both English and Gaelic was circulated by Dingwall's Chief Constable Finlayson, calling on the services of gamekeepers, ghillies, shepherds and Boy Scouts in assisting the authorities in 'the detection of spies, and of persons favourable to the enemies of the country, suspected of communicating information injurious to the Realm'.[45] The following month, Finlayson wrote to the Under-Secretary at the Scottish Office, informing him that:

The result of these notices is that, every hour of the day, the police are getting information from all quarters of the county, as to the alleged spies being seen, and in making enquiries into these keep the police constantly on the alert. The people everywhere throughout the county are fully alive to the possibility of there being spies, and the danger which might arise through them, hence their eagerness to give every sort of information they can, even of native strangers who visit their districts.'[46]

Similar concerns were evident in Elgin in October when the County Clerk drew the Scottish Secretary's attention to

the danger to the Country in this crisis owing to the number of alien enemies still at large in our midst. Serious apprehension is being felt all over the Country by the freedom with which these persons – in many cases believed to be paid spies – can move about without interference, and great expense is being caused to the Military and Local Authorities in guarding bridges and other vulnerable points ...[47]

At a time when the number of alien enemies in the prohibited areas around Elgin numbered only three males and eight females, the concerns of the local authorities highlight the disjuncture between the real and the imagined threat which Germans posed to Scotland's security.[48]

As in England, the first weeks of war in Scotland witnessed a heightening of the 'spy fever' which, in the years of the 'Naval Race' with Germany, had been fostered by the popular press and the developing genre of the spy thriller.[49] Reports of night signalling along the east coast, of hidden aerodromes in the Highlands, the enemy infiltration of Lerwick post-office, photographers 'snatched' at naval bases, German school teachers loitering near reservoirs and foreign strangers in 'out of the way' places, all encouraged a suspicion of the enemy aliens who remained in the community.[50] In August, the *Highland Times* regretted the region's pre-war hospitality: 'We in the north have been in the habit of extending the glad hand to hordes of Teutons ... We have been far too lax with these urbane strangers from the fatherland.'[51] And in September 1914, the *Glasgow Herald* reported a 'general feeling of suspicion against foreigners amongst us'.[52]

Such general suspicions, however, do not explain the 'isolated' incidents of rioting in May 1915. By November 1914, the total enemy alien population of all the districts where rioting occurred totalled around 66 persons. In no area did enemy aliens even approach 0.5% of the local populations recorded in 1911.[53] Of course, such small groups made the individuals concerned more conspicuous, more obvious targets. Yet such an argument does not account for the quietude which marked communities with similar proportions of enemy aliens.

Similarly, other plausible explanations can be discounted. Except for the Feyerabend family, none of the aliens attacked could have been considered strangers or 'new arrivals' in their respective communities, and the Feyerabend's themselves had been in Annan for over two years when they came under attack. The Egners in Leith had occupied their shop in Great Junction Street since at least the turn of the century, John Frenz had been a pork butcher in Perth since at least 1905, and Charles Kumerer, it seems, had moved to Perth from Edinburgh around 1908.[54] In Dumfries, Charles Cleeberg had arrived as a sausage skin manufacturer as early as 1895 and H. C. A. Ramsdorf, the High Street jeweller, had worked as a watchmaker in the area since at least 1897.[55]

Additionally, while war, rather than the empirical measurement of length of residence, may have re-made these individuals as 'strangers' to the re-formed sense of community which the consensus of war generated in most localities, few – if at all – had exhibited explicit pro-German sentiments. Indeed, the *Perthshire Constitutional* printed a letter from Hugh Liebow, a naturalised German resident, which recorded his 'disapproval of the dastardly methods being employed in this war.'[56] In Alloa, Albert Becher, whose shop was the focus of serious rioting in May 1915, was described as a 'quiet and peaceable citizen' by the local press and had been one of the first subscribers to the National Relief Fund, Red Cross Funds and the Arnsbrae Auxiliary Hospital.[57] In Dumfries, the manager of a shop attacked by the mob, while of German extraction, had a brother fighting for the Allies in France and a brother-in-law recuperating in hospital from war wounds.[58] And, admittedly emerging after the rioting in Dumfries which saw his hairdresser' shop come under attack, Conrad Ahrweiler emphasised that his sympathies were 'entirely with Britain', and maintained that he 'all along strongly protested against the brutal way in which the war ha(d) been carried on by Germany ... particularly against ... the diabolical crime of sinking the *Lusitania*.'[59]

Further explanations conventionally employed to explain the anti-German outbursts in England – the loss of local lives suffered in the sinking of the *Lusitania*, and the role of riot as a popular forum through which government was encouraged to enact more stringent anti-alien legislation – also seem to stand in need of qualification when applied to Scotland. The Scottish riots began one week after the *Lusitania* was torpedoed and, while many communities lost high profile local citizens, no area in which rioting occurred suffered disproportionately. In this regard, Panayi is correct that loss of lives sustained after the loss of the *Lusitania* is an 'unconvincing' explanation for the riots which – although it may have some credence in relation to the Liverpool dis-turbances – 'cannot apply to other parts of the country, unconnected with the *Lusitania*'.[60] The majority of the Scottish riots, furthermore, took place *after* 13 May, when – at the height of the English disturbances – the government sought to appease popular opinion and announced its intention to intern all non-naturalised male aliens.[61] The contention that, like the earlier English riots, the Scottish riots operated as a popular warning to the government of discontent with its policies is thus unfounded. While protests were still heard from many Unionist papers for more reactionary measures, it appears that most Liberal organs in areas affected by rioting in Scotland were favourable to these new measures.

It seems that the closer one gets to explaining the causes of the Scottish riots, the more one is drawn further from the universals of a national drama to the independent dynamics of the localities involved. The matrix of local issues which is evidenced in the nature of the Scottish riots highlights how, in the creation of the image of 'the enemy', the separation of the local and the national, the home and fighting fronts, and truth and falsehood are ambiguous distinctions.

Casualties and competition

In addition to the factors already analysed, three contributory discourses shaped the Scottish riots of May 1915: an economic discourse, a generational discourse and a geographical discourse, generated by patterns of military recruitment.

It is immediately apparent when one looks at the individuals who comprised the focus of the mob's attention, that all are traders, either of goods or services, whose Germanic origins would have been emblazoned on their shop fronts. Comprising the 'class' who conventionally form the focus of mob anger in strained economic conditions, one would not be surprised to uncover economic motives encouraging the rioters.

In the case of Annan and Dumfries, the evidence of economic causes is particularly strong. Christian Feyerabend's pork butcher's business on Annan's High Street had attracted considerable interest in the community. Various local papers recorded that, 'there being no other pork butchers in the town, Mr Feyerabend's business quickly developed, and by up-to-date methods and a pleasant counter-manner he soon had a large trade, and was considered to be doing extremely well'.[62] Business had been so good that before the war, he had taken on an assistant – another German, Carl Niggerman, age twenty-two – who was interned in October 1914.[63] Explicit allegations that the causes of Feyerabend's persecution were economic emerged in May 1915 when, under the heading 'The Annan Pogrom', a letter from Harry Llewelyn Davies of Newbie, appeared in the *Annandale Observer*, suggesting that 'the raid was fomented by the desire to remove by violence a trade competitor whose only crime was that he was supplying cheap food to the people of Annan'.[64] Large advertisements for W. G. Dixon's grocer's business in the local free newspaper that month announcing 'Special Value in Hams and Bacon' would seem to support the idea that local Annan traders were alert to local competition.[65] However, at the monthly sitting of the Annan Burgh Court in June, the Prosecutor, George Mitchell, maintained that 'there was not the slightest foundation for [Davies'] insinuation' which he considered 'uncalled for', 'unfair', 'absurd and untrue'.[66] Later allegations regarding Mitchell's sympathy with the local Traders' Association, nevertheless, would seem to call into question his impartiality.[67]

Following the Armistice, further evidence of anti-German sentiments in Dumfries with regard to business interests were also evident when the 440-strong Dumfries branch of the Comrades of the Great War passed a vote of censure on the Town Council for not debarring Charles Cleeberg, whose house had suffered damage in the riots of 1915, from bidding for a renewal of his lease on the local slaughter-house. In moving the vote of censure, Mr Stevenson, a postman, declared that it was 'high time this German monopoly was knocked on the head, and the whole show of them cleared out, so that our own countrymen could get a chance.'⁶⁸ In the end, Cleeberg did not turn up at the exciting public roup in the Town Hall, and in an article entitled 'The German Monopoly', the *Dumfries and Galloway Standard* reported how the slaughter-house was let to the Universal Casing Co. at a rent over twelve times that paid by Cleeberg in the pre-war period.⁶⁹

War also encouraged many to think again of Britain's liberal pre-war trading policies. In May 1915, the *Dumfries and Galloway Courier and Herald*, promised that once hostilities were over, we 'shall no longer allow [the Germans] to over-run us and to spy upon us, nor shall we permit our markets to be made the dumping ground of their cheap and nasty goods.'⁷⁰ In more general terms, war-time inflation meant that prices were increasing during the days of the riots in May 1915. In this context, the rioting could, perhaps, be interpreted as an expression of 'hunger politics'. But wages were also rising in this period, making such an argument somewhat untenable. Moreover, the Scottish riots did not involve the looting which marked much of the English experience. In none of the incidents of riot recorded in Scotland did riot incorporate the looting of goods. Thus, whilst economic discourses were clearly influential, they cannot form a monocausal explanation.

In almost every report on the Scottish riots, commentators remarked on the youth of the crowds which threatened the German shop-keepers. Often dismissed as childish hooliganism, it might be suggested that the composition of the crowds highlights a generational discourse within the narrative of the riots. According to the *Greenock Telegraph*, in Greenock the crowd which attacked William Gaze's shop on 13 May was composed 'mostly of young people' and the crowd which attacked Mrs Sieger's licensed premises on West Blackhall Street 'for the most part comprised boys and young men, with a good sprinkling of girls, curious to see what might happen'.⁷¹ After the rioting in Perth, the *Perthshire Constitutional* sought solace in the fact that the activists in the crowd comprised no 'responsible citizens', but rather, a 'tipsy man, and a few score of irresponsible youths from ten to fourteen'.⁷² Similarly, the *Perthshire Courier*, referred to the 'mythical' angry mobs which had been reported in Perth, and claimed that the crowd 'was mostly composed of young men and women, whose conduct was certainly not favourably commented upon by the citizens in general'.[73]

In a total war, perhaps the only groups in society whose war-time roles are ill-defined are children and young adults, as yet too young to fight or take an active role in the war-time economy. Whilst it is perhaps a supposition, the high profile of these groups in the crowds who rioted, ironically reflects the limits of the 'totality' of the Great War in absorbing and re-forming all levels of society in the interests of a higher purpose. May 1915 offered young girls an opportunity to play an active role in the war narrative, aside from the knitting of socks and balaclavas, and offered young men the chance to fight the German which military rules had denied them.

Yet even these factors do not explain the timing and the geographical specificity of the Scottish riots. Rather, perhaps the critical factors influencing the riots are not to be found in the press reports of the riots themselves, but on the adjoining pages, in the reports from the front, which form the interface between the wars of the locality and the nation.

In May 1915, and indeed throughout the period of hostilities, the 'provincial' press 'localised' the war. In reporting the sinking of the *Lusitania*, the immediate horror of the numbers lost was enhanced by reports of those community members whose friends and families had been drowned. Beneath a large photograph of the *Lusitania*, Aberdeen's *Weekly Free Press* carried reports of 'LUSITANIA SURVIVOR IN ABERDEEN', 'KEITH MAN'S STORY OF THE DISASTER' and two photographs of a north-east emigrant couple who had been 'lost in the Lusitania disaster'.[74] The *Perthshire Courier* reported how, on hearing rumours of the loss of the ship, 'hundreds awaited in the High Street' for the 'arrival of the latest news' and mourned the loss of 'a well-known and highly respected citizen' who had been on board.[75] In this way, the international became national; the national, local; and the local, personal.

The publication of the Bryce Report on German atrocities on 12 May enhanced this sense of the human losses and indignities which war engendered, and extracts were published widely in the Scottish local press.[76] The first rioting in Scotland coincided with the publication of the report, and its influence can be seen in the riots in Dumfries three days later where, on the gate-post of Charles Cleeberg's house, 'Rheinstein', on Lockerbie Road, one of the rioters chalked the word 'Louvain' – the scene of many alleged German atrocities.[77]

Yet the most telling evidence is in the reports of the casualties sustained by local regiments from the areas affected by rioting. By the time of the riots, the press had been reporting the Germans' use of

poisoned gas for some weeks: it had first been used at the end of April
on the Western Front. Such a weapon found no accommodation in
'received wisdom' regarding the 'rules' of war and threatened commonly-
held ideas of warfare premised on the 'cult of the offensive', and an
'understanding of warfare as structured, ordered and therefore potentially decisive'.[78] Yet, while the impact of such warfare affected many
British localities, the events on the continent in April-May 1915 were
particularly tragic for many of the Scottish localities where rioting
occurred in May 1915.

On the same day it reported the anti-German riots in Alloa, the *Alloa
Circular* carried the following in a column entitled 'THE WAR':

> The all-absorbing topic of conversation in Alloa and district during
> the past and present weeks has again undoubtedly been the part
> played by the 7th Argyll and Sutherland Highlanders in the recent
> fighting in the neighbourhood of Ypres. The news of the gallant
> part which the battalion played in the severe engagement of Sunday
> 25th April, has created a profound impression throughout the entire
> community; and that impression has been greatly intensified by the
> heavy losses which the battalion has sustained. As yet no official list
> of casualties is available and the only means of ascertaining the
> condition of individuals in the battalion has been by communications
> received from them personally or from friends in the ranks who
> happen to know how it fared with them in the battle ...
>
> The scarcity of reliable news as to the casualties has naturally
> caused the keenest anxiety throughout the County of Clackmannan,
> from which a proportion of the battalion was recruited. Every day
> the advent of the official casualty list has been eagerly awaited, and
> the visits of the postman have been anticipated with mingled hope
> and fear ...[79]

The fighting in the area around St Julien at the end of April cost
Clackmannan dearly, but news of the county's losses only began to
emerge some weeks after the engagement. Similarly, in Perth – an area
whose Black Watch battalions had already suffered serious casualties at
Neuve Chapelle in March – May 1915 brought news of heavy losses.
On the day of the anti-German riots in Perth, the *Perthshire Advertiser*
carried the following news:

> There is unfortunately good reason to believe that the gallant Black
> Watch have suffered severely in the recent fighting on the continent.
> The glorious traditions of the regiment have been fully sustained

but it has been at the sacrifice of hundreds of grand young lives ...
... there are numerous anxious homes and the suspense of wives
and children is particularly poignant in the meantime.[80]

Both the 1st and 2nd Battalions of the Black Watch saw action at Aubers
Ridge in May 1915 and sustained heavy casualties. Indeed, the 1st
Battalion lost fourteen of its officers in this engagement and 462 other
ranks, either dead, wounded or missing, and of the 450 of the 2nd Battalion
involved in the battle, 270 were lost.[81] Further anxiety, no doubt, was
caused by the departure for France of the 6th Battalion at this time.

May 1915 also found many Dumfriesshire soldiers in action as the
King's Own Scottish Borderers (KOSB) saw action in Gallipoli and
Ypres. In the fighting around Hill 60, the Battle of Gravenstafel Ridge
and the Battle of St Julien, the KOSB suffered tremendous casualties.
Indeed, one regimental historian comments: 'somehow or other the
conviction comes to readers of the events of 1914–15 that highly trained
officers and men were hurriedly and prodigally sacrificed for insufficient
military ends.'[82] In May and June, two further KOSB battalions were
dispatched to the theatres of war.

On 15 May, in a column entitled 'EDINBURGH IN WAR TIME', the
Edinburgh Evening News highlighted a further dimension to the losses
suffered that May:

> We are talking more about the war during the past two or three
> weeks. It has never been out of our thoughts since August, but at
> times the great subject has not impressed the imagination with the
> strength of recent days. In the early days of the war, the losses in
> Edinburgh to a large extent fell on the classes which give us our
> officers and our professional soldiers; but in April and May, with the
> Territorial casualties, all sections of the community have been in-
> volved.[83]

A riot had been whispered of that day in Edinburgh, and in various parts
of the city, 'large numbers of people congregated in the vicinity of pork
butchers' shops', although no riots actually took place. In Leith 'considerable crowds' gathered outside a shop in Junction Street, causing its
German proprietor to close early.[84]

May 1915 had a peculiar and tragic resonance for many of the areas
affected by anti-German rioting which is not immediately apparent if a
narrow interpretation of the home front encompasses one's sphere of
interest.[85] The interface between the home and fighting fronts was, for
non-combatants, a literary as much as a personal experience mediated

by the telegram, the letter and, particularly, the press. At a time before official casualty lists were available, the press was *the* public forum, shaping a community's sense of loss. In this sense, its power – while often intangible – was profound.

Conclusion

'We are living in times to which the experience of peace offers no guide.'[86]

Both in material and ideological terms, newspapers rely on their ability to create 'readerships' in order to communicate their message. Through the appeal to the 'we' for which they pose to speak, they create imagined communities – communities of the mind. Similarly, 'total war' relies upon the press to foster a supportive national consensus, a united public opinion. As Harold Lasswell explained in 1927, 'the communization of warfare necessitated the mobilisation of the civilian mind'.[87] In a very real sense, the totality of the Great War demanded a 'surrender of the self', whether to battle, industry or motherhood in the interest of the war effort, and the surrender of those values which divided society along class, geographic and political lines. As Eric Leed has suggested, the 'declaration of war declared the arrival of a field of endeavour and rendered collective life coherent and unidirectional'.[88]

Yet public opinion did not exist outwith the lived experiences of individual communities and personalities and very often the 'nation' created by war excluded many who were contained within its physical borders. It was through the forum of the local press that the real and imagined battle-fields of the home and fighting fronts encountered one another and it was at the level of the locality that the popular status of the enemy – in human form – was negotiated.

Many features of the national and local environment suggest explanations for the Scottish riots of May 1915 – the loss of the *Lusitania*, the revalations of the Bryce Committee Report, the high profile of local enemy aliens, the local economic situation, the role of young adults in war-time and the heavy losses sustained by Scottish regiments on the Western Front. Yet the role of the press in mediating these discourses is crucial. Total war could not exist in any other way than as a discursive textual entity. Through its processes of signification, new 'cognitive worlds' were created, nations were refashioned and new enemies were identified.[89]

Appendix 1

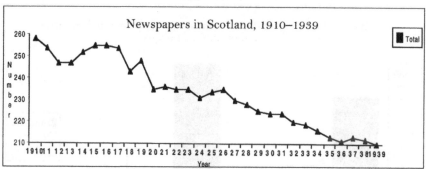

Newspapers in Scotland, 1910–1939

Source: *Newspaper Press Directory,* 1910–1939.

Appendix 2

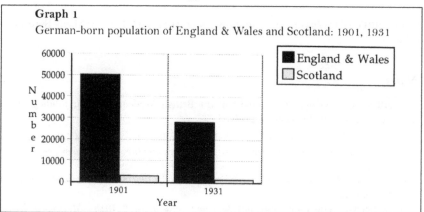

Graph 1

German-born population of England & Wales and Scotland: 1901, 1931

Source: P. Panayi, *Immigration, Ethnicity and Racism in Britain, 1815–1945* (Manchester, 1994)

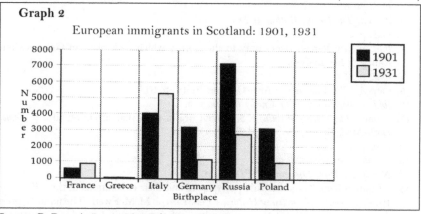

Graph 2

European immigrants in Scotland: 1901, 1931

Source: P. Panayi, *Immigration, Ethnicity and Racism.*

Appendix Three

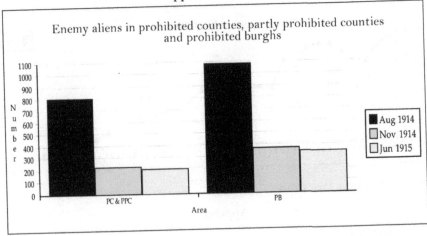

Enemy aliens in prohibited counties, partly prohibited counties and prohibited burghs

Source: SRO, HH31/37/1, Aliens Returns, Nov. 1914; HH31/37/2, Aliens Returns, 3 Jun. 1915.

Notes

The author acknowledges the support of the British Academy in their funding of the research from which this chapter evolved.

1. None of these individuals was killed as a result of the rioting of May 1915, but many suffered physical injuries and their homes and business premises came under attack.
2. P. Panayi, *The Enemy Within: Germans in Britain During the First World War* (Oxford, 1991), p. 223.
3. P. Panayi, 'The Lancashire anti-German riots of May 1915', *Manchester Region History Review* (1988–89), p. 5.
4. *Ibid.*, pp. 6–7
5. Panayi, *The Enemy Within*, p. 243.
6. *Ibid.*, p. 248.
7. *Ibid.*, p. 223. Panayi refers only to the rioting which took place in Greenock and Annan in his analysis.
8. *Ibid.*, p. 253.
9. Panayi, 'The Lancashire Anti-German Riots', p. 10.
10. *Ibid.*, p. 10; Panayi, *The Enemy Within*, p. 3.
11. Panayi, *The Enemy Within*, p. 3. Panayi draws particular attention to *The Times*, *Daily Mail*, *Evening News* and *Weekly Dispatch*.
12. *Ibid.*, p. 4.
13. See *ibid.*, pp. 232, 233.
14. *Newspaper Press Directory [NPD]* 1914.
15. J. Cunningham, 'National daily newspapers and their circulations in the UK, 1908–1978', *Journal of Advertising History*, 4 Feb. 1981; J. M. McEwen, 'The national press during the First World War: ownership and circulation', *Journal of Contemporary History*, xvii (1982), p. 468.

16. See Appendix 1.

17. Cunningham, 'National daily newspapers', p. 16.

18. A. P. Wadsworth, 'Newspaper circulations, 1800–1954', *Manchester Statistical Society*, 9 Mar. 1955, p. 1.

19. J. Grant, *The History of the Newspaper Press, Vol. Three: The Metropolitan Weekly and Provincial Press* (London, 1872); A. Reid, 'How a provincial paper is managed', *Nineteenth Century*, xx (1886), pp. 391–402; *Royal Commission on the Press 1948*, Minutes of Evidence, Cmd. 7398, Q. 7324, Response from Sir William Robieson (George Outram & Co. Ltd), p. 18; M. Macdonald, 'The Press in Scotland', in D. Hutchison (ed.), *Headlines* (Edinburgh, n.d.), pp. 8–21.

20. *NPD*, 1914, 1921; *Census of Scotland, 1921*.

21. *NPD*, 1913, 1914, 1916.

22. *NPD*, 1910, 1923.

23. A. J. Lee, *The Origins of the Popular Press in England, 1855–1914* (London, 1976), p. 287.

24. McEwen, 'The national press during the First World War', p. 468.

25. *Ibid.*, pp. 471, 474.

26. *Ibid.*, p. 471.

27. J. M. McEwen, 'The press and the fall of Asquith', *Historical Journal*, xxi (1978), pp. 863–83; S. Inwood, 'The Role of the Press in English Politics during the First World War, with special reference to the period 1914–16' (University of Oxford, D. Phil thesis, 1971).

28. Lee, *The Origins of the Popular Press*, p. 75.

29. J. Buchan, *The Battle Honours of Scotland, 1914–18* (Glasgow, 1919), p. 5.

30. See Introduction to this volume. Also, for Buchan's period in the Department of Information, see P. Buitenhuis, *The Great War of Words: Literature as Propaganda, 1914–18 and After* (London, 1989) and G. S. Messinger, *British Propaganda and the State in the First World War* (Manchester, 1992).

31. M. Cooke and A. Woollacott, 'Introduction', in M. Cooke and A. Woollacott (eds), *Gendering War Talk* (West Sussex, 1993), p. xi.

32. See: A. Ponsonby, *Falsehood in War-Time* (Southam, 1980 ed.); C. Haste, *Keep the Home Fires Burning: Propaganda in the First World War* (London, 1977); T. Wilson, *The Myriad Faces of War: Britain and the Great War, 1914–18* (Cambridge, 1986); H. D. Lasswell, *Propaganda Technique in World War 1* (Mass., 1971 ed.); M. L. Sanders and P. M. Taylor, *British Propaganda During the First World War, 1914–18* (London, 1982); E. Demm, 'Propaganda and caricature in the First World War', *Journal of Contemporary History*, xxviii (1993), pp. 163–92; A. G. Marquis, 'Words as Weapons: propaganda in Britain and Germany during the First World War', *Journal of Contemporary History*, xiii (1978), pp. 467–98.

33. See D. Hopkin, 'Domestic censorship in the First World War', *Journal of Contemporary History*, iv (1970), pp. 151–69; N. P. Hiley, 'Making War: The British News Media and Government Control, 1914–16' (Open University, PhD thesis, 1984); C. J. Lovelace, 'Control and Censorship of the Press During the First World War' (Kings College London, D. Phil thesis, 1982).

34. Buchan, *The Battle Honours of Scotland*, p. 6.

35. P. Meech and R. Kilborn, 'Media and identity in a stateless nation: the case of Scotland', *Media, Culture and Society*, ii (1992), p. 255.

36. See Appendix 2.

37. P. Panayi, *Immigration, Ethnicity and Racism in Britain, 1815–1945* (Manchester, 1994), p. 106.

38. Scottish Record Office [SRO], HH/31/37, 25478/1444.

39. SRO, HH/31/37/2, Aliens in Scotland – Statistical Tables, 6 Jan. 1915.
40. 'His opponents, at least those who trespassed into the open, were few; but they compensated in audacity for what they lacked in numbers.' S. Koss, *Lord Haldane: Scapegoat for Liberalism* (London, 1969), p. 163.
41. *Daily Record*, 13 May 1915.
42. *Ibid.*
43. *Glasgow Herald*, 17 May 1915.
44. *Perthshire Constitutional and Journal*, 10 May 1915.
45. SRO, HH/31/6, 25478/267.
46. SRO, HH/31/6, 25478/267, Letter, 7 Sept. 1914.
47. SRO, HH/31/10, 25478/686, Letter, 6 Oct. 1914.
48. SRO, HH/31/6, 25478/686, Letter, E. Holt Wilson (War Office) to P. J. Rose (Scottish Office), 10 Oct. 1914. Wilson notes that, of the three enemy alien males recorded in the area, two were over sixty years of age.
49. See D. French, 'Spy fever in Britain, 1900–1915', *Historical Journal*, xxi (1978), pp. 355–70.
50. See SRO, HH/31/10, 25478/1007; HH/31/10; HH/31/17. Also, a variety of reported incidents may be found in most newspapers. See, for example, *Glasgow Herald*, 6, 7, 8, 10, 11, 15, 19, 28 Aug., 12 Sept. 1914.
51. *Highland Times*, 27 Aug. 1914.
52. *Glasgow Herald*, 15 Sept. 1914.
53. SRO, HH/31/37/1, Aliens Returns, Nov. 1914. (As no aliens other than the Feyerabend family have, as yet, come to light, the number of enemy aliens for Annan has been estimated at five.)
54. Post Office Directories: Edinburgh and Leith, Perth.
55. Post Office Directories: Dumfries.
56. *Perthshire Constitutional and Journal*, 17 May 1915. (Letter was received *before* the riots in the town.)
57. *Alloa Advertiser*, 22 May 1915; *Alloa Circular*, 19 May 1915.
58. *Dumfries and Galloway Courier and Herald*, 16 May 1915.
59. *Dumfries and Galloway Standard*, 19 May 1915.
60. Panayi, *The Enemy Within*, p. 230.
61. *Ibid.*, pp. 78–9.
62. *Dumfries and Galloway Courier and Herald*, 19 May 1915; *Dumfries and Galloway Standard*, 19 May 1915; *Annandale Observer*, 21 May 1915; *Dumfriesshire Free Press and Annan Advertiser*, 20 May 1915.
63. *Glasgow Herald*, 22 Oct. 1914.
64. *Annandale Observer*, 21 May 1915.
65. *Dumfriesshire Free Press and Annan Advertiser*, 13 May 1915.
66. *Annandale Observer*, 4 Jun. 1915.
67. *Ibid.*, 11, 18 Jun. 1915.
68. *Dumfries and Galloway Standard*, 30 Apr. 1919.
69. *Ibid.*, 17 May 1919.
70. *Dumfries and Galloway Courier and Herald*, 8 May 1915.
71. *Greenock Telegraph and Clyde Shipping Gazette*, 14 May 1915.
72. *Perthshire Constitutional and Journal*, 17 May 1915.
73. *Perthshire Courier*, 18 May 1915.
74. *Weekly Free Press*, 15 May 1915.
75. *Perthshire Courier*, 11 May 1915.
76. See T. Wilson, 'Lord Bryce's Investigation into alleged German atrocities in Belgium, 1914–15', *Journal of Contemporary History*, xiv (1979), pp. 369–83.

77. *Dumfries and Galloway Courier and Herald*, 16 May 1916. See also Ponsonby, *Falsehood in War-Time*, p. 83.

78. T. Travers, *The Killing Ground: The British Army, The Western Front and the Emergence of Modern Warfare, 1900–1918* (London, 1987), p. 37.

79. *Alloa Circular*, 19 May 1915.

80. *Perthshire Advertiser*, 15 May 1915.

81. See: C. Grant, *The Black Watch* (Oxford, 1971); A.G. Wauchope, *A History of the Black Watch in the Great War, 1914–18* (London, 1925); B. Fergusson, *The Black Watch: A Short History* (Glasgow, 1955).

82. Captain Stair Gillon, *The K.O.S.B. in the Great War* (London, c.1930), p. 67.

83. *Edinburgh Evening News*, 15 May 1915.

84. *Glasgow Herald*, 17 May 1915.

85. See also Ian S. Wood, 'Be Strong and of a Good Courage', in this volume.

86. *Glasgow Herald*, 30 Nov. 1914.

87. Lasswell, *Propaganda Technique*, p. 10.

88. E. J. Leed, *No Man's Land: Combat and Identity in World War One* (Cambridge, 1979), p. 53.

89. See T. Bennett, '"Media", "reality", "signification"', in M. Grevitch, T. Bennett, J. Curran and J. Woollacott (eds), *Culture, Society and the Media* (London, 1982), p. 287. See also, J. Hartley, *Popular Reality: Journalism, Modernity, Popular Culture* (London, 1996). Both of these works have informed the approach adopted here.

February, 1910. One Halfpenny

The Morning Watch.

VOL. XXIII.   Edited by Rev. J. P. Struthers, M.A., Greenock.   No. 2.

Britain's "First Line of Defence."

CHAPTER EIGHT

Piety, Gender and War in Scotland in the 1910s

Callum G. Brown

I N 1910, THE Scottish evangelical magazine, *The Morning Watch*, carried a drawing of a woman with children at her knee on its front cover, bearing the caption 'Britain's "First Line of Defence"'. The image was powerful and already well-understood in Scotland and indeed Britain as a whole. It encapsulated a pervasive and persistent discourse on the nature of piety – pervasive within the religious-dominated definitions of the family, respectability and virtue, and persistent from the early nineteenth century to the middle of the twentieth. This familiar discourse focused on female piety and purity which, located in the domestic sphere of home and child-rearing, was perceived as the moral heart of the Christian nation and its empire. A parallel discourse on male religiosity existed in symmetry to it. As Tom Johnston, Secretary of State for Scotland, recalled of his childhood in Kirkintilloch in the late nineteenth century:

> One great institution of our childhood was the Band of Hope. It met on Friday evenings and provided an occasion for the appearance of old gentlemen with magic lanterns showing entrancing pictures of mice being poisoned in beer, and dipsomaniacs, wife and child beaters, being ultimately buried in paupers' graves, or hanged for murder committed under the influence of the demon Rum.[1]

Johnston's memory was shared by hundreds of thousands of other Scots who were exposed in the early twentieth century to similar narratives in magic lanterns and silent movies at Band of Hope, League of the Cross, Sunday school and home-mission events. Virtue and piety were endlessly paraded as 'female', while drunken dissipation and irreligion were represented as 'male'. This chapter will explore how these discourses were affected by the First World War and in what manner they survived into the inter-war period.

Historians of religion have long assumed that war has a profound impact upon religiosity. Evidence of an interruption to church connection arising from total war and the failure of large numbers of combatants to return to church membership and religious observance after the twentieth century's two world wars, is used to support notions of war as an engine of religious change – and especially of secularisation. John Wolffe has recently likened the Great War to 'the effect of a serious illness on the life an individual'. He writes:

> British society during the war, and religious organisations in particular evoke the image of a fitness and health-food fanatic who, after a long period of life afflicted by nothing worse than colds and migraines, has to face up to the awareness that he has a disabling cancer.[2]

Many ecclesiastical historians have documented the problems of the churches during and after the First World War. Churchmen were shaken by what appeared to be public indifference to the churches as institutions, but they were also racked with doubt concerning the theological implications of the war. The Church of England, for instance, became engrossed with whether the Bible stipulated repentance as the dominant theme of the Christian's response.[3] The response in Scotland matched many of the features of ecclesiastical reaction throughout Britain. As Jay Brown has shown, the war had severe consequences for the social vision of the Presbyterian churches. Initially filling them with self-confidence regarding their place in a society that required moral and spiritual direction in the midst of crisis, by 1916 and 1917 the experience of war had led to a failure of the hope for a religious revival in Scotland. Many clergy perceived a moral shift; as one military chaplain said: 'Self-indulgence, riotous living, theft, obscenity, violence – these seem no longer wrong, and he who disclaims them seems unintelligible if not amusing.'[4] By the end of the war, the social gospel of Christian socialism which had brought a consensual approach to social politics in the 1890s and 1900s in Scotland, and which had brought church and labour close together in the pursuit of a fairer society, was in tatters. Not only had the advent of rent strikes and 'Red Clydeside' produced a politicisation of social improvement which alienated church leaders, but the churches themselves took a surge to the political right under the influence of an ecumenical leadership in both the Church of Scotland and the United Free Church.[5] The First World War heralded a profoundly confrontational era for inter-war Scottish religion, characterised by classism and eugenics, and incorporating an hostility to the Labour movement and Irish Catholics.

The ecclesiastical landscape concerning the Presbyterian churches and the War is now better drawn. Where historians of religion have yet to delve in any depth is into the place of the war in the religious culture of either Scotland or Britain. As with other areas of religious history in the modern period, there has also been a neglect of the gender dimensions of piety. The study of women and piety in late modern Britain has yet to develop to any meaningful extent, and the study of masculinity is still in its infancy. Yet Joanna Bourke has already focused attention on the impact of the Great War on male identity. She focuses on the male body, the ways in which it was perceived, and on the manner in which it was revered during and after the conflict. She writes:

> The male body was subjected to callous treatment during the war and then to the renewed sanitising disciplines of peace. At the same time, the ceremonies honouring male bodies remained inadequate. The spiritualists as well as the hoaxer were all too willing to exploit sorrow as a commodity.[6]

Here Bourke picks up a common theme of historians' treatment of religion during the war – the shortcomings of both conventional religious ceremony and of the churches, and the popularity of spiritualism in filling the gap at the end of the war. This rise in spiritualism – amongst both men and women – has attained a prominent place in the religious historiography of the war – indeed, in many cases, the most prominent place of all.[7] The circumstances within which it arose relate to very different circumstances of male and female experiences of the war. For women, it seems to have been closely related to the non-return of loved ones from the Front. For men, it was linked to what a Scottish officer in the war called 'trench religion'.

'Trench religion'

The effect of the war upon British male combatants was the subject of many inquiries and reports by clergy and laity of individual denominations, but in addition to these there was a major multi-denominational study by British Protestant churches between 1917 and 1919. A committee of twenty-six church-people, predominantly clergy, were drawn from a wide variety of churches and church organisations, jointly convened by the Bishop of Winchester and the Rev. David S. Cairns, Professor of Dogmatics and Apologetics at the United Free Church

College in Aberdeen. The committee received written and oral evidence from chaplains and army officers. It was Cairns who wrote the committee's report which was published in 1919 as *The Army and Religion*. David Cairns (1862–1946) was a prominent figure in the United Free Church and became its moderator in 1923. Before the War he had shown considerable interest and sympathy in the social gospel of Christian socialism.[8] This background shaped a key theme in the 1919 report on soldiers and religion – the issue of the war's impact on social class and the churches. But Cairns had another concern in his report: the nature of men's religious beliefs.

One of the fundamental presumptions behind this report was that a large proportion of the men who fought during the war had been, at its outset, in poor contact with the churches or religious organisations. A questionnaire issued to chaplains by the churches during the war showed that in the Scottish regiments, 20% of troops 'are in a vital relationship' with a Church, compared to 11.5% of men in English regiments. A Church of Scotland enquiry across the army as a whole came up with a figure of 30%, though we do not know the precise nature of the question asked.[9] Further examination concluded that men from Scottish urban regiments were on a par for church connection with men from English regiments. With women acknowledged to be more church-connected than men, the conclusion of the statistics was that 'at this moment the Churches are in danger of losing the vigorous manhood of the country'.[10]

This perception was nothing new to the churches. In the nineteenth century, piety became perceived in highly gendered ways, especially by the Scottish Presbyterian churches. The whole vast evangelical enterprise of the 'home mission' – incorporating Sunday schools, mission day-schools, tract distribution societies, city missionaries, district visitors and the massive side-arm of the 'Gospel Temperance Reformation' – was dedicated to reclaiming what, by the late Victorian period, were casually referred to as 'the sunken portion', 'the submerged tenth', and 'the lapsed masses'. The working classes were systematically portrayed by the Protestant churches as 'the home heathens', devoid of Christianity and morality to the same extent as the natives of Africa and Asia. But the home heathens were pictured in two distinct discourses: one male and one female. These two differed substantially, for while women were perceived as angels in need of training, men were 'pagans'.

'We are apt to think that Churches are prospering,' the Rev. Thomas Chalmers, the leading light of the Free Church, told English MPs in

1847, 'but if they are so, then it would appear that that prosperity is consistent with a phenomenon altogether contemporaneous with it, and that is the palpable increase, from year to year, of a profligate, profane, and heathen population.'[11] Chalmers was responsible, more than any other individual in Britain, for cultivating the notion that urbanisation caused the decline of religion. When preaching in Glasgow in 1817, he had warned that:

on looking at the mighty mass of a city population, I state my apprehension, that if something be not done to bring this enormous physical strength under the control of Christian and humanized principle, the day may yet come, when it may lift against the authorities of the land, its brawny vigour, and discharge upon them all the turbulence of its rude and volcanic energy.[12]

In 1821 he wrote in his most influential book, that 'in our great towns, the population have so outgrown the old ecclesiastical system, as to have accumulated there into so many masses of practical heathenism'.[13] His alarmist language of 'home heathens', 'paganism' and 'dense irreligion' conveyed his central idea that in cities the working classes were alienated from the churches, morality and social order. To Thomas Chalmers, the face of the nineteenth-century city was infected with 'frequent and ever-enlarging spots of a foul leprosy, till at length we have spaces in many a town ... comprehensive of whole streets, nay, of whole parishes, in a general state of paganism.' Chalmers pioneered the churches' social-scientific study of what he described as 'the deep and dense irreligion which, like the apathy of a mortification or paralysis, has stolen imperceptibly on the great bulk of our plebeian families.'[14] If the rise of the modern city seemed to Chalmers and his many acolytes to challenge piety, then it was men who were the foundations of urban social breakdown. It was 'the brawny vigour' of the mob, as he put it in 1817, that was to be feared the most. As an agent of the Glasgow City Mission reported in the 1850s: 'Out of the twelve families I visited today, I do not think that more than one woman is living at peace with her husband. The men ... are all drunkards and abuse their poor wives when under the influence of strong drink.'[15]

This discourse was perpetually broadcast throughout the Victorian and Edwardian periods. Religious tracts and teetotal propaganda invariably portrayed family life as being corrupted by male violence, drink and roughness. In the 1910s, one oral respondent from Stirling recalled how at her local Mission Hall, the traditional magic lantern slides depicting abusive and drunken fathers were replaced by celluloid representations: 'This is where they used to show films, sort of Christian films like "The man that drunk too much and never gave his wife the money for to feed the children".'[16] This type of representation of men as irreligious drunks remained a constant feature of evangelical and temperance propaganda between the 1850s and the 1930s, and was used especially intensely in the training of children in religious, temperance and militaristic organisations. In the Boys Brigade (BB), founded in Glasgow in 1883, the taking of the pledge of total abstinence was a common feature, combined with a requirement to attend week-day prayer meetings prior to qualifying to play with BB football teams on Saturdays. The militarisation of male adolescence in the quarter century before the outbreak of the First World War was a dominating strategy of many evangelicals, and it met with enormous success. But the discipline being imposed was perceived very much in a moral context of restraining the natural 'temptations' to which boys and men succumbed – irreligion and drink.

The discourse on the male 'home heathen' persisted into the Great War. Indeed, it lay at the base of the churches' perception of the impact of war in the 1910s. The 1919 report explicitly regarded the issue as not being one of men losing their Christianity at the Front, but of them confronting a new form of religious experience. The ordinary soldier was perceived by many church informants as ill-educated about Christianity and faith, and the war was seen as a 'rude awakening' of base spiritual feelings. One officer from a Scottish regiment described a typical 'irreligious man' and his confrontation with war in the trenches:

As he [the irreligious man] draws near the Line for the first time, he becomes growingly aware that he had missed something vital in life, something that if he had it now would fill the void in his spirit, and bring him through the time that awaits him. He becomes aware of this need for God, but he does not know how to find Him, and often there is nobody to tell him. He resolves that if he comes through alive, he will seek till he finds. He prays in the hour of battle. But when he goes back to the rest camp or the base he forgets, and often yields to temptation. The void seems to have been filled by earthly things. But the want is felt again when he goes back to the front. This may happen again and again.[17]

Cairns noted that the evidence taken from the inquiry's informants 'indicate that the men who had been in the trenches had experienced an awakening of the primitive religious convictions – God, Prayer, Immortality, but that they did not associate these with Jesus Christ, that their thought of God was not Christianised.'[18] The shock of war in the trenches was seen as forcing men to return to an 'elemental faith', and in the process weakening the conventional 'religion of our days'. The same Scottish officer wrote:

The religion of ninety per cent of the men at the front is not distinctively Christian, but a religion of patriotism and of valour, tinged with chivalry, and at the best merely coloured with sentiment and emotion borrowed from Christianity.[19]

In this manner, as another observer remarked, 'The soldier has got religion, I am not so sure that he has got Christianity'.[20] Cairns felt that 'the evidence shows conclusively that at the front the impact of danger awakens the religious consciousness even of the most unlikely men'.[21] He went on:

It is very remarkable that the whole materialistic and anti-religious propaganda, which made so much noise, and apparently had so much vogue among our labouring classes a few years ago, seems to have simply withered away in the fires of the Line. The men of the British armies, however dim their faith may be, do in the hour of danger, at least, believe in God, "the great and terrible God." Most men we are told pray before they go over the parapet, or advance in the face of machine guns, and they thank God when they have come through the battle. It is possible to make too much and too little of this. Granting that it is at best a very elementary form of religion, and that is usually evanescent enough, it is none the less very significant ... However brief and transient, it is an implicit repudiation of that material view of life which is being judged in the thunder and flame around the men who pray.[22]

This male rejection of materialism was considered very important by the churches during and immediately after the war. The later Victorian and Edwardian periods were ones in which materialism was becoming manifest – as far as the churches were concerned – in the working classes' rejection of the churches in favour of socialism, secular recreation and sport. Equally, there was concern that the middle classes and the capitalistic classes were doing the same – even within church life. One Church of Scotland minister, for example, lambasted the 'millionaire congregations' of the United Free Church.[23]

During the war, some churchmen started to speak of a 'trench religion' – a form of soldiering spirituality produced by the hellish conditions and the constant proximity of death. This was perceived as an unsophisticated religiosity, little more than a basic feeling dominated by fatalism. One officer in a Highland regiment described it as the subduing of the human spirit by the display of mechanical power:

> The comradeship with Death is the most potent but not the only circumstance of the battlefield which alters the spiritual balance. The limbo of the soldier's vaguer feeling is intensely coloured by a sense of unspeakable impotence in the face of gigantic forces of destruction. Nowhere, as in a great army, does a man's littleness and unimportance stare on him so startlingly. Nowhere, as on a battlefield, is there such evidence of the powerlessness of the mightiest human organisation to protect his own small individuality. A millimetre's deflection in the laying of a gun is the difference between life and death to him.[24]

The powerlessness of the individual was interpreted by chaplains as bringing the ordinary soldier into a feeling of contact with God. One officer said:

> In times of danger men cry out to God. In spite of the fact that very often stark fear may be at the bottom of their prayers, yet it must be remembered that these cries have been wrung out from the utmost depths of their hearts. In many cases they have never really been absolutely in earnest before in their lives, they have been brought face to face with death, and while they have spoken to God, they will never be quite the same afterwards. They have had, perhaps for the first time, a certain definite religious experience; it is a foundation for further building.[25]

Yet the underlying materialistic foundations of working-class experience were acknowledged by the churches. The 1919 report quoted at length the testimony of a chaplain from a city regiment in the west of Scotland:

> What strikes me, however, about nearly all the men and women of the working classes is that the question of money is terribly constantly present with them ... When heavy bereavement falls on them, even then they think at once of how it will affect their pockets. The same question is uppermost when they are asked to let their sons go to the war. They are far more angry with Government for not dealing justly or quickly in the matter of allowances and pensions than because they have dragged the country into war. In talking about careers they do not consider the honour of them or

the usefulness of them ... But even though this charge is true of the poorer men as a whole, it does not mean that they really take a material view of life. It is the inevitable result of their position ... There is real pathos if not tragedy in this. For it is true that finer elements in their natures have not had a real chance to grow owing to the constant presence of the economic factor in life.[26]

The language in *The Army and Religion* report of 1919 is, not surprisingly, heavily drawn from the values and discourses of the officer class. As such, it is important to note the incredulity of such men when trying to understand working-class life. They see it as something different, something almost zoological, to deconstruct and understand. The chasm between their own social experience and that of 'their' men is clearly profound. The officers' and chaplains' incomprehension with the primacy given by working-class soldiers to survival – both economic survival in peace and life survival in war – was not eroded by the shared experiences of the line, but withstood the exigencies of a common threat of death. There is an implicit duality of discourse in these accounts concerning religiosity: the 'base' religion of men confronting their maker for the first time, and the refined and experienced personal faith of the better educated and the socially superior. In this context of perceiving a 'materialist' ethos devoid of religious refinement, the officer class find it interesting, even puzzling, that there was even an elemental religious experience amongst the men at the Front.

With this elemental religious experience came other 'fine qualities'. An officer in a Scottish regiment said: 'The war has created a new tenderness between man and man, a new sense of fellowship and social sympathy, i.e. within a circle embracing the nation and friendly aliens.'[27] As well as humanity, a new 'real man' was anticipated from the war. The west of Scotland chaplain cited earlier wrote:

As to their characters, there can be no doubt that it [the war] has put stiffening into them. Most show signs of nervous strain ... And most have been hardened – though not necessarily in a bad sense. You cannot remain the same when you have GOT TO become accustomed to having your pals knocked out, and men who become familiar with death in that way inevitably become hard ... But at the same time some sterling virtues may have been ingrained into them. Boys who were "nice" and polite and delicate in feeling, and reverent in bearing, may come home swearing like troopers, and with all the bloom brushed off their manners, but at the same time they may have more real backbone than in the days when they were so nice.[28]

Another Scottish chaplain said:

Sympathy and mutual regard, mutual understanding, have found a new scope and a new inspiration. Comradeship is the most real thing in their experience and opens up a way straight to the heart of the Gospel, to the comradeship of Christ, the ideal Friend, the Saviour. So strong is this sense of comradeship that it submerges even hereditary antagonism.[29]

The rudimentary nature of the soldiers' religious experience in war brought its downside for the Christian churches. The lack of knowledge of Scripture, of Jesus Christ, of church doctrine were 'paraded' in many churches' reports. But more frightening to the churches was the apparent continued immoralities of male life – notably drinking and sexual immorality. They were particularly alarmed by the sexual freedom of troops at base camps where they made relationships with French women. Because of the 'monstrously abnormal conditions', many churchmen argued that 'what we are considering is not only moral evil but human pathology'. The same west of Scotland chaplain said:

As to the question of purity, I have a very sad impression. They argue that sexual indulgence is natural and therefore legitimate. They combine a very affectionate and respectful attitude to their own women with this utterly different attitude to the women who are available for indulgence. Their minds are pretty filthy. They have never been schooled to the battle for chastity, and their talk is pretty often disgusting. In fact we have not yet learnt the way in which to train our young men in purity, and it is time we faced the fact. Moreover, I do not think that there is anything to pick and choose between the classes in this matter. 'Varsity men seem to me quite as bad as labourers.[30]

The churches looked for solutions to bring men back into the fold of the churches, and to make the nation fit to be described as Christian. The problem was seen as immense:

The heart of the situation is that the bare Theism of the men has in it neither the intellectual strength to solve the questions that they are already asking as to God and the war, nor the moral force to lift them above the temptations of the flesh ... The faith that they had was emotional and intuitive. The dangers around them suddenly awakened men to God. Their past conventional unbelief shrivelled up in a moment, and they felt the reality of God.[31]

The innate shortcomings of masculinity still lay at the heart of the problem. Cairns listed the factors which bedevilled men, and top of his list came 'the unruly heart of man'. 'A man's conduct,' he explained, 'cannot always be explained simply as the outcome of his circumstances and training.' It was 'the man himself – the man who is quite capable of saying "I will do evil."' This he regarded as 'the root difficulty', the essential ability of man to be ultimately untrainable, unquellable in his choice of evil. To this was added drink, but just as important in Cairns' estimation was 'sheer ignorance regarding the body and its functions'.[32] A few such cryptic references to 'the body' seem to be derived from unrecorded evidence given to the inquiry committee. Ignorance of 'the sexual facts' was highlighted by Cairns as something requiring remedial attention. Knowledge of such things, he said, was 'usually picked up in furtive and undesirable ways – ways which themselves militate against real purity.' This was a failing of church and school: 'The ethics of reproduction are too sacred for casual speech.' New teaching of men was required to take sex-talk out of common discourse and replace it with teaching that demonstrated how 'all the facts about life as God ordained it are holy, happy and beautiful.'[33]

As far as the churches were concerned, the male experience of war affirmed alienation from organised Christianity. Trench warfare and life at the base camps separated men from the wholesome influence of their mothers, sweethearts and wives, and threw them into a comradeship which, in the constant face of death, operated within an atmosphere of 'wet' canteens and brothels. It affirmed the irrelevance of not just the churches but also 'respectability', and created an unintellectual and probably temporary 'trench fatalism' which perceived God as 'luck'. This threw men upon superstition and further away from an acceptable Christianity, leading them to seek comfort from a wide variety of talismans and to regard even the Bible as just another good luck charm to be carried into battle. As Hugh McLeod has observed, for the churches 'this grasping for supernatural help implied no acceptance of the regime of moral discipline and formal religious observances encouraged by their chaplains.'[34] Supernatural experiences, including visions of the Virgin Mary, Jesus, Angels and God Himself, were widely reported.[35] A Highland regiment's officer noted: 'A very dangerous belief in spiritualism is gaining ground, and a tendency towards dabbling in it.'[36] Bill Hanlan, a First World War serviceman from Dalkeith, recalled that at Albert on the Somme in 1916 the statue of the Virgin Mary had fallen across the German trenches and that the local French people thought that she was keeping the Germans back.[37] Another officer from a Highland regiment said:

> The war has changed the men radically; but they are not too conscious of the change. It has not made them think more deeply. On the contrary, it has made them place thinking below emotion and instinct. The war seems to have revived something ancestral in these men – something elementally religious. This has made it even more impossible for them to harbour the old popular versions of Christianity (taboo), etc., but rendered them far more open to vital religion ... The war has undoubtedly widened the gulf between the men and the Churches. They think the latter utterly divorced from real life. The great fact which has been burned into my mind is that, while almost every man goes through times of intense religious emotion in the trenches, very few seem to have the faintest conception that the emotion which has gripped them has anything to do with Christianity.[38]

In these ways, the war affirmed both church and elite views of the working-class 'home heathen'. The trenches re-emphasised the flimsiness of male piety, and the innate conflict between masculine weakness and a 'true' faith. The Victorian discourse on masculinity was reawakened in war, re-anointing the denizen of the slums as the grave weakness of the nation's Christianity.

The angel on the Home Front

The war at home was a different context. The 'Home Front' developed a femininity, the product of the loss of men to serve in the armed forces. A notion of a male vacuum developed in civil society, and the opportunity was widely taken to strip Britain of as much male immorality as possible. The result was that the war introduced an intensification of puritanism in British society. This was perceived as curtailing male immoralities and male 'rough culture', and encouraging a more female form of piety and morality to prevail. The war brought a wide variety of measures in this moral crusade: drink prohibition around munitions bases, early closing of public houses, state take-overs of some pubs and breweries, and the closing down of many sporting and recreational events. As we shall see, it also brought other measures. But, in so doing, it ironically cast a closer light upon female susceptibility to immorality, and produced some startling 'revelations'.

The Scottish people were already well-versed in the discourse on female purity and piety. From the early nineteenth century much of the literature of evangelical mission work and the vast literature of religious reading was centred on female usefulness and the key role that women played in maintaining the morality of the family. The extensive religious press of the nineteenth century – journals, magazines, tracts and books, much of it distributed as Sunday-school prizes – developed in Scotland from the 1840s, a concentration on the female's role in family life. In stories and vignettes, historical biographies and in straight exhortation, a pious femininity was portrayed as the basis of the nation's greatness. The Scottish revivalist magazine, *The Day-Star*, stated in 1856:

WOMAN AND RELIGION. It has been eloquently and truly said, that if Christianity were compelled to flee from the nations of the great, the academies of philosophers, the halls of legislators, or the throngs of busy men, we should find her last retreat with woman at the fireside. Her last audience would be the children gathering round the knee of a mother; the last sacrifice, the secret prayer, escaping in silence from her lips, and heard perhaps only at the throne of God.[39]

'The best qualities to look for in a wife,' the same journal advised in 1855, 'are industry, humility, neatness, gentleness, benevolence, and piety.' It went on: 'When you hear a lady say, "I shall attend church, and wear my old bonnet and every-day gown, for I fear we shall have a rain-storm," depend upon it she will make a good wife.'[40] According to *The Day-Star*, woman was the moral linchpin of society as a whole:

The character of the young men of a community depends much on that of the young women. If the latter are cultivated, intelligent, accomplished, the young men will feel the requirement that they themselves should be upright, and gentlemanly, and refined; but if their female friends are frivolous and silly, the young men will be found dissipated and worthless. But remember, always, that a sister is but the guardian of a brother's integrity. She is the surest inculcator of faith in female purity and worth.[41]

The Free Church Magazine in 1844 published an article on 'Female Methods of Usefulness'.

Female influence should shed its rays on every circle, but these ought to be felt, rather in their softening effects, than seen by their brilliancy. There are certain duties which sometimes call Christian women out of their quiet domestic circle, where both taste and feeling conspire to make them love to linger; such duties will, we humbly think, be best performed by those who enter this enlarged field, not from any desire of a more public sphere, but because, in obedience to the precepts of their divine Lord, the hungry are to be fed, the sick comforted, the prisoners visited.[42]

The organising and campaigning role of women in evangelical and temperance work in the second half of the nineteenth century took the evangelical message from the private world of personal conduct into the public world.[43] In campaigns for temperance reform, prohibition, the rescue and reform of prostitutes and 'wayward' girls, women social reformers took a step out of women's traditional role into the public sphere. 'If every woman in the country would take one family and look after them and bring them and themselves to Christ's feet, we should have a better and happier world', wrote one Scottish female campaigner in 1911.[44] The temperance movement was a place where women had an active role through organisations like the British Women's Temperance Association – the 'White Ribboners'. Women were also the particular target of temperance propaganda:

If then, O mothers of Britain, you will only sweep your own hearthstones, and each one cleanse their own from this insidious foe, and firmly resolve it shall never cross your threshold more, the homes of Britain will blossom as the rose. The mother and child will sing songs of joy and gladness. The father will go forth in the morning strong, well fed, and well clad to his daily toil, and will return in the evening with pleasure and gratitude, to his now happy home.[45]

The experience of the Home Front during the war challenged this discourse. While there was some commentary on the sexual and moral failings of soldiers at the front, especially at the war's end, this was often 'explained away' as the result of both the extreme conditions of trench warfare and the failings of church and education at home. Women's immorality during the war, on the other hand, was a shock to contemporary 'respectable' society and something that could not be excused. The moral failings of women were widely lambasted. An officer from a city regiment in the East of Scotland reported:

The opinion of Society on these matters, judging from my experience in the Army, I should say is frankly pagan, and not Christian at all. The lack of restraint and reserve since the war among women who were previously modest and respectable is an especially conspicuous and regrettable fact. It appears that there is need that the Church should head a crusade to purge the nation of its impurity and vice, and should insist above all things that the problem of prostitution and venereal diseases should be drastically dealt with.⁴⁶

Coupled with sexual immorality amongst women during the war was what was perceived to be a new level of alcohol abuse by women. The Scottish National Society for the Prevention of Cruelty to Children (SNSPCC) had been familiar for nearly forty years with men as the active agents in child neglect and cruelty. With the outbreak of war, two very shocking things happened. Firstly, though the number of cases did fall, it was not as large as might have been expected with men away from their families. In 1914 the Edinburgh branch investigated 1,790 cases, and in 1915, 1,277. Secondly, there was a considerable rise in child abuse and neglect by mothers. In 1905, out of forty-five cases that led to convictions, twenty were by men and twenty-five by women. In 1915, forty-six of the fifty-four cases in Edinburgh led to convictions of drunken mothers for neglect of their children. In 1916, it was thirty-three cases out of forty. In 1917, twenty-one cases out of twenty-five, and in 1918 seventeen cases out of twenty-one. Then things changed. In 1920, out of the thirty-nine cases, nineteen were the result of father's neglect and twelve of mother's neglect, the rest shared neglect.⁴⁷ In short, the war propelled woman to the forefront of perceptions of child cruelty and neglect, raising questions about the 'natural' attributes of women as mothers.

This issue arose especially in relation to women and drink during the war. Intemperance amongst women was widely noted in Scotland by the summer of 1915. In Edinburgh during the second quarter of that year, 181 children of serving soldiers were placed in shelters 'owing to intemperance amongst women'. Interestingly, it was reported that thirteen of the children had been voluntarily handed over by the soldiers – implying that some men were now in a more responsible role than their wives. In Glasgow, the rise of female drinking was one factor behind the Licensing Court in January and March of 1916 passing resolutions in favour of prohibition for the duration of the war.⁴⁸ In the absence of men, women were developing social habits of a rough 'male' character. The SNSPCC reported in Edinburgh in 1917:

In the course of their work the Men Inspectors find that there is a determination amongst a large number of women to go their own way and live as they like in the absence of their husbands ... The moral surroundings in these homes is as bad as it can be and the children's minds are being poisoned by the atmosphere in which they live ... One point that presents difficulty is that of children being left alone for long periods, often from an early hour in the evening to the early morning. A common practice is for women to lock children in and take the key away so that the Inspectors cannot get access to the children. The early part of the night is spent in public houses, picture houses and theatres and it is often not till the early hours of the morning that they return home.[49]

The shock was not just that women had shown a loosening of morals, but that they were *capable* of such levels of immorality. It had been widely assumed that women's moral sensibilities were innate; as the *Free Church Magazine* had put it in the 1840s, women were 'benevolent from natural sensibility, active from constitutional inclination, amiable from temper'. The failure of church missions during the war – missions aimed overwhelmingly at women – was another depressing outcome for the churches. The evangelical discourse on female virtue and piety was facing a serious crisis.

Puritanism and the war

The impact of the war upon concepts of piety in Scotland was dramatic. The Protestant churches, religious charities, and the temperance movement united with many town councils and the Scottish Office in a massive campaign of puritan revival.

This started even before the war ended. In 1916 and 1917, a moral panic erupted over the growth of gambling, with the Chief Constable of Glasgow reporting that as many as sixteen bookies' offices were operating in the business quarter of the city centre. At the same time, there was even greater panic over the use of slot machines of chance that were being installed in grocers' shops and ice-cream shops, enticing women to spend their household money on gambling. As a result, the Scottish Office rushed through the Gaming Machines Act 1917 which banned all forms of automatic machines in Scotland.[50]

The panic over drinking was even greater. By May 1918 there had already been a large number of municipal plebiscites on prohibition, mostly in the west of Scotland in areas such as Clydebank, Cowdenbeath, Lesmahagow, Carluke, Barrhead and Paisley. The results of these seemed to show support for prohibition or state purchase of the licensed trade – in the case of Clydebank, by a factor of eight to one.[51] This was no hypothetical issue, for prohibition was now a real possibility in Scotland. Under the terms of the Temperance (Scotland) Act of 1913, local pleb-iscites on the prohibition or restriction of the number of public houses were permitted from June 1920. As the United Free Church Temperance Committee put it in May 1918, 'The forces are mustering for the great battle of 1920. The propaganda is well begun.'[52]

By the spring of 1919, canvassing for the local veto polls was well under way, and the extension of the vote to women was seen as absolutely critical to the temperance cause. It was noted that the municipal votes had shown women to be more strongly in favour of prohibition: in Clydebank, for instance, only five out of seven men were in favour of prohibition while nine out of ten women were.[53] The veto polls of June 1920 were a notable moral struggle for the churches in Scotland, involv-ing massive campaigning on the streets, the picketing of pubs, and parades by children in Bands of Hope and by the White Ribboners. One woman recalled that as a child in the late 1910s or early 1920s – possibly around the time of the local veto polls – she was marched in a white pinafore at the head of a White Ribboner parade in Fallin in Stirlingshire, posing as the victim of her father's drinking habits. She recalled that her father was watching, not knowing of her involvement, and remem-bered how he got angry with her mother for letting her join that organisation.[54] The war was a critical factor in the rise of puritan evan-gelicalism in the depressed conditions of the 1920s and 1930s. With the mainstream Protestant churches out of favour with many sections of the working class as a result of the war (notably those who had been at the Front), independent evangelical churches and small mission or-ganisations thrived alongside teetotal organisations like the Bands of Hope, the Good Templars and the Rechabites.[55] The war instigated the last cathartic gasp of evangelical puritanism in Scotland, and although there was to be a strong recruitment to the churches after the Second World War, in reality it was already in its death-throes by the end of the 1930s.

In December 1918, the Church of Scotland and the United Free Church joined forces in calling a 'National Mission of Rededication'. It completely failed in its objectives and was regarded suspiciously by politicians and even church members.[56] Nonetheless, levels of Scottish church membership recovered from the war very strongly, reaching levels in the mid 1920s higher than at the outbreak of the war. Indeed, while it is clear that per head of population in the early 1910s church membership was falling, the war and its immediate aftermath resulted in a strong recovery. One vital element was the strength with which both religious and temperance organisations broadcast the discourse on female piety in the 1920s and 1930s. Female oral respondents recall with great vividness the portrayal of innate female virtues and male susceptibility to drink and 'rough' behaviour.[57] The war had instigated a shock to a widely-perceived gendered piety in Scotland, but it revitalised the promotion of that discourse – especially amongst the female young – and helped to sustain church affiliation in Scotland for several decades to come.

Notes

1. T. Johnston, *Memories* (London, 1952), p. 17.
2. J. Wolffe, *God and Greater Britain: Religion and National Life in Britain and Ireland 1843–1945* (London, 1994), p. 237.
3. See R. Lloyd, *The Church of England in the Twentieth Century*, vol. 1 (London, 1946), pp. 222–53.
4. Quoted in S. J. Brown, '"A solemn purification by fire": responses to the Great War in the Scottish presbyterian churches 1914–19', *Journal of Ecclesiastical History*, xlv (1994), p. 82.
5. C. G. Brown, *Religion and Society in Scotland since 1707* (Edinburgh, 1997), pp. 132–42.
6. J. Bourke, *Dismembering the Male: Men's Bodies, Britain and the Great War* (London, 1996), p. 250.
7. See for instance H. McLeod, *Religion and the People of Western Europe 1789–1970* (Oxford, 1981), pp. 94–6; Wolffe, *God and Greater Britain*, p. 241; J. Winter, *Sites of Memory, Sites of Mourning: The Great War in European Cultural History* (Cambridge, 1995), pp. 54–77.
8. See for instance D. S. Cairns, *Christianity in the Modern World* (London, 1906).
9. D. S. Cairns (ed.), *The Army and Religion* (London, 1919), pp. 189–90.
10. *Ibid.*, p. 192.
11. *Free Church Magazine*, Aug. 1847, p. 250.
12. T. Chalmers, *A Sermon delivered in the Tron Church on the occasion of the death of Princess Charlotte* (Glasgow, 1817), p. 31.
13. T. Chalmers, *The Christian and Civic Economy of Large Towns* (Glasgow, 1821), p. 342.
14. T. Chalmers, *The Right Ecclesiastical Economy of a Large Town* (Edinburgh, 1835), p. 21.
15. Quoted in E. King, *Scotland Sober and Free: The Temperance Movement 1829–1979* (Glasgow, 1979), p. 17.
16. Scottish Oral History Centre Archive [SOHCA], University of Strathclyde, SOHCA/06/C.1 (born 1907).
17. Quoted in Cairns (ed.), *Army and Religion*, pp. 13–14.
18. *Ibid.*, p. 9.
19. *Ibid.*, p 10.
20. *Ibid.*, p. 9.
21. *Ibid.*, p. 7.
22. *Ibid.*, pp. 7–8.
23. M. McCallum, *Religion as Social Justice* (Glasgow, 1915), p. 6.

24. Quoted in Cairns (ed.), *Army and Religion*, p. 162.
25. *Ibid.*, p. 12.
26. *Ibid.*, pp. 79–80.
27. *Ibid.*, p. 93.
28. *Ibid.*, p. 97.
29. *Ibid.*, p. 131.
30. *Ibid.*, p. 144.
31. *Ibid.*
32. *Ibid.*, pp. 371–2.
33. *Ibid.*
34. McLeod, *Religion and the People*, p. 95.
35. Bourke, *Dismembering the Male*, pp. 231–3.
36. Quoted in Cairns (ed.), *Army and Religion*, p. 20.
37. I. MacDougall (ed.), *Voices from War* (Edinburgh, 1995), p. 19.
38. Quoted in Cairns (ed.), *Army and Religion*, pp. 62–3.
39. *The Day-Star*, xii (1856), p. 97.
40. *Ibid.*, xi (1855), p. 266.
41. *Ibid.*, x (1854), p. 112.
42. *Free Church Magazine*, vi (1844), p. 171.
43. See for instance B. Aspinwall, *Portable Utopia: Glasgow and the United States 1820–1920* (Aberdeen, 1984), pp. 86–150.
44. Griselda Cheape, quoted in L. Mahood, 'Family ties: lady child-savers and girls of the street 1850–1925', in E. Breitenbach and E. Gordon (eds), *Out of Bounds: Women in Scottish Society 1800–1945* (Edinburgh, 1992), p. 42.
45. *The Day-Star*, xii (1856), p. 13.
46. Quoted in Cairns (ed.), *Army and Religion*, pp. 144–5.
47. Scottish Record Office [SRO], GD409/6/1, Scottish National Society for the Prevention of Cruelty to Children [SNSPCC] Conviction Book. 1902–34.; GD409/1/5, SNSPCC Edinburgh District Committee Minute Book 1912–22. I am grateful to Lynn Abrams for providing me with references to the SNSPCC material.
48. *Reports to the General Assembly of the United Free Church of Scotland*, Temperance Committee, 1917, p. 10.
49. SRO, GD409/1/5, SNSPCC Edinburgh District Committee Minute Book, Report of 1 Jul.–30 Sept. 1917.
50. SRO, HH 1/1841, Mechanical Games in Use at Fairgrounds.
51. *Reports to the General Assembly of the United Free Church*, Temperance Committee, 1918, p. 21.
52. *Ibid.*, p. 33.
53. *Ibid.*, p. 33.
54. SOHCA/006/Mrs U.3 (born 1913).
55. Brown, *Religion and Society*, pp. 147–54.
56. *Ibid.*, p. 140.
57. *Ibid.*, pp. 196–204.

Contributors

CALLUM G. BROWN is Professor of Late Modern European History at the University of Glasgow. He has published ten books, the latest being *Religion and the Demographic Revolution: Women and Secularisation in Canada, Ireland, UK and USA since the 1960s* (Boydell & Brewer, 2012)

EWEN A. CAMERON is the Sir William Fraser Professor of Scottish History at the University of Edinburgh. His books include *Land for the People? The British Government and the Scottish Highlands* (1996) and *Impaled Upon a Thistle: Scotland since 1880* (2010).

I.G.C. HUTCHISON is a former Senior Lecturer in History at the University of Stirling and a former editor of the *Scottish Historical Review*. His books include *A Political History of Scotland, 1832–1924* (1986), *The State and the University: The Case of Aberdeen, 1860–1963* (1993) and *Scottish Politics in the Twentieth Century* (2000).

WILLIAM KENEFICK is a Senior Lecturer in Modern History at the University of Dundee. He has published widely on Scottish maritime and labour history, the impact of the Great War and the Russian Revolution on the Scottish working class, Irish and Jewish relations in Scotland from c1870 to present, and labour politics and the Dundee working class. He edited (with A. McIvor) *Roots of Red Clydeside, 1910–1914* (1996), and is author of *Rebellious and Contrary: The Glasgow Dockers, 1853–1932* (2000), and *Red Scotland! The Rise and Fall of the Radical left, c.1872–1932* (2007).

CLIVE LEE* was Professor of Historical Economics, and Head of the Department of Economics, at the University of Aberdeen. He wrote extensively on the modern economic history of Britain, and his publications include *Scotland and the United Kingdom: The Economy and the Union in the Twentieth Century* (1995) and *The Service Sector and Economic Growth: Recent Findings in Economic and Social History* (1996).

CATRIONA M. M. MACDONALD is Reader in Late Modern Scottish History at the University of Glasgow. She is Editor of *Unionist Scotland* (1998), and author of *The Radical Thread* (2000) and *Whaur Extremes Meet* (2009). She is currently editor of the *Scottish Historical Review*.

ELAINE W. MCFARLAND is Professor of History at Glasgow Caledonian University. Her publications include *Protestants First: Orangeism in Nineteenth Century Scotland* (1990); *Ireland and Scotland in the Age of Revolution* (1994) and *John Ferguson 1836–1906: Irish Issues in Scottish Politics* (2004). She has also published a number of articles on death, mourning and commemoration in modern Scotland, and on the post-war Church of Scotland. She is currently

* Now deceased.

working on a biography of the Great War commander Lieutenant General Sir Aylmer Hunter-Weston.

IAIN J. M. ROBERTSON is Reader in Historical Geography at the University of Gloucester. He has published widely on historical geography of the Highlands of Scotland and on expressions of social protest. His publications include *The Later Highland Land Wars* (2013) and *Landscapes of Protest in the Scottish Highlands after 1914* (2014).

GORDON URQUHART* had a wide-ranging career as an archivist, aerial photograph salesman and researcher, who carried out extensive work in the arts and heritage in the Highlands. He had a degree in cultural history from the University of Aberdeen and continued his studies by distance learning when he moved to Zambia with his family. He had a special interest in the Great War in relation to the Highlands and Highland symbolic culture.

IAN S. WOOD is a former lecturer in history at Edinburgh Napier University and with the Open University. His extensive writings focus largely on the social and political history of Scotland, and his recent books include *Winston Churchill* (2000), *Ireland: The Second World War* (2002), *God, Guns and Ulster* (2003), *Crimes of Loyalty: A History of the UDA* (2006) and *Britain, Ireland and the Second World War* (2010).

* Now deceased.

Index

Aberdeen 17–18, 21, 24, 28, 43,
    49–50, 53, 54, 70, 156, 163, 176
Aberdeen Evening Express 69
Admiralty 12, 18, 121
Advertisements 152–4; *see* Press
Agriculture 15–17, 22, 85, 91–2
Ahrweiler, C. 160
Aisne 86
Aliens Restriction Act (1914) 155
Alloa 145, 156, 160, 164
Alloa Circular 164
Anderson, W. C. 69
Andrews, Linton 6
Annan 145, 161
Annandale Observer 161
Anti-German riots
    England 145–6
    Scotland 157, 158–166
Anti-German sentiment 62, 72, 84,
    109, 115, 119, 146–7, 150, 157–9
Arbroath 20
Argyll and Sutherland Highlanders
    84–5
    7ᵗʰ Bttn. 164
    10ᵗʰ Bttn. 125
    19ᵗʰ Bttn. 125, 137
Argyll, Duke of 84
Armistice 9, 55
Army and Religion, The 176, 181
Asquith, H. 41, 49, 51, 52, 53, 156
Aubers Ridge 165
Ayrshire 49, 53, 62

Band of Hope 173, 189
Banff 18, 75
Barr, Rev. James 44, 64–5
Beaton, Captain (North Uist) 94
Becher, A. 145, 160
Beith, J.H. *see* Ian Hay

Bell, J. J. 125
Berwick 156
Berwickshire Fox Hounds 71
Bethune, E. 106–7
Black Watch 1, 164
    1ˢᵗ and 2ⁿᵈ Bttns. 165
    4ᵗʰ Bttn. 6
    6ᵗʰ Bttn. 165
Blackwood's Magazine 125–7, 130
Board of Agriculture 16–17, 92–4
Boer War 37, 45, 82, 104, 157
Bonar Law, A. 51, 52
Bone, Muirhead 7
Boys Brigade (BB) 117, 122, 178
British Expeditionary Force (BEF)
    86
British Socialist Party (BSP) 62–3,
    67, 70, 71
British Women's Temperance
    Association 186
Brown, James 49
Bryce Committee Report (1915)
    163, 166
Buchan, John 3, 9, 149–10
Buckie 18

Cairns, Rev. D. S. 175–6, 183
Caithness 90
Cameron, Allan of Erracht 81
Cameron of Lochiel 81, 83, 84, 86
Cameron, Captain Allan 86
Cameron, Col. John 86
Cameronians (Scottish Rifles)
    2ⁿᵈ Bttn. 4, 128
    5ᵗʰ Bttn. 9n.
    7ᵗʰ Bttn. 112, 113
Campbell, R. W. 125, 136
*Carrying On – After the First
    Hundred Thousand* 140

Casualties 1, 20, 87–8, 114–18
Cave, Sir George 75
Central Iron Moulders 70
Chalmers, Rev. Thomas 176–7
Chamberlain, W. J. 60, 75, 76
Chemicals 26
Churches
    and First World War 174–5, 178, 184
    and 'Red Clydeside' 174
    inter-war 174–5, 189
    secularisation 179
    see specific denominations,
        Evangelicalism, Spiritualism,
        Trench religion
Church of England 174
Church of Scotland 47, 68, 174, 176, 189
Churchill, Winston 37, 41, 111, 121
Cleeberg, C. 162, 163
Clyde Dilution Commission (1916) 23
Clyde Workers Committee (CWC) 42, 48, 49
Clydebank 189
Clydebank Trades Council 70
Clydebridge Steel Company 14
Coal industry 25
Colquhoun, Sir Iain 87
Conscientious objection, *see* war resisters
Conscription 20, 41, 42, 49, 60, 65, 69–70, 76, 118
Considine, Lieut. P. F. 116
Consumption 31
Cooperative movement 50, 105
Corporatism 55
Crawfurd, Helen 71
Croft, Lieut. Col. 126–7

Daily Chronicle 151
Daily Record 44, 61, 65, 147, 157
Dalziel, Sir H. 41, 151
Dardenelles *see* Gallipoli

David Colville & Sons 14
Day-Star, The 185
Debt 31
Defence of the Realm Act [DORA] (1915) 73, 91–2, 120, 151
Dilution Scheme 23
Dingwall 86, 158
Drumnadrochit 92
Dublin Fusiliers 115
Dumbarton 84
Dumfries 145, 148, 159, 160, 161–6
Dumfries and Galloway Standard 148, 162
Dundee 1, 19, 25, 27, 36, 67, 70, 72
Dundee Advertiser 61

Economic consequences (of war) 30–2
Edinburgh 1, 7, 21, 45, 51, 53–4, 74, 116, 145, 156, 159, 165, 187
    class 107, 115
    losses 114–8
    recruitment 109, 118–121
    territorial regiments 103, 104–110 see Royal Scots
Edinburgh Evening Dispatch 69
Edinburgh Evening News 115, 118, 165
Edinburgh Trades Council 104–5, 118
Egerton, Maj. Gen. 113–4
Elections (parliamentary)
    general elections (1900) 45, (Jan. 1910) 44–5, (Dec. 1910) 36, (1918) 41, 44, 46, 47, 49, 50, 51, 52, 53, 55, (1922) 41, 52, 53, 54
    by-elections (N.E. Lanarkshire 1901, 1904, 1911) 40, (Dundee 1908) 37, (Govan 1911) 40, (Midlothian 1913) 41
Elger, William 55
Elgin 72, 158
Empire loyalty 2, 4, 7, 55, 89, 106, 150, 156–7
Employment structure 21–3

Esslemont, G. B. 42
Evangelicalism 174, 176–7, 184–6,
    188, 189
Evening Dispatch 69, 115–6
Evening Times 148
Ewing, Dr William 111–2, 114,
    116–117

Feyerabend, C. 145, 159, 161
Fife 25, 32, 39, 46, 70
Findhorn 18
First Hundred Thousand , The 7
    as 'letter home' 133–7
    disobedience 129–130
    metaphor and humour 126–132
    military etiquette 128–9, 131
    morale 128
    readership 127, 130, 131, 142
    sales 126
    Scottish identity 132, 140–141
    see Ian Hay
Fishery Board 17
Fishing 17–19, 85
Food production 15–19
Football 84, 103, 106, 147
Fort William 19
Forward 59, 61, 62, 63, 64, 66, 67,
    71, 74, 75, 77
Franchise 45, 52, 54, 189
Fraserburgh 18
Free Church Magazine 185, 188
French, General Sir John 87
Friends Ambulance Unit 73

Gallacher, Willie 71
Gallipoli 3, 110–18, 121, 165
Gambling 188
Gaming Machines Act (1917) 188
Gasworkers Union of Scotland 70
George Heriot's 107
George Outram & Co 149
George Watson's 107, 115
German community 145, 155–6,
    159–161

traders 145, 157, 159, 161–2, 165
Glasgow 13, 16, 21–2, 25, 40, 45,
    48, 49, 50, 52, 54, 63, 67, 70–71,
    76, 84, 85, 107, 156, 177, 187, 188
Glasgow Herald 7, 62–3, 65, 71, 147,
    151, 154, 157, 159
Glasgow Labour Party 70
Glasgow Observer 43
Glasgow Stock Exchange 85
Glasgow Study Group 68
Glasgow Trades Council 50, 54
Glasier, Bruce 67–8
Glengarnock Iron and Steel
    Company 14
Good Templars 189
Gordon Highlanders 1
Govan 40, 49, 53
Granton 19
Gravenstafel Ridge 165
Greenock 52, 84, 145, 156, 162
Greenock Telegraph 162
Gretna disaster 107, 110

Haig, Sir Douglas 8, 47
Haldane, Robert 104–5, 108
Hamilton, Sir Ian 113
Happy-go-lucky 126
Harmsworth, R.L. 41, 44
Harris Tweed 85
Hawick 156
Hay, Ian [John Hay Beith] 7,
    125–6; 132–3 *see The First
    Hundred Thousand*
Heart of Midlothian FC 103
Hebrides 17, 86, 90–1
Henderson, Maj. J. N. 116
Highland Land League 54, 90
Highland Land Settlement
    Association 89, 90
Highland News 71, 159
Highlands 6, 82, 84, 85, 91, 159
    changing attitudes 85–88
    evictions 68–9
    land protest 17, 88–96, 98

military identity 6, 81–2, 85–6, 97
recruitment 17, 81–85
regiments 82, 83, 84, 85–6, 87–8
see Highland Land League, Land
  reform, Identity
'Hill 60' 165
Home Rule
  Ireland 38, 45; *see* Irish
  Scotland 55
Housing 48–9, 68
Hunter-Weston, General Sir Aylmer
  113–4

Ibrox Football Stadium 84
Identity
  Highland 6, 81–2, 83–4, 85, 96,
    97 *see* Highlands
  local 8, 83, 92–3, 95, 97–8, 115
  Scottish 1, 2, 7, 55, 61, 88, 132,
    140, 154, 166
If 64
Independent Labour Party (ILP) 5,
  36, 40–1, 48, 49
  and conscription/recruitment
    59–60, 64, 67, 69, 70–71, 72,
    73, 74, 77
  and Labour Party 63, 64, 69, 74
  and wartime discontent 68–69
  attitudes to war 59–64
  membership 37, 40, 61, 63, 67, 73,
    74–5, 77
International Workers of the World
  (IWW) 67
Inverness Courier 85–6, 87, 88
Inverness Liberal Association 89
Irish
  in literature 133–4
  nationalism 38, 40, 44–5, 52,
    133–4
  recruitment 45, 85

Japan 31
John Bull 156
Johnston, Tom 173

Justice 62
Jute industry 25, 27–8, 32

Keir Hardie 39
Kelp 85
Kessack, J. O'Connor 49
Kilmarnock 40
Kilsyth 68
Kiltarlity 94
King's Own Scottish Borderers
  (KOSB) 165
Kirkintilloch 70, 173
Kitchener, Lord 64, 108, 113, 121,
  137

Labour Leader 63, 66, 70, 71, 74
Labour Party 40, 43, 44, 45, 48–49,
  51–2, 66, 69, 70; *see* Independent
  Labour Party, Labour Represent-
  ation Committee, Scottish
  Workers Representation Com-
  mittee
Labour Representation Committee
  (LRC) 39
Lairg 95
Lanarkshire 13, 40, 41, 46, 65
Land reform 36, 37, 54, 88–96
Land Settlement (Scotland) Act
  (1918) 96
League of the Cross 173
Leith 7, 16, 25, 52, 67, 70, 107, 110,
  145, 159, 165
Leslie, William 72–3
Liberal Unionists 39
Liberal War Committee 42
Liberals 5, 36–7, 41–5, 48, 50, 52,
  53, 148, 157
Liebow, Hugh 145, 159
Lloyd George, David 36, 41, 43–4,
  52
Local tribunals 69–73
Loch Carron 19
Locomotives 26
Lodge, Prof. Richard 109

Loos 7, 87–8, 133, 134, 137–140
Lothians 25, 32, 40–1, 144
Lovat, Lord 86
Lovat Scouts 82
Lusitania 157, 160, 163, 166
Lutyens, Sir Edwin 2

MacCallum, Rev. Malcolm 68
Macdonald, J. Ramsay 49
Macdonald of Clanranald 84
Mackay, J. G. 89
MacKinnon Wood, 51, 156
Mackintosh, E.A. 120–121
Maclean, John 62–3, 71
Maclean, Rev. Norman 117
Making of Mickey McGhee, The 135–6
Masculinity 173, 175, 176, 178,
    181–4, 185
Maxton, James 48, 68, 71, 73
McCallum Scott, A. 37, 41, 44, 46,
    52, 58
McCrae, Sir George 103–4, 105–6,
    109–10, 116
Military production 12–14
Military Service Acts (1916) 60, 69,
    70, 75
Miners Federation 39, 49
Mons 86, 136
Morison, T. B. 89–90
Morning Watch, The 174
Mull 91, 93, 94
Munitions of War Act (1915) 12–13
Munition levy 29
Munro, Robert 89–90
Murray, William 111

National Federation of Women
    Workers (NFWW) 24
National identity *see* Identity
'National Mission of Rededication'
    189
National Registration Act (1915) 69
National Service League 104–5
Nationalisation 53–4

Neuve Chapelle 4, 164
New Liberalism 36–7
No-Conscription Fellowship 60, 66, 70
North British Locomotive Company
    26

Oban Times 85, 87

Paisley 20, 50, 52
Parkhead Ordnance Works 13, 23
Peace Society 63, 64
Perth/Perthshire 90, 145, 156,
    159–160, 164
Perthshire Advertiser 164
Perthshire Constitutional and Journal
    157, 159, 162–4
Perthshire Courier 162, 163
Peterhead 18
Poison gas 164
Political effects (of war) 52–55
Ponsonby, Arthur 37, 41–2, 44
Population 21, 32
Port Glasgow 84
Press
    and local/national experiences
        150, 151, 163, 165
    and Scottish identity 151–4, 166
    circulation 147–9
    English press 146, 147, 148–9, 151
    political persuasion 148, 156
    Press Bureau 151
    readerships 151
    Scottish press 61, 74, 146, 148,
        149, 151–4, 156, 165, 166 *see*
        circulation
Pringle, W. M. R. 42, 51–2
Puritanism 188–190

Queen's Own Cameron Highlanders
    (QOCH) 81, 84–5, 86–8
    5th Bttn. 85
    7th Bttn. 87–8

Railways 54

Rechabites 189
Recruitment 6, 20, 45, 61–2, 65, 69,
    76, 81–85, 96, 97, 109, 118–121,
    157
    eighteenth-century 81, 96
Red Cross 45
'Red Clydeside' 3, 48, 174
Religion *see* Churches, 'Trench
    religion', Evangelicalism
Rent strikes 48
Reserve Forces Bill (1907) 104
Roberts, Field Marshal Lord 105
Roman Catholic Church 54
Rosebery, Lord 2, 109, 154
Ross-shire 86
Royal Commission on the Militia
    and Volunteers (1903) 104
Royal Naval Volunteer Reserve 18
Royal Scots 1, 103–22
    4th Bttn. 107, 109, 110, 111–4,
        115–6, 121–2
    5th Bttn. 107, 111, 113, 116, 118–9
    7th Bttn. 107, 110, 111–114
    9th Bttn. 107, 109
    16th Bttn. 103, 110

St Andrews 21
St Cuthbert's Cooperative Society
    105
St Julien 164, 165
Savings 31
Scotsman 115, 118
Scottish Conservative Club 46
Scottish identity *see* Identity
Scottish Labour Party 39, 70
Scottish Land Court 89
Scottish Landowners Federation 37
Scottish Liberal Association 43
Scottish National Society for the
    Prevention of Cruelty to Children
    (SNSPCC) 187
Scottish National War Memorial 1–2
Scottish Trades Union Congress
    (STUC) 49, 50, 53, 55, 70

Scottish Workers Representation
    Committee (SWRC) 39–40, 50
Seaforth Highlanders 85
Second Socialist International 62
Seely, Sir John 105–6
Sheep 15–16, 92
Shells and Fuses Agreement (1915) 23
Shetland 18–20
Shinwell, Emmanuel 71
Shipbuilding 12–13
Shop Assistants Union 70
Shop stewards movement 48, 51–2
Skye 19, 91, 95
Small Landholders (Scotland) Act
    (1911) 17, 89, 92, 96
Smith, Very Rev. G. A. 68
Socialism 48, 53, 63, 66, 71 *see*
    relevant political parties
Socialist Labour Party 67, 76
Socialist Party of Great Britain 67
Somme 114, 140, 183
Spies 158–9
Spiritualism 175, 183
Steel manufacture 13–14, 22, 32
Stewart, William 63–4, 69, 70, 71,
    74, 75
Stirling 43, 46, 49, 51
Stornoway 19
Sugar 26
Sunday school 173, 185
Sutherland 17, 68–9
Sutherland Echo 68

Tariff reform 38, 53
Taxation 28–30
Temperance 173, 177–8, 184, 186,
    188–9
Temperance (Scotland) Act (1913)
    188
Territorial Army 7, 20, 103
    and class 105–7
    and Kitchener 108
    Edinburgh regiments 104–110,
        115

Imperial Service Obligation 108,
109–110, 118
recruitment 104, 105, 108
see Edinburgh, Royal Scots
Textiles 27
Tillet, Ben 62
Times, The 105, 147
Tiree 90, 96
Trade disruption 24–8, 31
Trade unionism 39, 55, 62, 70
Tramways 24, 28
'Trench religion' 175–84
and class 180–181

Uists 84, 91, 95, 96
Unemployment 25, 61
Uniforms 82
Union for Democratic Control
(UDC) 49, 71
Unionists 37–41, 45, 46–7, 52, 53
United Free Church 44, 47, 109,
111, 174, 176, 179, 189
Universities 21
Aberdeen University 47
Edinburgh University 104
Glasgow University 85

Vimy Ridge 139
Volunteers 103–4

Wages 25–6
War finance 28–30
War resisters 59–61, 67, 71–4,
75–77 *see* ILP

Wartime politics 41–51
Waterloo House 126
Watt, Rev. Maclean 118
We Did Not Fight 73
Weekly Free Press 163
Weekly News 148
Wheatley, J. 53
William Beardmore & Co 12, 22, 47
Winchester, Bishop of 175
Women
and child neglect 187–8
and marriage 177, 187, 189
and politics 48
and temperance 177–8, 186, 187,
188, 189
British Women's Temperance
Association 186
employment 22–4, 27
female piety 173, 175, 176, 184–8,
189–190
in literature 136
National Federation of Women
Workers (NFWW) 24
soldiers' attitudes towards 182,
183, 187
see masculinity
Woollen industry 27
Workers' Union 70
'Writer-fighters' 1

Young Scots 37
Younger, George 38
Ypres (second battle) 86–7, 164,
165